IDEOLOGY AND
PRACTICE IN
SCHOOLING

IDEOLOGY AND PRACTICE IN SCHOOLING

EDITED BY

Michael W. Apple
AND Lois Weis

Temple University Press

PHILADELPHIA

Temple University Press, Philadelphia 19122
© 1983 by Temple University. All rights reserved
Published 1983
Printed in the United States of America

Library of Congress Cataloging in Publication Data
Main entry under title:

Ideology and practice in schooling.

Includes index.
1. Education—Economic aspects—United States—
Addresses, essays, lectures.   2. Educational sociology—
United States—Addresses, essays, lectures.   3. Labor
and laboring classes—Education—United States—Addresses,
essays, lectures.   I. Apple, Michael W.   II. Weis, Lois.
LC66.I33   1983   370.19   83-1139
ISBN 0-87722-295-9
ISBN 0-87722-313-0 (pbk.)

Contents

Acknowledgments

Volumes such as this are often the result of discussions with many individuals over long periods of time. Many people at Wisconsin, the State University of New York at Buffalo, and elsewhere contributed ideas, criticisms, and support. Among them are Philip Altbach, Rima D. Apple, Tereffe Asrat, Gail Kelly, Michael Olneck, Sheila Slaughter, and Geoff Whitty.

Perhaps our greatest debt of gratitude is to the progressive students, teachers, and other educators who have been in our classes over the years. Not only did they respond sensitively to the chapters included in this volume, but they continuously document the possibility of a more democratic and enlightened educational theory and practice by their own ongoing struggles in the institutions in which they work.

We want to thank Kenneth Arnold of Temple University Press for his encouragement and support during this project. Barbara Seffrood, Dian Jensen, and Mildred Young demonstrated once more why they are some of the best secretaries with whom one could work.

Contributors

Jean Anyon is an Associate Professor of Education at Rutgers University, Newark.

Michael W. Apple is Professor of Curriculum and Instruction and Educational Policy Studies at the University of Wisconsin, Madison.

Landon E. Beyer is an Assistant Professor of Education at Knox College.

Robert B. Everhart is an Associate Professor of Education at the University of California, Santa Barbara.

Andrew Gitlin is an Assistant Professor of Education at the University of Utah.

Nancy King is an Assistant Professor of Education at the University of Maryland, College Park.

Linda M. McNeil is a Research Associate at the Center for Educational Research at the University of Wisconsin, Madison.

Joel Taxel is an Assistant Professor of Language Education, The University of Georgia, Athens.

Linda Valli is a Lecturer in the Department of Educational Policy Studies at The University of Wisconsin, Madison.

Lois Weis is an Assistant Professor of Social Foundations of Education at the State University of New York, Buffalo.

INTRODUCTION

CHAPTER 1

Ideology and Practice in Schooling: A Political and Conceptual Introduction

MICHAEL W. APPLE
and LOIS WEIS

The daily life of teachers, administrators, parents, and students in our schools is filled with political and ideological pressures and tensions. The turmoil caused by budget cuts and layoffs, by class, race, and gender antagonisms, and even by the internal politics of complex bureaucratic institutions, is part of what one experiences when one works within the institution. At a time of fiscal crisis and, often, great ideological differences about what schools should do, it is hard not to think of education as part of a larger framework of institutions and values. While this has been recognized for years by many who either work in or engage in research on schools, the dominant tradition of educational research, unfortunately, has been overly psychological. It has tended to be individualistic and to ignore the political and economic reality of schools. By focusing primarily on how to get students to learn more mathematics, science, history, and so forth (surely not an unimportant problem), educational research has neglected to inquire into the larger context in which schools exist, a context that may actually make it very difficult for them to succeed.

Actually, this dominant research model—what has been called the "achievement tradition"—has been weakened by its neglect of two things.[1] Because of a positivistic emphasis and an overreliance on statistical approaches, it has been unable to unravel the complexities of everyday interaction in schools. Its focus on product has led to a thoroughgoing naiveté about the very process of education, about the internal dynamics of the institution. Second, its tendency toward atheoreticism has made it difficult for us to link these internal dynamics to the larger ideological, economic, and political context. Schools sit isolated from the structurally unequal society (and the conflicts this inequality engenders) of which they are a part.

In their exceptionally clear discussion of the major approaches to research in education, Karabel and Halsey state that among the most important research programs now required is one that will connect interpretive studies of schools with structural analyses. That is, an approach that combines an investigation of the day-to-day curricular, pedagogic, and evaluative activities of schools with generative theories of the school's role in society is needed to move us forward.[2]

This volume takes up their recommendation. Its central concern is to fill much of the gap. The individual chapters all share a fundamental interest. What actually happens at the level of practice in educational institutions? In what ways should our understanding of these practices be informed by current theoretical appraisals of the role of education in advanced capitalist societies such as our own? The authors treat Karabel and Halsey's argument seriously. Each seeks to integrate an analysis of the level of practice (that is, what the social relations, curriculum, teaching, and so on are) in our institutions with a critical structural appraisal of how such practices illuminate the relationship of the school to the surrounding socioeconomic order.

What Schools Do

As David Hogan notes, it is difficult to separate educational issues from larger political issues. He identifies four categories into which these issues have fallen. Though no more than ideal types, these include:

> structural politics centered upon the nature and strength of the alignment of the school with the economy (for example, conflicts over differentiated and vocational education) and conflicts over the structure of authority relations within schools (for example, conflicts over the centralization of administrative authority, unionization and professionalism); human capital politics generated by the efforts of parents or communities to enhance the rates of return to their children or school population relative to other children or school populations; cultural capital politics created by conflicts over competing definitions of legitimate knowledge, that is, conflicts over the distribution of symbolic authority in the society (for example, conflicts over curricular content or textbooks); and finally, displacement politics, in which educational issues (often, though not always, conflicts of a cultural capital kind) become proxies for other non-educational conflicts in the community.[3]

Hogan's points are significant. Conflicts over knowledge, over economic goods and services, and over power relations within and outside the school are all of considerable moment. In order to understand these complex issues, we need to step back from thinking about schools as places that seek only to maximize the achievement of students. Instead of this psychological and individualistic perspective, we need to interpret the school more socially, culturally, and structurally. A number of questions organize these interpretations. What is it that education does in this larger context? When it does this, who benefits?

In general, recent research on the social, ideological, and economic role of our educational apparatus has pointed to three activities schools engage in. Though clearly interrelated, we can distinguish these "functions" as those assisting in accumulation, those assisting in legitimation, and those assisting in production.[4] First, schools assist in the process of capital accumulation by providing some of the necessary conditions for recreating an unequally responsive economy. They do this in part by internally sorting and selecting students by "talent," a process that by integrating students into a credential market and a system of urban segregation, roughly reproduces a hierarchically organized labor force.[5] It has been argued that, as students are hierarchically ordered—an ordering often based on the cultural forms of dominant groups—students of different race, class, and sex are taught different norms, skills, values, knowledge, and dispositions.[6] In this way, schools help meet the economy's demand for a stratified and at least partially socialized body of employees.[7]

We have to be quite cautious here. One can easily make it seem as if everything pertaining to education can be reduced to the needs of the division of labor or of economic forces outside the school. Such a perspective—commonly called a base/superstructure model—is too simplistic and mechanistic.[8] While a number of the chapters in this volume will argue with such models, it is crucial, though, to keep in mind that there are some very real ties between an economy and the sorting and selecting activity of education.

Second, schools are important agencies for legitimation.[9] That is, they are part of a complex structure through which social groups are given legitimacy and through which social and cultural ideologies are built, recreated, and maintained. Thus, schools tend to describe both their own internal workings and society's as a whole as meritocratic and as inexorably moving toward widespread social and economic justice. In this way, they foster the belief that the major institutions of our society are equally responsive by race, class, and sex. Unfortunately, the available data suggest that this is less the case than we might like to think. In fact, as a number of investigators have demonstrated, slogans of pluralism aside, in almost every social arena from health care to anti-inflation policy, the top twenty percent of the population benefit much more than the bottom eighty percent.[10] Given the emerging politics of rightist regimes in advanced capitalist societies, this disparity may be exacerbated even further.[11] In essence, while pluralism does exist in "late capitalist society," its extent has been greatly exaggerated, and its character has changed markedly, as both the corporate-managed and the state-operated sectors have increasingly gained control of more and more segments of our lives.[12]

Yet the school's role in legitimation is not limited to making our socioeconomic system seem natural and just or to demarcating groups from one another. Since schools are also part of the political institutions of our society, part of the state, they must legitimate themselves as well. That is, not just the economy, but the educational apparatus and the state bureaucracy and government in general have their own needs for legitimacy. They too must generate consent from the governed. Since the need for political legitimacy may not always resonate with the requirements of the economy, matters are complicated considerably.

Finally, the educational apparatus as a whole constitutes an important set of agencies for production. Our mode of production, distribution, and consumption requires high levels of technical/administrative knowledge for the expansion of markets, defense, the creation and stimulation of new consumer needs, the control and division of labor, and for communicative and technical innovations that will increase or hold a market share or profit margin, and just as importantly for cultural control.[13] Schools and universities ultimately help in the production of such knowledge. As research and development centers whose costs are socialized (that is, spread among all of us so that capital need not pay the bulk of the cost) and as training grounds for future employees of industry, universities, for example, play an essential role in making available the technically useful knowledge on which so much of our science-based industries depend and on which the culture industry is based.

At the same time, technical/administrative knowledge plays another, less economic, role in education. Schools themselves are increasingly dominated by technicist ideologies. The major curricular, teaching, and testing programs in use are nearly all strikingly behavioral and reductive in orientation. Yet, by attempting to reduce all curricular knowledge to atomistic behaviors, as is so often the case currently, many school practices also reduce the cultural sphere (the sphere of democratic discourse and shared understandings) to the application of technical rules and procedures. In essence, questions of "why" are transformed into questions of "how to." The result of this, combined with the fact that serious conflict is usually absent from the curriculum itself, is that instrumental ideologies replace ethical and political awareness and debate.[14] Here, the ideological and economic roles of schools often intersect.

When this is said, though, we need again to be careful of falling into the trap of economism. The very notion that the educational system assists in the production of economically and ideologically useful knowledge implies that schools are cultural as well as economic institutions. By defining the knowledge of certain groups as legitimate for production and/or distribution, while other groups' knowledge and traditions are considered inappropriate as school knowledge, schools help not only in the production of useful technical/administrative knowledge but in the reproduction of the culture and ideological forms of dominant groups.

As research such as Paul Willis's analysis of working class youth culture demonstrates, however, students in schools may often reject dominant knowledge and ideologies.[15] The school, in this instance, serves as a site for the production of alternative and/or oppositional cultural practices. These practices may not serve in any straightforward way the accumulation, legitimation, or production needs of the state or capital. There is no simple one-to-one correspondence between economics and culture. Thus, just as in institutions of the state where there is a relatively autonomous need for legitimacy, in schools, too, there is a partially autonomous cultural dynamic at work, one that is not necessarily reducible to the results and pressures of the capital accumulation process.

This brief description does not exhaust what schools do, of course. However, our major claims are these: We cannot fully understand the way our educational institutions are situated within a larger configuration of economic, cultural, and political power unless we attempt to examine the different functions they perform in our unequal social formation. Further, while we need to unpack the various roles schools perform, we cannot assume that educational institutions will always be successful in carrying out the three functions of accumulation, legitimation, and production. These reflect structural pressures on schools, not foregone conclusions. In part, the possibility that education may be unable to carry out what is "required" by these pressures is made even more of a reality by the fact that these three functions are often *contradictory*.

Perhaps a current example will be helpful here. In a time of fiscal crisis, industry requires fewer highly paid and highly credentialed employees. The declining need for credentialed employees and the problems of declining revenues brought about by the current economic crisis are creating a concomitant crisis in educational institutions and the government. Powerful classes and industry have begun to question whether so many liberally trained students are needed. The very basis of the acceptance of education's usual modes of operating is threatened. In order to cope with the problems of falling monetary support and the questioning of its operations, the state bureaucracy and its educational apparatus (stimulated by economic pressures and by higher officials in the government itself) have introduced highly centralized cost-benefit and accountability mechanisms, tightened "standards," reduced funding for higher education and "frills," reintroduced "basics," and so on. In the process, however, other elements of the public may lose faith in the authority and legitimacy of the government, since they see the tightening up as actually creating inequality and narrowing the avenues they need to get ahead. Here, two of the functions of schools clash. Educational policy is truly caught in a contradictory situation. It must assist in recreating a relatively tight economic and ideological ship and, at the same time, keep its legitimacy in the eyes of others. The state's need for consent, therefore, is sometimes at odds with the pressures being placed upon it by changing economic conditions.[16]

While this is a relatively simple example, it does serve to highlight the fact that the educational apparatus is often caught between a number of potentially competing imperatives. Solving one set of problems may exacerbate another. Responding overtly to the problems of economic inequality may create tensions because of the other functions that education must perform.

Therefore, focusing on a single supposedly dominant requirement of the educational system—such as, say, its ideological and economic role in helping to reproduce the social division of labor—cannot provide an adequate account of its position as a site for other activity. As Roger Dale has pursuasively argued, any particular demand on education can only be fully comprehended in relation to the other structurally generated demands on the school. And these relationships are often fundamentally contradictory.[17] Returning to our quote from Hogan, we can see that economic forces and conflicts do not provide a complete description of what education does. Conflicts over knowledge and power, over culture and politics, intersect with economic determinations. A major focus of this volume will be how these interact at the level of practice and how they reproduce or contradict the larger relations of inequality outside the school.

Status Attainment and Class

Although those who study education have not focused primarily on the contradictory roles of schools, the relationship between schooling and the amelioration or recreation of inequality has not been ignored. The sociology of education, in particular, has a long tradition of dealing with this area, both through studies of the status attainment process and through the more recent ethnographic investigations of school culture that have grown in response to some of the weaknesses of status attainment research. Both of these areas of the sociology of education, unfortunately, have been less structurally inclined than they might be. They too have been challenged for some of the same reasons that the dominant, more psychological, "achievement" model has been. While they have taken some of Hogan's points about the political and economic nature of the institution seriously (in, for instance, the persistent attempts by status attainment researchers to link achievement in school to the occupational structure outside of it), they have been less successful in recognizing the other conflicts about and functions of our educational system. Inequality cannot be seen as a proxy for relations of structural domination and exploitation. Occupational choice by individuals underrepresents class dynamics and class structure. In fact, the occupational structure is not the same as class structure.[18] And, as we have argued, schools do more than link one to an occupational status in the first place.

Let us examine this in somewhat more detail, since the conceptual and empirical strengths and weaknesses of this tradition provide some of the context for the arguments by the authors of the various chapters in this volume. Perhaps the best way of seeing these issues is to counterpose the status attainment and ethnographic research programs against each other and examine the arguments about each one. As we shall see, there is often a relatively large divide between, and within, these two approaches.

Though it is unfortunate, the division between a sociology of education concerned with large-scale and statistically complex studies of status attainment, on the one hand, and smaller-scale, more intense studies of the internal characteristics, on the other, is currently rather large. It is almost as if the "soft" folks never read the "number crunchers" and vice versa. One need only read two journals to find evidence of this split: *Sociology of Education* in the United States and the new and interesting *British Journal of Sociology of Education*. The former is filled with relatively atheoretical but statistically sophisticated studies; the latter mainly contains theoretical, historical, and ethnographic papers.

Of course, there are other significant divisions within the literature. The debate between Marxist theorists and those who take more usual stratification approaches to the study of the benefits one might get from education is beginning in earnest. The intense arguments between symbolic interactionists and more Marxist, structural analysts of the internal characteristics of schools are continuing.[19] Many of our comments in this section of our introductory chapter will have to do with these multiple divisions and how they have led to a substantive and fruitful program of research on the more general problem of the relationship between education and the economic and cultural reproduction of class relations.

The basic question that research on status attainment seeks to answer is this. What is the balance between ascribed and achieved characteristics in the determination of someone's future educational and occupational success?[20] Status attainment researchers also investigate this question with respect to adult income. Many of the longitudinal studies that have emerged from this approach have sought to investigate the relationship between differential educational attainment and social stratification. The underlying idea on which such studies are based is that longitudinal investigations of the relationship between academic attainment and, say, future occupation or income level "will help us understand not only 'who ends up where' but 'how they get there?' "[21]

The tradition on which this research is based should be applauded for its statistical sophistication, which has grown markedly in the last decade or so. It should be commended for both its emphasis on reanalysis of its prior work in the light of new methodological advances and its attempt to build upon previous research.[22] Finally, it should be recognized as having played an important part (though perhaps less than it might like) in policy deliberation at a national level. However, when all of this is said, and it should be, it is clear that the research is undertheorized in important ways. What it all *means* is opaque, since its theoretical grounding remains problematic. Whether it fully answers the question of "how they got there" or how we are to think about who "they" are remains open to question.

For example, any study, no matter how elegant, that is confined to the relationship between educational attainment and occupational structure, relies on a particular unarticulated vision of our economy that underrepresents and undertheorizes class as an essential variable. Here we mean class not as a position on a particular occupational scale (such as the widely known Duncan scale), but as a complex assemblage of cultural and economic relationships that help constitute the production, consumption, and control of labor and of economic and cultural capital.[23]

The significance of these kinds of questions about class and the control of labor and production are partly documented by Wright in his interesting criticism of the tradition of status attainment research. He argues that the theoretical underpinnings of this approach rest on a particular unit of analysis. This is the atomistic individual. That is, "outcomes which are attached to individuals are the essential objects of investigation, and the causes of these outcomes are largely seen as operating through individuals."[24]

Wright goes on, arguing that while, in status attainment theory,

the metric for discussing occupational positions is based on social evaluations of positions, and thus has a supra-individual character . . . the essential dynamic of the theory, however, is conceived almost entirely at the level of atomistic individuals. Social structures have their consequences because they are embodied in individuals, in the form of personal characteristics. The class structure is seen as relevant in the analysis . . . only insofar as it constitutes one of the factors which shape the individual's own achievements and motivations. The preoccupation of the theory is with ascription vs. achievement as determinants of individual outcomes, *not* with the structure of the outcomes themselves. . . . The point is that in . . . status attainment theories . . . social structures are viewed as interesting largely as determinants or constraints on individual actions and outcomes. With few exceptions, they have little theoretical relevance in their own right.[25]

Thus, Wright claims that the lack of an adequate theory of social structure and political economy, one that is specific to our kind of economic formation, makes it difficult for stratification researchers to fully understand the relationship between education and differential benefits. An improved understanding requires a different unit of analysis, a fully developed perspective on social class, not the atomistic individual.

In sum, important criticisms of current work have been based on its underdeveloped notion of class, its choice of the individual rather than social structure and classes as the basic unit of analysis, and its atheoretical assumptions about occupations and the division of labor.[26]

These are not merely theoretic points. They have provided the background for an interesting and more structurally oriented empirical program as well. Recent research has documented some rather important conclusions here. For example, class compares favorably with status in predicting even individual success.[27] When class is a major unit of analysis, it is clear that in the current class structure of the United States, managers receive greater income returns from their education than do workers.[28] Furthermore, some data indicate that "class position is at least as powerful an explanatory variable in predicting income as occupational status."[29]

But what about advantages that are the result of race and gender? While it would be historically inaccurate and conceptually naïve to reduce all gender and racial issues to those of class, it seems to be the case empirically that when class (defined more fully and adequately than is usual in the stratification and status attainment literature) is controlled, the differential benefits gotten from education for, say, blacks and whites largely tend to disappear.[30] Similar results have been found concerning men and women. Again, generally speaking, when class is held constant, the substantial differences between the sexes in the benefits gained from education tend to lessen considerably.[31] The real issue here is why there is such a large concentration of women and minority members within the working class and, more specifically, within particular fractions of that class. How do gender, race, and class interpenetrate each other in contemporary capitalism?[32] It is difficult to fully understand, given the theoretic gaps in much of the current literature.

This is not to say that the results of this traditon of research are inconsequential. Indeed, many of the results, and the technical procedures employed to generate them, are quite interesting. An example is found in the recent report by Jencks and his colleagues, *Who Gets Ahead*? The findings there (largely by Michael Olneck in his analysis of the effects of education) are often provocative. Olneck argues, for instance, that there are few substantial returns to blacks if they complete only high school, and that relatively higher returns accrue only to those blacks who make it through college. Such data raise important questions about our attempts at ameliorative curricular reform. Added to this is the fact that high-school graduation seems to have greater pay-off for those people who already come from relatively advantaged backgrounds. "Men who come from disadvantaged backgrounds must attend college to reap large occupational benefits from their education."[33] Surely these findings are interesting. But, again, without a more serious analysis of the political economy of our kind of social formation, they lack a coherent framework that would enable us to put these and other data together into a viable structural program. Their meaning is, in fact, unclear.

Status attainment research, even in its more interesting empirical work, has been subject to at least one other serious criticism that is close to the concerns of this volume. It has tended to treat schools as black boxes. It relies largely on questionnaires, tests of various kinds, official records, occasionally interviews, and so on, but it almost never enters into schools to find out how the results that appear on these records, tests, and so forth are actually produced. The flesh and blood of real students, teachers, and administrators accomplishing all this is never seen. Even those researchers who—like Bowles and Gintis—are critical of existing research in that tradition and who are on the political left, still treat schools as if the internal characteristics of these insitutions are relatively unimportant sociologically or, even when discussed, not to be probed first hand.[34] In Bowles and Gintis's case, this proved to be a particular problem, since, as recent Marxist ethnographies have demonstrated, the correspondence between what is allegedly taught in schools and the needs of a hierarchical labor market is not that clear. As we stated, working-class students, for instance, often expressly reject the credentials, the overt and hidden curriculum, and the norms that are purportedly taught in schools.[35] The reliance on "external" and "objective" data made it hard for Bowles and Gintis to do other than treat the school like a black box, in the same way as previous stratification researchers were apt to do.

Unfortunately, in this way what is actually taught, what is actually learned, what is rejected, and how the lived experience of class, race, and gender actors acts as a mediating force in producing the outcomes so well studied by stratification researchers are missed in this kind of analysis.

To be sure, the need for research inside the school has not gone unrecognized within the status attainment tradition. Two of the most sophisticated investigators within it have recently argued strongly that in order to go substantially further in our understanding what schools actually do, we need to know much more about what goes on within the walls of the institution itself.[36] They are clearly suggesting an ethnographic program of analysis.

Inside the Black Box

By examining one side of the divisions in the sociology of education and by exploring some of the debates within that side, we do not want to give the impression that ethnographic analyses can answer all of our questions. Neither do we want the reader to assume that there is no equally contentious division within this side.

A good deal of ethnographic research is theoretically indebted more to a sociology that is phenomenologically inclined than to the procedures and linguistic styles of stratification research. Rather than using large-scale sampling techniques, one acts as a participant observer. Rather than examining the ensuing occupations and incomes, one examines the level of cultural practices within the schools themselves. The researcher spends long periods within the school, examining the "negotiated" informal and implicit social rules and meanings that actors in the particular setting apply. As Woods puts it:

> The sociological approach which informs [this] work derives from symbolic interactionism. This concentrates on how the social world is constructed by people, how they are continually striving to make sense of the world, and assigning meanings and interpretations to events, and on the symbols used to represent them. It puts emphasis on pupils' and teachers' own subjective constructions of events, rather than sociologists' assumptions of them, and elevates the process of meaning-assignation and situation-defining to prime importance. Hence the emphasis on "perspectives," the frameworks through which we make sense of the world, and on different "contexts" which influence the formation and operation of these perspectives. These perceptual frameworks are then linked to action. The action is thus impregnated with the meanings assigned to it by the participants, and is revealed as a mixture of strategies, adaptations and accommodations. Wherever they go

in the school, pupils and teachers are continually adjusting, reckoning, bargaining, acting, and changing.[37]

Such adjusting, bargaining, acting, and changing does go on, of course. And it is important to know how it occurs, how the reality of school life is ongoingly produced by our continuous meaningful interaction. Yet, the mere fact that reality is socially constructed does not indicate "how and why reality comes to be constructed in particular ways and how and why particular constructions of reality seem to have the power to resist subversion."[38] What is too often missing from ethnographic studies is exactly what Karabel and Halsey realized was essential—not only a recognition of the differential power of economic and cultural capital within the school, but a structural theory that accounts for it.

This is not to say that all activity in institutions such as schools should be reduced to abstract theoretical formulations. It does mean, however, that one important weakness of much ethnographic research is that it does not take seriously enough the fact that class and culture, reproduction, contestation and resistance, and contradiction *are* found in the everyday lives of teachers, children and parents. They *are* all members of class, gender, and racial groups as well as being individuals. Contradictions and tensions between and within classes, between the country and the city (and hence within particular local political economies), between sexes and races, and so on, are all lived out in local communities and schools like the ones investigated by most participant observers. With all of the richness and value of these ethnographic descriptions, with all of their help in enabling us to get inside the black box of the institution, they too often leave us wondering what it all means. How can we understand elementary schools, for example, in the United States without considering the dynamics of class and gender: a huge majority of teachers are women, an overwhelming majority of principals are men, and this employment pattern is part of the sexual and social division of labor? This situation is structural. Yet it is not abstract, but is lived out in schools every day.[39]

In many ways, much ethnographic research in education falls prey to problems that in some ways are similar to those found in the literature on social stratification. These studies too have an underdeveloped notion of social class, one that is not sufficiently linked to the political economy of the areas being studied.[40] Their appraisals of the cultural form and content of the students and the school, while clearly going beyond a good deal of the status attainment research because of their very interests, are still less strongly linked to the literature on class, race, and gender cultures than they should be.[41] And finally, their approach lacks an important historical element. It is not connected fully enough to changes over time in the division and control of labor, to ongoing alterations in class composition, and to the changing historical functions of the state in education. This last point, as we saw earlier, is especially critical in times of what has been called the fiscal crisis of the state. Like the dominant psychological tradition of research in education, schools still too often are not consciously situated within the historically changing dynamics of the society of which they are a part.

We are left here with a predicament. Status attainment research has been strongly criticized for not getting inside the black box of the school. A tradition of ethnographic investigation has grown rapidly, offering an important counterbalance to these more statistically oriented studies. Yet, while both complement each other in this way, they are equally subject to other important criticisms. Both have pursued less than vigorously the connections between their questions and data and structural issues related to the organization and control of the particular kind of social formation in which we live. Both have employed theoretically weak notions of economy, class, and culture. Both, finally, have systematically neglected the complex dynamics and interrelationships *among* class, economy, and culture. It is this nexus—the dialectical interconnections among relations of domination and exploitation, cultural form and content, and dominant modes of production—that has become the focus of culturalist research on the reproductive role of education. This has come to be called the sociology of school knowledge.

The Sociology of School Knowledge

The issues surrounding economy, class, and culture within the school did not appear suddenly. They followed more than a decade of conceptual and empirical investigations that have firmly established what might be called a critical culturalist problematic within sociological studies of the school.

There has been a dual focus in these culturalist studies. Culture has been analyzed as both *lived experience* and as *commodity*. The first examines culture as it is produced in ongoing interaction and as a terrain in which class, gender, and racial meanings and antagonisms are lived out. The second looks at culture as a product, as a set of artifacts produced for use. Both are necessary, and both have been present in the scholarship that has evolved. We shall not present a detailed history of the growth of the traditions these studies represent. Such analyses are available elsewhere.[42] We shall, however, briefly lay out some of the historical, conceptual, and political foundations upon which they have rested.

In the late 1960s and early 1970s, when structural analyses of the actual cultural form and content inside schools remained relatively unexplored in the sociology of education in the United States, perceptible inroads were being made into this area elsewhere. In England, for instance, the publication of Michael F. D. Young's collection, *Knowledge and Control*, signaled a growing interest in the social origins and effects of the organization and selection of curricular knowledge. Young, Bernstein, Bourdieu, and others in Europe argued that the organization of knowledge, the form of its transmission, and the assessment of its acquisition are crucial factors in the cultural reproduction of class relationships in industrial societies.[43]

In the United States, often in reaction to the positivistic and technical orientation (what we earlier called the "achievement" tradition) that dominated the field, similar kinds of questions emerged. Yet, they emerged less from the sociology of education than from the curriculum field itself. Strongly influenced by critical theory and the sociology of knowledge, as well as the rebirth of Marxist and neo-Marxist dialogue, attempts were made to link the actual knowledge—both hidden and overt—found in schools to the relations of domination and subordination outside the institution.[44]

In the United States, England, and France, it was argued that the questions most sociologists of education and curriculum researchers asked concealed the fact that assumptions about real relations of power were already embedded in their research models and the approaches from which they drew. As Young put it, sociologists were apt to "take" as their research problems those questions that were generated out of the existing administrative apparatus, rather than "make" them themselves.[45] In curriculum studies, it was claimed that issues of efficiency and increasing meritocratic achievement had almost totally depoliticized the field. Questions of "technique" had replaced the essential political and ethical issues of what we should teach and why.[46]

The interests that guided this research program as it emerged in the prior decade were threefold: to replace the "individualistic, meritocratic analysis of the relationship between education and social inequality" with a more historical and structural appraisal; "to displace the objectivist, psychologized" approaches to research on academic achievement and school curriculum with a "socio-political analysis" of what counts as legitimate school knowledge; and to raise challenges to the managerial, efficiency, and technically oriented approaches to the organization and control of classrooms and schools and replace them with a "socially interactive and culturally based critical view."[47]

Schools were seen as places that not only "processed people," but as institutions that "processed knowledge" as well.[48] One of the primary foci, in fact, was on the interrelationships between these two kinds of "processing." In terms of the concepts we previously introduced, it was recognized that school practices needed to be related not only to problems of individual achievement, occupational choice, and mobility, but to the processes of capital accumulation and legitimation and production as well. Taking a key concept from Gramsci, the program around which this research centered was that of determining how "ideological hegemony" was maintained. How was the control of culture and meaning related to the reproduction of (and, later, resistance to) our socioeconomic order? The intellectual work of this period was primarily devoted to ideology critique.[49]

Ideology was usually understood in an Althusserian manner. The individual was not "the originating source of consciousness, the irruption of a subjective principle into objective historical process." Instead, consciousness and meaning are made up of ("constituted by") ideological practices that are independent of individual human subjects and that actually "produce subjectivity." Thus, "ideology is a practice producing subjects."[50]

For critical researchers on both sides of the Atlantic, then, the symbolic resources organized and transmitted in the school were not neutral. Instead, they were better thought of in ideological terms, as the cultural capital of specific groups which—though this culture did have a life of its own—functioned to recreate relations of domination and subordination by "positioning" subjects within larger ideological discourses and relations. The culture of the school, hence, was a terrain of ideological conflict, not merely a set of facts, skills, dispositions, and social relationships that were to be taught in the most efficient and effective way possible.

For Bernstein, for example, the emphasis was on how a particular segment of the middle class reproduced itself by controlling the curricular and pedagogical apparatus of the school. In Bourdieu's work, one saw how the cultural capital of elite groups worked in schools and universities to reproduce class boundaries both within and outside of ruling groups. This was accomplished in part because the educational system was relatively autonomous from the needs of production, and this very autonomy enabled it to do its ideological work.[51] Other investigators pursued similar paths, examining how the major forms of curriculum, pedagogy, and evaluation contributed to the recreation of the ideological hegemony of dominant classes in equally subtle and complex ways. What bound these people together, though, was a persistent concern not only with economy but with culture and with the relationship between what actually happens within the educational system and the structure of exploitation and domination outside of it. The attempt—which grew in sophistication over the years—was to blend together serious structural analysis with studies of the lived and commodified culture of the school. The problem was to integrate micro and macro in a coherent way.

This integrative intent was summarized by one of us in an earlier work. There it was suggested that three areas had to be interrogated if we were to go further than previous research into what schools do and who benefits from their current organization and content.

> We need to examine critically not just "how a student [can] acquire more knowledge" (the dominant question in our efficiency minded field) but "why and how particular aspects of the collective culture are presented in school as objective, factual knowledge?" How, *concretely*, may official knowledge represent ideological configurations of the dominant interests in a society? How do schools legitimate these limited and partial standards of knowing as unquestioned truths? These questions must be asked of at least three areas of school life: (1) how the basic day to day regularities of schools contribute to students learning these ideologies; (2) how the specific forms of curricular knowledge . . . reflect these configurations; (3) how these ideologies are reflected in the fundamental perspectives educators themselves employ to order, guide, and give meaning to their own activity.
>
> The first of these questions refers to the hidden curriculum in schools—the tacit teaching to students of norms, values, and dispositions that goes on simply by their living in and coping with the institutional expectations and routines of schools day in and day out for a number of years. The second question asks us to make educational knowledge itself problematic, to pay much greater attention to the "stuff" of the curriculum, where knowledge comes from, whose knowledge it is, what social groups it supports, and so on. The final query seeks to make educators more aware of the ideological and epistemological commitments they tacitly accept and promote by using certain models and traditions—say, a vulgar positivism, systems management, structural-functionalism, a process of social labeling, or behavior modification—in their own work. Without an understanding of these aspects of school life, one that connects them seriously to the distribution, quality, and control of work, power, ideology, and cultural knowledge outside our educational institutions, educational theory and policy making may have less of an impact than we might hope.[52]

While such a critical interrogation of the knowledge, social relations, and ideological commitments would not by itself alter either education or society, such a program of criticism was seen as an essential first step in generating both more emancipatory research and practice. The interest was in initiating the process of rigorously scrutinizing what was taken for granted so that the actual social and cultural outcomes of our theories and practices could be illuminated, at the same time keeping in mind the interests both of ethnographers in day to day life inside the black box of the school and of the stratification researchers in the institutions beyond the school. Instead of merely describing the way actors socially construct and interpret reality, however, these studies examined critically that reality itself, treating it as an ideological construction related to class, race, and gender hegemony. And instead of individual occupational selection the studies used class and the reproduction of class relations as a major organizing concept.[53] Such criticism involved, as Wexler put it, "removing the cloak of neutrality by reversing the cognitive social process of converting values to facts."[54] Without reversing this process, we would have nowhere to begin.

There were problems, of course, with some of these early critical formulations. They assumed that it was relatively simple to read a text ideologically, that social interests were always represented in curriculum and teaching in some straightforward fashion, much as a mirror reflects an image. Sometimes this is the case; often, it decidedly is not.[55] They too at times embodied a position that schools were necessarily successful in teaching a hidden curriculum that reflected (again the mirror analogy) the requirements of the division of labor in society. And, finally, they neglected the reality of contradications and struggle. They posited too passive a model. As has become much clearer over the past few years, people—including teachers and students—can act against dominant ideological forms. The ultimate results might not be either what schools intended or what a simple ideological reading might imply. Ideological hegemony wasn't something that either existed or did not exist at any particular moment. It was (and is) a constant struggle, the conclusion of which can not be known in advance.[56]

This is a crucial point. Because hegemony requires the "consent" of the dominated majority, it can never be permanent, universal, or simply given. It needs to be won continually. Whatever stability it possesses is a "moving equilibirum containing relations of forces favorable or unfavorable to this or that tendency."[57] If hegemony is neither fixed nor guaranteed, it can be fractured and challenged. These challenges, in fact, have to arise because of the tensions, contradictions, and increasingly visible inequalities produced by our dominant mode of production, distribution and consumption. Resistance to it, even when less than conscious, cannot always be incorporated back into dominant ideological forms.[58] Thus, even the educational system itself, in both its internal culture and its relations to the wider society, is not simply an instrument of domination in which powerful groups control less powerful ones. It is the *result* of a continuing struggle between and within dominant and dominated groups.[59]

Such internal criticism was not without impact. One participant in the debates over the past decade describes part of the changes in outlook in the following way.

> The dominant theoretical tendency in the critical social theory of education . . . stressed the extent to which education is social structurally determined, the depth of the operation of cultural domination through schooling, and the ways in which the culture and the microstructure of the school enable perpetuation of the macrostructural functions of capital accumulation and social legitimation. These initial insights [were] then modified. The central tenets in the model of political economy of schooling and of class cultural rule by the transmission of ideology as educational knowledge [were] significantly qualified. The concept of [economic] totality [was] replaced by an awareness of relative institutional autonomy. Structural integration [gave] way to the description of internal contradictions. Domination [was] mitigated by study of class conflict and student resistance within the school.[60]

Let us examine Wexler's historical points in somewhat more detail. While the history of this kind of critical work in the sociology of school knowledge has not necessarily been linear, it has in essence gone through a number of phases. The first was the introduction of the idea of the importance of studying the role of ideas and consciousness, not just the occupational outcomes of the school. In England, in particular, some of the more extreme versions of what was then called the "new sociology of education" seemed to assume that such "questioning of teachers' and others' taken for granted assumptions about prevailing curricular arrangements and pedagogical practices would not only transform education but also lead to wide-ranging changes in the wider society."[61] Though they were somewhat naïve politically, the impact of their analysis should not be dismissed. By legitimating the study of knowledge and consciousness, of culture, they set the stage for much that followed.

Stimulated in part by criticisms of such a "naïve possibilitarian" stand,[62] broader social theories were incorporated into the research program. These tended to be relatively crude correspondence theories, often based on or resembling that posited by Bowles and Gintis in *Schooling in Capitalist America*. This stressed the "determining effects of capitalist production relations on the nature of schooling and consciousness in capitalist societies."[63] As a consequence, somewhat less stress was placed on the power of cultural forms within the schools. Clearly, such a mechanistic theory could not be sustained for long, and in its place a more structuralist marxist orientation developed.[64] Rather than seeing the economy as determining everything else, with schools having little autonomy, theories of this kind described social formations as being made up of a *complex totality* of economic, political, and cultural/ideological practices. Unlike base/superstructure models, where "superstructural" institutions such as schools were seen as being wholly dependent upon and controlled by the economy, these theories held that these three sets of interrelated practices jointly create the conditions of existence for each other. Thus, the cultural sphere, for instance, has "relative autonomy" and has a "specific and crucial role in the functioning of the whole."[65]

This may seem quite abstract, but its implications proved to be quite consequential. It once again engendered a rapid increase in the study of cultural production and reproduction. For if ideology and culture are "conceived of as having a more real autonomy than merely that which is required for the reproduction of the relations of production," then the school curriculum and the day to day social relations in schools as sets of ideological practices become very significant in terms of possibilities for action[66] once again.

However, in the wake of the arguments made earlier about the possibly contradictory nature of the functions of schools and the nature of the conflicts within and about the institution, there was (and is) now a distinct difference. Whereas before one simply assumed a correspondence between economy and ideology, now it was realized that there might be disjunctions between the two. Reproduction was not all that was going on. Cuture could be, say, both reproducing *and* contradicting economic needs. Ideologies might be inherently contradictory

We want to stress the importance of the fact that there has been a rapid movement away from earlier dogmatic formulations.[67] As economism has been increasingly questioned, as simple base/superstructure models have come under closer scrutiny, a considerable degree of flexibility has resulted. This has been important in a number of ways. It has brought an element of serious self-criticism into the debate over the relationship among education, culture, and economy. By showing the relatively autonomous nature of culture, and by rejecting reductive approaches that merge everything into "functions" of a mode of production, we are much more able to unpack the specificities of each area we are studying. Finally, and perhaps most important for educators, these theoretical debates have had a crucial impact on what is seen as the efficacy of practical efforts.[68]

Let us be specific here. If education can be no more than an epiphenomenon tied directly to the requirements of an economy, then little can be done within education itself. It is a totally determined institution. However, if schools (and people) are not passive mirrors of an economy, but instead are active agents in the processes of reproduction and contestation of dominant social relations, then understanding what they do and acting upon them becomes of no small moment. For if schools are part of a "contested terrain," if they are part of a much larger set of political, economic, and cultural conflicts the outcomes of which are not naturally preordained to favor capital, then the hard and continuous day-to-day struggle at the level of curriculum and teaching practice is part of these larger conflicts as well. The key is linking these day-to-day struggles within the school to other action for a more progressive society in that wider arena.

This is notable tonic for the cynicism or sense that nothing can be done in schools that has pervaded a significant portion of the critically oriented educational community over the past decade or so. The very sense of the school's active role in recreating hegemonic relations that are constantly being threatened—and, hence, are in constant need of being rebuilt—instead opens up a whole arena for joint action with other progressive educators, parents, students, labor groups, women, people of color, and so on. Culture—commodified and lived—within the black box, then, takes an even more critical place. Investigating the role it plays and struggling to promote progressive elements of it becomes of great consequence.

Therefore, there has been even greater interest in culturalist studies. A large number of studies have begun again to pay considerable attention to how ideology works in cultural materials. This research focuses on commodified culture, on the "things" of culture, such as films, texts, novels, art, and so forth in an attempt to illuminate the ideological tensions, commitments, and contradictions in the material. Some of these investigations have been much more sophisticated than earlier approaches to ideological analysis and have sought to incorporate recent advances in cultural analysis drawn from work in semiotics and literary structuralism that has grown out of European work on ideology. A number of the chapters in this volume will exhibit some of this influence.

However, while these approaches are certainly better than what preceded them, we do need to remember that they study only one half of the cultural dynamic. As we argued, a thoroughgoing analysis of the relation between ideology and the knowledge and social relations of schooling must include not only investigations of the material of culture, but of subjectivity as well. Process must complement product. Without this dual focus, we run the risk of forgetting something very important, the actual activity of people.

Whitty directs our attention to some of these dangers.

Many post-Althusserian writers, engaged in an attempt to elucidate more clearly the specific characteristics of ideological practice, have drawn heavily on work in linguistics and semiotics and this has led to a variety of "structuralist" approaches to reading ideology, which focus on the ways in which texts produce meaning and position human subjects through their internal structures and rules rather than their overt content . . . Such studies often concern the ways in which texts address and position "ideal subjects," whereas [Richard] Johnson reminds us that the actual significance of the ideological work they do depends on their relationship to "attitudes and beliefs already lived. Ideologies never address ('interpellate') a 'naked subject.' . . . Concrete social individuals are always already constructed as culturally classed and sexed agents, already having a complexly formed subjectivity." . . . In structuralist analysis, there is always a danger of "remaining locked in the ideological forms themselves and *inferring* effects" [and] of underplaying the significance of the "*moment* of self creation, of the *affirmation* of belief or of the *giving* of consent." As such, they are in danger of producing too mechanistic a model of the formation of subjectivities.[69]

Thus, the active agent must take its place beside the subject who is "produced" by ideology. The tension between the two positions is constant and, in fact, is reproduced in the essays printed here. As a number of them demonstrate, there is a strong relationship between ideology and the knowledge and practices of education. Ideology does have power; it is shown both in what school material includes *and* in what it excludes. It does position people within wider relations of domination and exploitation. Yet, when lived out, it also often has elements of "good" as well as "bad" sense in it.[70] Side by side with beliefs and actions that maintain the dominance of powerful classes and groups, there will be elements of genuine (though perhaps incomplete) understanding; elements that see the differential benefits, power, and control and penetrate close to the heart of an unequal reality. Thus, while we must continue that part of our program that analyzes the ideological content of education, we should also remember that real people with real and complex histories interact with that content. The ideological outcome is always the result of that interaction, not an act of imposition.

This is a more dynamic way of looking at the question of ideological reproduction than has prevailed in the literature on ideology and schooling in the past. It provides the foundations for a more complete theory of how ideology functions. In the next section of this chapter we provide a concrete model that synthesizes the theoretical points we have just made.

Analyzing the Dynamics of Ideology

In the previous sections we pointed out the growing sophistication of our concepts of what schools do socially. We argued that approaches that focused only on economy and not on culture, or that dealt only with cultural products and not lived cultural processes, were incomplete. We also claimed that education was not a stable enterprise dominated by consensus, but instead was riven with ideological conflicts. These political, cultural and economic conflicts are dynamic. They are in something like constant motion, each often acting on the others and each stemming from structurally generated antagonisms, compromises, and struggles. In the context of our increased general understanding of the relationships between culture and the formation of, and/or resistance to, ideological hegemony, what does this mean for the more specific problem of ideology and education?

First, rather than an unidemensional theory in which economic form is determinate, society is conceived of as being made up of *three interrelated spheres*—the economic, cultural/ideological, and political.

Second, we need to be cautious about assuming that ideologies are only ideas held in one's head. They are better thought of less as things than as social processes.[71] Nor are ideologies linear configurations, simple processes that all necessarily work in the same direction or reinforce each other. Instead, these processes sometimes overlap, compete, drown out, and clash with each other. They are better represented, perhaps, by the "cacophany of sounds and signs of a big city street than by a text serenely communicating with the solitary reader, or the teacher or TV-personality addressing a quiet domesticated audience."[72]

That there may not be "a quiet domesticated audience" points to the dialectical character of ideology. This is brought out clearly if we think about the dual (actually opposite) sense of the word "subject." People can be both subjects of a ruler and the subjects of history. The word is used in different senses: the first passive, the second active. Thus, ideologies not only subject people to a preexisting social order. They also qualify members of that order for social action and change. In this way, ideologies function as much more than the cement that holds society together. They empower as well as depower.[73]

This process of empowering partly results from the fact that a number of elements or *dynamics* are usually present at the same time in any one instance. This is important. Ideological form is not reducible to class. Processes of gender, age, and race enter directly into the ideological moment.[74] It is actually out of the articulation with, clash among, or contradictions among and within, say, class, race, and sex that ideologies are lived in one's day-to-day life.

In order to unpack how ideologies work, then, we have to consider each of the spheres and the dynamics that operate within them. Figure 1 may be helpful in conceptualizing the intricate connections among these elements.

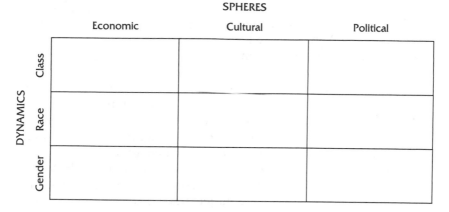

Fig. 1. Dimensions of ideological production.

As the figure shows, each sphere of social life is constituted by the dynamics of class, race, and gender. Each of these dynamics, and each of these spheres, has its own internal history *in relation to* the others. Each dynamic is found in each of the spheres. Thus, to give an example, it is impossible to completely comprehend class relations in capitalism without seeing how capital used patriarchal social relations in its organization. The current deskilling of women clerical workers through the introduction of word-processing technology and the overall loss of jobs that will result among working class women offers one instance where class and gender interact in the economy. In schools, the fact that elementary-school teachers are mostly women who historically have come from a particular segment of the population again illuminates the dual dynamics of class and gender. The rejection of schooling by many black and brown youths in our urban centers, and the sense of pride that many unmarried minority high-school girls have in their ability to bear a child are the result of complex interconnections among the histories of class, race, and gender oppressions and struggles at the level of lived culture.

Examples like these could be multiplied. Our major point is to document the relational quality of ideology. Schools are part of the economic, political, and cultural spheres. The needs of these may not always completely overlap. The dynamics that make up these spheres, therefore, also interact in everyday activity in schools. They, too, may not always reinforce each other. This makes ideological analyses a complicated endeavor since even unpacking one ideological process like that of gender is quite difficult. Integrating the others into it may be calling for something that is exceptionally hard.

Because of this complexity, no one study can fully incorporate all of the points we have raised here. Each of the following chapters, though, provides a detailed examination of how particular aspects of ideology work in schools. Yet, while we have been at pains to lay out a model of how one might best think about integrating various studies of the dynamics of ideology, it would be unrealistic to expect that all of the authors included here share a single, unified theory of how and why ideology functions in schools. Given the recent ferment within the literature on cultural and economic reproduction and given the fact that a number of the essays are meant to be suggestive and exploratory, any such consensus—except at the most general level—would be artificial.

Consensus may be lacking in another way, as well. If ideological outcomes are indeed the result of interaction between commodified and lived culture, between object and subject, then this book should reflect that. Some readers may disagree with the arguments presented by certain authors. Total agreement would be a surprise; and it would not necessarily be good. We began this chapter with a recognition that education itself is a contested terrain, an arena of intense and varied conflicts. We believe that if these areas of conflict are illuminated, if theoretic, empirical, and political disagreements are generated by the studies included in this volume, then it will have served part of the purpose for which it was published—to continue the critical process of placing the practices and theories that dominate schooling at the very center of educational debate.

There is, of course, a real danger that should not go unexplored. While we have argued here that it is very important to investigate the ideological "presence" in the official knowledge and the official and the unofficial social relations in schools, it is all to easy to transform these issues into wholly academic ones. Academic study of the problems we face is often both stimulating and necessary and we would be the last to deny its value. Yet, unlike many other fields, as well as being an area of scholarship education entails a practice. We are called upon to act—to act responsibly and with all of the wisdom we can gather, but to act nonetheless.

This has significant implications for how we should read the chapters included here. All of them choose one portion of how the knowledge and practices of schools work to produce ideological meanings and forms of consciousness. Some devote their attention to the reproductive power of ideology, to how it may subject people and incorporate them into relations of exploitation and domination. Others highlight the way ideological processes also empower people, and how resistance, contestation, and contradiction may operate in that setting. Some stress one dynamic; others show connections among, say, class and gender. At the same time, however, each and every one of the authors is interested in more than merely understanding what schools do and in who benefits in what ways from them. They have a fundamental interest in identifying political and cultural struggles that are emerging from these practices now, or that may do so in the future.[75] Hence, even though answers to how and what schools do ideologically are not preordained in the minds of these researchers, an interest in emancipatory practice guides them. They are all engaged. The issues that they want us to deal with are not, and should not be, only of scholarly import. Raising them is seen as part of the long and hard political work of contesting dominant relations of power and control and of finding points where action by progressive educators, women, people of color, and others can be effective. Criticism of existing practices is done not for criticism's sake, but to develop the conceptual, empirical, textual, historical, and ethnographic tools necessary to begin to see what needs to be done.

Research at the Level of Practice

As we argued earlier, there has been a dual focus in what might be called a critical culturalist problematic within sociological studies of the school. Culture has been analyzed as both a lived experience and as a commodity. Lived culture refers to culture as it is produced in ongoing interactions and as a terrain in which class, race, and gender meanings and antagonisms are lived out. Here the school is seen as an arena where tensions and contradictions are worked through, rather than as a place where individuals who fit neatly within an unequal social structure are produced. Ethnographic investigations allow us to capture the creation of ideologies by enabling us to explore on a day-to-day basis the context within which practices, meanings, and social relations are lived. The idea of lived culture is more dialectical than earlier notions of the hidden curriculum. By focusing on culture as it is produced, investigators analyze the way in which class, race, and gendered persons potentially act back on meanings embedded within institutions rather than passively accept such meanings. As we argued earlier, the lived culture of teachers and students in schools provides a key to how reproduction occurs as well as pointing to elements of resistance that may have emancipatory potential. Chapters by Everhart, Gitlin, Valli, Weis, and King in this volume focus specifically on the lived culture of teachers or students within classrooms and schools.

The second focus in culturalist studies has been on culture as a commodity, as a set of artifacts produced for use. The starting point of most of these analyses is articulated by Michael F. D. Young. He argues that there is a "dialectical relationship between access to power and the opportunity to legitimate dominant categories, and the processes by which the availability of such categories to some groups enable them to assert power and control over others."[76] In other words, what counts as school knowledge (here we are speaking of knowledge in its commodified form) tends to embody the interests and culture of the group or groups who have the power to distribute and legitimate their world view through educational institutions. With Young, Bernstein, Bourdieu and others, then, the studies in the next section of this book argue that the organization of knowledge, the form of its transmission, and the assessment of its acquisition are factors in the reproduction of class relationships in advanced industrial societies. Chapters in this section by Anyon, Taxel, Beyer, McNeil, and Apple examine commodified culture as it exists in educational institutions.

We do not mean to suggest here that social interests are always represented in the curriculum in a straightforward fashion. As argued earlier, this is sometimes the case; often it is not. Furthermore, commodified and lived cuture, although they may be separated for analytical purposes, are, in fact, linked. Lived culture *must* be understood at least in part as a response to particular forms of commodified culture and to the way in which this culture is distributed differentially to students of different races, classes, and gender. While the authors in this book tend to concentrate on either lived or commodified culture, they share a concern for both focuses.

While we separate the two focuses of cultural study for analytic purposes, we urge investigators to consider carefully the dialectical relationship between them. Not to do so is to risk missing how the way in which groups struggle against particular meanings opens up possibilities for action. We must be careful, however, not to romanticize resistance. While many of the authors stress the potential for class, race, and gendered persons to act back on meanings embedded within educational institutions, the implications of such practices for the reproduction or transformation of broader social and economic relations deserves further study. As Willis has shown, resistance can be progressive on one level and yet can serve to reproduce at an even deeper level the social relations of production that maintain a capitalist economy. As one of us has demonstrated elsewhere, this is as true for the lived culture of workers as it is for students.[77]

For those reasons, we have argued here that cultural and economic reproduction, insofar as it occurs in schools, is a complex and tentative process. There are reproductive and nonreproductive tendencies in both commodified and lived culture and little is totally reproductive regardless of its intent. Ideological hegemony is not and cannot be fully secure.

Since we believe that the cultural sphere is relatively autonomous and does embody both reproductive and transformative elements, we are optimistic that culture in schools and elsewhere can be worked on, and with, to encourage a more just and humane society. No serious action in schools is possible, however, without a more thorough understanding of life inside the black box and the connections that exist between that life and structures of domination and exploitation outside the school. The chapters that follow provide significant steps on the path toward such informed action.

Notes

1. For a more extensive analysis of this and other research approaches, see Michael W. Apple, *Ideology and Curriculum* (Boston: Routledge and Kegan Paul, 1979).

2. Jerome Karabel and A. H. Halsey, eds., *Power and Ideology in Education* (New York: Oxford University Press, 1977), p. 61.

3. David Hogan, "Education and Class Formation: The Peculiarities of the Americans," in Michael W. Apple, ed., *Cultural and Economic Reproduction in Education: Essays on Class, Ideology and the State* (Boston: Routledge and Kegan Paul, 1982), pp. 52–53.

4. Michael W. Apple and Joel Taxel, "Ideology and the Curriculum," in Anthony Hartnett, ed., *The Social Sciences in Education* (London: Heinemann, 1982). We have purposely set off the word "functions," given the debate over the utility of the concept of functionality itself, since it often implies an endlessly reproductive process that is relatively conflict-free with little chance of change. As will be seen later in this chapter, we have fundamental disagreements with this position. For criticisms of functionalist logic in education, see Apple, *Cultural and Economic Reproduction*. A sophisticated version of functionalist analysis is defended in G. A. Cohen, *Karl Marx's Theory of History: A Defense* (Princeton: Princeton University Press, 1978).

5. See, for example, Randall Collins, *The Credential Society* (New York: Academic Press, 1979); John Ogbu, *Minority Education and Caste* (New York: Academic Press, 1978); and Manuel Castells, *The Economic Crisis and American Society* (Princeton: Princeton University Press, 1980).

6. Pierre Bourdieu and Jean Claude Passeron, *Reproduction in Education, Society and Culture* (London: Sage, 1977), and Basil Bernstein, *Class, Codes and Control*, vol. 3 (Boston: Routledge and Kegan Paul, 1977).

7. This has been most systematically argued in Samuel Bowles and Herbert Gintis, *Schooling in Capitalist America* (New York: Basic Books, 1976). There are a number of inadequacies, both theoretical and empirical, in this position. See, for example, Michael W. Apple, *Education and Power* (Boston: Routledge and Kegan Paul, 1982) and Michael R. Olneck and David B. Bills, "What Makes Sammy Run: An Empirical Assessment of the Bowles-Gintis Correspondence Theory," *American Journal of Education* 89 (November 1980): 27–61.

8. Apple, *Education and Power*; Apple, *Cultural and Economic Reproduction in Education*, especially chap. 1; and Stuart Hall, "Rethinking the 'Base and Superstructure' Metaphor," in Jon Bloomfield, ed., *Class, Hegemony and Party* (London: Lawrence and Wishart, 1977), pp. 43–72.

9. John Meyer, "The Effects of Education as an Institution," *American Journal of Sociology* 83 (July 1977): 55–77.

10. Vicente Navarro, *Medicine Under Capitalism* (New York: Neale Watson, 1976), p. 91. See also James O'Connor, *The Fiscal Crisis of the State* (New York: St. Martin's Press, 1973).

11. Manuel Castells, *The Economic Crisis and American Society*, especially chaps. 3–5.

12. C. B. Macpherson, "Do We Need a Theory of the State?" in Roger Dale, et al., eds., *Education and the State, Volume 1* (Sussex: Falmer Press, 1981), p. 65.

13. We are indebted to Walter Feinberg for part of this argument. See also David Noble, *American By Design* (New York: Knopf, 1977); Apple, *Ideology and Curriculum*; and Apple, *Education and Power*, chap. 2.

14. Apple, *Ideology and Curriculum*.

15. Paul Willis, *Learning to Labour* (Westmead, England: Saxon House, 1977).

16. Apple, *Education and Power*.

17. Roger Dale, "Education and the Capitalist State," in Apple, ed., *Cultural and Economic Reproduction in Education*, p. 137.

18. Erik Olin Wright, "Class and Occupation," *Theory and Society* 9 (January 1980): 177–214.

19. Michael W. Apple, "The New Sociology of Education: Analyzing Cultural and Economic Reproduction," *Harvard Educational Review* 48 (November 1978): 495–503.

20. Erik Olin Wright, *Class Structure and Income Determination* (New York: Academic Press, 1979). p. 77.

21. Alan C. Kerckhoff, ed. *Research in Sociology of Education and Socialization: Longitudinal Perspectives on Educational Attainment* (Greenwich: JAI Press, 1980), p. viii.

22. Much of the recent work is summarized in Kerckhoff, *Research in Sociology of Education and Socialization*, a valuable book within the context of this research program.

23. The interested reader might want to follow up the argument about how class should be interpreted by looking at, say, recent Marxist criticism of status attainment research such as the work of Erik Olin Wright or some of the historical and empirical work on class formation, culture, and the labor process in Europe and the United States. See, for example, Nicos Poulantzas, *Classes in Contemporary Capitalism* (London: New Left Books, 1975); Richard Edwards, *Contested Terrain* (New York: Basic Books, 1979); and John Clarke, Chas Critcher, and Richard Johnson, eds., *Working Class Culture* (London: Hutchinson, 1979). For an historical analysis of the role of education in class formation in the United States, see David Hogan, "Education and Class Formation: The Peculiarities of the Americans," in Apple, *Cultural and Economic Reproduction in Education*, pp. 32–78.

24. Wright, *Class Structure and Income Determination*, p. 70.

25. Ibid.

26. Wright, "Class and Occupation."

27. Wright, *Class Structure and Income Determination*, p. 126.

28. Ibid., p. 165.

29. Ibid., p. 225.

30. Ibid., p. 195.

31. Ibid., p. 216.

32. Ibid., p. 201. See also, Women's Studies Group, *Women Take Issue*

(London: Hutchinson, 1978) and Michael Reich, *Racial Inequality* (Princeton: Princeton University Press, 1981).

33. Christopher Jencks, et al., *Who Gets Ahead?* (New York: Basic Books, 1979), pp. 174–75. It is important to note that nearly all of these studies have been of *men*. They, therefore, underrepresent and in part reproduce the structure of patriarchal domination in society.

34. Bowles and Gintis, *Schooling in Capitalist America*.

35. This point has been discussed at much greater length in Apple, *Education and Power*.

36. See William Sewell and Robert Hauser, in Kerckhoff, *Research in Sociology of Education and Socialization*. See also the interesting article by Alan C. Kerckhoff, "The Status Attainment Process: Socialization or Allocation?" *Social Forces* 55 (December 1976), 368–81. See also Lois Weis, "Educational Outcomes and School Processes," in Philip Altbach, Robert Arnove, and Gail Kelly, eds., *Comparative Education*: New York: Macmillan, 1982).

37. Peter Woods, *The Divided School* (Boston: Routledge and Kegan Paul, 1979), p. 2.

38. Geoff Whitty, "Sociology and the Problem of Radical Educational Change," in Michael Flude and John Ahier, eds., *Educability, Schools and Ideology* (London: Croom Helm, 1974), p. 125.

39. See Gail Kelly and Ann Nihlen, "Schooling and the Reproduction of Patriarchy," in Apple, *Cultural and Economic Reproduction in Education*, pp. 162–80.

40. A similar point is made by Anthony Green. See his "Extended Review," *British Journal of Sociology of Education* 1 (March 1980), 121–28.

41. Important here are Clarke, Critcher and Johnson, *Working Class Culture*, and Women's Studies Group, *Women Take Issue*.

42. See Karabel and Halsey, *Power and Ideology in Education*, especially chap. 1; Apple, *Ideology and Curriculum*; P. C. Grierson, "An Extended Review of *Knowledge and Control, Explorations in the Politics of School Knowledge*, and *Society, State and Schooling*," *Educational Studies* 4 (March 1978): 67–84; Michael W. Apple, "Curriculum as Ideological Selection," *Comparative Education Review* 20 (June 1976): 209–15; and Michael W. Apple, "The New Sociology of Education: Analyzing Cultural and Economic Reproduction," *Harvard Educational Review* 48 (November 1978):495–503.

43. Michael F. D. Young, ed., *Knowledge and Control* (London: Macmillan, 1971), Basil Bernstein, *Class, Codes, and Control*, vol. 3, and Bourdieu and Passeron, *Reproduction in Education, Society and Culture*.

44. Apple, *Ideology and Curriculum*.

45. Young, *Knowledge and Control*.

46. Michael W. Apple, "The Process and Ideology of Valuing in Educational Settings," in Michael W. Apple, Michael Subkoviak, and Henry Lufler, Jr., eds., *Educational Evaluation: Analysis and Responsibility* (Berkeley: McCutchan, 1974), pp. 3–34.

47. Philip Wexler, "Change: Social, Cultural and Educational," in *New Directions in Education: Critical Perspectives*, Department of Social Foundations and Comparative Education Center, State University of New York, Occasional Paper no. 8, (Buffalo, 1981), p. 2.

48. Young, *Knowledge and Control*.

49. Philip Wexler, "Body and Soul: Sources of Social Change and Strategies for Education," *British Journal of Sociology of Education* 2, no. 3 (1981): 259.

50. Chantal Mouffe, "Hegemony and Ideology in Gramsci," in Chantal Mouffe, ed., *Gramsci and Marxist Theory* (Boston: Routledge and Kegan Paul, 1979), p. 171. See also Louis Althusser, "Ideology and Ideological State Apparatuses," *Lenin and Philosophy, and Other Essays* (London: New Left Books, 1971). As we shall see later, this position has been strongly criticized both politically as well as conceptually.

51. See especially Bernstein's final chapter in *Class, Codes, and Control, Volume 3*. He has recently published an even more ambitious attempt to develop a theory linking class, culture, and ideology. See Basil Bernstein, "Codes, Modalities and the Process of Cultural Reproduction," in Apple, *Cultural and Economic Reproduction in Education*, pp. 304–55.

52. Apple, *Ideology and Curriculum*, p. 14.

53. We shall argue later that ideology is *not* reducible to class dynamics. Any attempt to do so neglects the impressive contributions made by feminist criticisms of orthodox Marxist research and theories. See Women's Studies Group, *Women Take Issue*, and Madeleine Arnot, *Class, Gender and Education* (Milton Keynes, England: The Open University Press, 1981).

54. Philip Wexler, *Critical Social Psychology*.

55. For further discussion of the complicated issue of ideological "representation" in a text, see Michele Barrett, et al., eds., *Ideology and Cultural Production* (New York: St. Martin's Press, 1979), and Colin Sumner, *Reading Ideologies* (New York: Macmillan, 1979).

56. These criticisms have been discussed at much greater length in Apple, *Education and Power*, and Wexler, "Structure, Text and Subject." See also Henry Giroux, *Ideology, Culture and the Process of Schooling* (Philadelphia: Temple University Press, 1981).

57. Dick Hebdige, *Subculture: The Meaning of Style* (London: Methuen, 1980), p. 16.

58. We do not mean to imply that such challenges will always be progressive. The possibility that they will not be is raised in David Plotke, "The United States in Transition: Toward a New Order?" *Socialist Review* 10 (November-December 1980): 71–123, and David Plotke, "The Politics of Transition: The United States in Transition, II," *Socialist Review* 11 (January-February 1981): 21–72.

59. It is important to stress the fact that educational policies and practices often result from conflict between segments of dominant classes. The way the state is acting to rebuild hegemonic control in the current economic, political, and cultural crisis is examined in Apple, *Education and Power* and Michael W. Apple, "Common Curriculum and State Control," *Discourse* 2, no. 4 (1982): 1–10.

60. Wexler, "Body and Soul," p. 248. While Wexler has been involved in this tradition of critical culturalist analysis, he is critical of a number of tendencies within it and argues that they must be superseded given current economic, political and cultural conditions. See also Philip Wexler and Tony Whitson, "Hegemony and Education," unpublished paper, University of Rochester, 1981.

61. Society, Education and the State Course Team, *The Politics of Cultural Production* (Milton Keynes, England: The Open University Press, 1981), Introduction, p. 3.

62. For criticisms of the political position of the new sociology of education, see Whitty, "Sociology and the Problem of Radical Educational Change"; Jack Demaine, "On the New Sociology of Education," *Economy and Society* 6 (May 1977): 111–44; Rachel Sharp and Anthony Green, *Education and Social Control* (Boston: Routledge and Kegan Paul, 1974); Grierson, "An Extended Review";

and Gerald Bernbaum, *Knowledge and Ideology in the Sociology of Education* (New York: Macmillan, 1977).

63. Society, Education, and the State Course Team, *Politics of Cultural Production*, Introduction, p. 3.

64. Bowles and Gintis themselves have since criticized their initial work. See Herbert Gintis and Samuel Bowles, "Contradiction and Reproduction in Educational Theory," in Len Barton, Roland Meighan, and Stephen Walker, eds., *Schooling, Ideology and the Curriculum* (Barcombe, England: Falmer Press, 1981), pp. 51–65.

65. Society, Education and the State Course Team, *Politics of Cultural Production*, Introduction, p. 3.

66. Ibid., p. 4.

67. The conceptual and political roots of this movement are described in greater depth in Apple, *Cultural and Economic Reproduction in Education.*

68. Apple, *Education and Power*, especially chaps. 1 and 6.

69. Geoff Whitty, "Ideology, Politics and Curriculum," in Society, Education and the State Course Team. *The Politics of Cultural Production*, p. 16. See also Wexler, "Structure, Text and Subject."

70. Richard Johnson, "Histories of Culture/Theories of Ideology" in Barrett, et al., eds., *Ideology and Cultural Production*, p. 43.

71. Goran Therborn, *The Ideology of Power and the Power of Ideology* (London: New Left Books, 1980), p. vii.

72. Ibid., p. viii.

73. Ibid., p. vii.

74. Ibid., p. 26. See also Therborn's interesting discussion of the necessity of linking analyses of class ideologies with those of male chauvinism, ibid., p. 38.

75. That this interest extends well beyond the contributors to this book is documented in Society, Education and the State Course Team, *Politics of Cultural Production*, Introduction, p. 4.

76. Michael F. D. Young, "An Approach to the Study of Curricula as Socially Organized Knowledge," in Young, *Knowledge and Control*, p. 8.

77. Apple, *Education and Power*, pp. 66–90.

IDEOLOGY AND COMMODIFIED CULTURE

CHAPTER 2

Workers, Labor and Economic History, and Textbook Content

JEAN ANYON

It has often been argued theoretically that school knowledge contributes to the reproduction of an unequal social system. Pierre Bourdieu, for example, put forth the view that school knowledge expresses and legitimates the interests of powerful groups in society. He argued that elite knowledge and culture are forms of symbolic capital. The unequal distribution of this capital in society reproduces on a cultural level the unequal distribution of capital on the economic level and thus increases the power of elites. Intellectual traditions and patterns of thought that provide competence in elite culture are not only legitimated but transmitted unequally by school. Curriculum knowledge contains, moreover, ideologies that misrepresent and conceal inequalities in the structure of relationships on which social and cultural power is based, and disguises the contribution of schools to the reproduction of these relations and to the power of dominant groups.[1]

The purpose of this chapter is to investigate empirically—through an analysis of United States history textbooks—the possibility that an ideology is expressed in the curriculum content that might, despite the claim of objectivity, serve the interests of some groups in society over others. Ideology is defined here as an explanation or interpretation of social reality that, although presented as objective, is demonstrably partial in that it expresses the social priorities of certain political, economic, or other groups. Ideologies are weapons of group interest; they justify and rationalize; they legitimate group power, activities and needs. An ideological version of a historical period, for example, involves the selection and organization of information to provide an interpretation of social events and hierarchies that will predispose attitudes and behaviors in favor of certain groups.[2] When an ideological description is presented as objective or socially neutral, it is more convincing. Ideological descriptions and definitions—if believed—influence one's view of reality and facilitate the use of power by the groups favorably presented. Group interest can be reflected in textbooks by obvious distortions or hidden assumptions. Ideological selection can be a matter of omitting facts or of subtle distinctions and emphases. If a single ideological perspective governs school history textbooks, it can acquire the status of truth, and will be less likely to be subjected to scrutiny in classrooms, or compared with other points of view.

The political importance of an assessment of curriculum content and social ideology is that any attempt to counteract the contribution of schools to the reproduction of an unequal social order must be grounded in an understanding of objective and subjective conditions. A struggle against the ideological domination of students by curriculum knowledge, therefore, must include an accurate assessment of what school knowledge is commonly made available to students, and what ideological predispositions regarding attitudes and behavior it may imply. The possible ideological effects on students will be assessed after the textbook content has been examined.

Methodology

This study used seventeen well-known, secondary-school United States history textbooks that appear on board of education lists of "Books Approved for Use"'in both of two large, urban school systems in the Northeast (see appendix). The school systems were chosen because they have substantial numbers of both minority and white students from poor and working-class families. For many of these students, these history textbooks are likely to be the major source of information concerning United States history.

The seventeen textbooks vary little from publisher to publisher and from year to year. Although some have more information on blacks and women than others and some include reproductions of primary source documents while others do not, all of them cover about the same set of persons, places, and events. All use a common descriptive vocabulary when they discuss political and economic leaders, institutions, and social events. Finally, the judgments they make about what constitute social problems and solutions are also remarkably similar.

The content areas of the history textbooks to be analyzed are economic and labor union developments during the period of rapid industrialization and social change from the Civil War to World War I. These developments involved substantial conflicts of interest and struggles for social power. In reports of historical developments that involve group conflict it is possible to ascertain whose viewpoint is provided, and to assess if that viewpoint legitimates the prerogatives of any group at the expense of any other.

Although it would have been equally appropriate to have analyzed the treatment of black history, women's history, or any other topic involving conflict between groups, I have chosen to analyze economic and labor history, partly because it has been largely ignored by those who have recently examined curriculum content, and partly because the relationships and social conflicts between employers and employees reveal basic configurations of resource and power.

In each textbook, all the chapters that pertained to the period between 1865 and 1917 were examined to determine whether the information they contained was in any way biased. Those years constituted a crucial period in the growth of the United States economy. Mechanization and expansion of the productive forces, and the consolidation of industries into large corporations (for example, Standard Oil, Western Electric, and U.S. Steel) transformed an agricultural, entrepreneurial economy into a powerful corporate one. By the beginning of World War I, industrialization and incorporation had produced considerable wealth for some, an affluent middle class, and economic and social problems that have endured: the urban poor, and persistent unemployment; labor-management conflict; low wages and poor working conditions for many of the nonunionized;[3] and the control of a major portion of the economic resources by a relatively small number of corporations.[4]

Economic Developments

All the textbook discussions of this period of expansion include the extension of the railroads, communications, and industry, new inventions, and the contributions of the industrialists to the cheap and efficient production of consumer goods. The aspects of these developments considered salutary are emphasized, and their discussion consumes substantial portions of the chapters.[5] Other developments, such as economic concentration and workers' problems, are only briefly discussed and the solutions proposed for them support the activities of some social groups and not others.

All the books consider business monopolies and trusts to be a problem.[6] The way they treat social responses to this problem, however, actually disguises and rationalizes the continuation of economic concentration. Several books grossly overestimate the effectiveness of antitrust and similar legislation. The following passage, for example, does not mention that many of the legal steps alluded to failed:

During the seven years he served as President [Theodore] Roosevelt brought 44 lawsuits against the trusts. The two Presidents who followed him rolled up even better records. William Howard Taft took 90 monopolies to court. Woodrow Wilson busted even more trusts. . . . But it was Teddy Roosevelt who blazed the trail. . . . Trusts and monopolies were broken up. Then the great good that industry had done for our country carried us forward to better times for everybody.[7]

While this and two additional textbooks make exaggerated claims,[8] the fourteen remaining books are more circumspect.[9] Each provides several pages of description (very often in favorable terms, as in the quotation above) of the activities and intentions of "trust-buster" Teddy Roosevelt and the legislation passed under Woodrow Wilson.[10] These descriptions are usually part of, or accompanied by, passages in which the Progressive Era itself is lauded as a period of social progress and reform. Only a few lines mentioning that the trust-busting laws were either narrowly construed by the courts or largely unenforced can be found interspersed with descriptions of implied good intentions, and these brief statements are offered without any comment about implications or consequences.[11]

By attaching value to only partly successful legislation, and by omitting discussion of the actual results, the textbooks encourage belief in the notion that industrial concentration—monopolies, holding companies, and trusts—will be prevented or controlled through legislation. In this way, they indirectly facilitate economic concentration.

All but one of the textbooks describe the laws and the period itself in terms of reform and progress.[12] This vocabulary is common in descriptions of the politics of the time, but it does not represent the only interpretation, nor is it politically neutral. With respect to trust-busting, for example, the labels "progress" and "reform" suggest responsive political institutions and good intentions on the part of political and economic leaders, and so serve to rationalize the failure of the legislation to control powerful economic groups. These consequences of the textbook vocabulary become clear when other, contrasting labels that might have been used are considered.

Some historians have suggested that the antitrust legislation was not intended to radically alter the activities of big business, but was a politically conservative response by political and economic leaders to popular pressure for more fundamental change.[13] They argue that the new laws were not imposed on business, but were designed with the explicit cooperation and advice of various national business groups.[14] Further, since the laws did not remove power from big business, and since other laws of the period did not change unpopular economic inequities, the primary purpose of these laws can be seen not as reform, but as the maintenance of social and economic inequality. The legislation was designed to ensure the legitimacy, and thus the stability and survival, of industrial capitalism and the power of the large corporation.

One need not agree with this whole argument. However, the use of the words "conservative" and "maintenance" to describe trust-busting activities and their consequences highlights the ameliorative connotations of the labels "reform" and "progress." Selective use of vocabulary, then, provides ideological support for the activities of powerful economic and political groups.

The textbooks discuss only briefly economic developments detrimental to the industrial worker of the period, including low wages and poor working conditions.[15] While most of them do express or imply sympathy for the plight of the worker during the period of industrialization, the explanations they offer actually justify the workers' position of suffering. The most commonly used explanations are along the following lines:

> After the Civil War several developments influenced the position of workers. First . . . millions of immigrants settled in large cities. These immigrants formed a ready supply of unskilled labor and were willing to work for low wages under poor working conditions. Second, the relation between employer and employee was changing . . . [A]s Theodore Roosevelt observed: "A few generations before, the boss had known every man in his shop. . . . In the small establishment there had been a friendly human relationship between employer and employee. . . . There was no such relation between the great railway magnates . . . and the one hundred and fifty thousand men who worked in the mines. . . . In addition, work became increasingly mechanized, with the worker tending to function like a machine.[16]

These explanations are not inaccurate, but they tell only one side of the story. For example, attributing low wages to the willingness of unskilled immigrants blames the victims of low wages for their own plight. Some scholars have argued, to the contrary, that immigrant workers were used by employers to keep wages as low as possible, just as blacks, women, and other underemployed groups of workers are today. They argue that industrialists at the turn of the century were aware of the benefits of an abundant supply of immigrant workers and took steps to increase the number available.[17]

By alleging a causal relationship between the attitudes of immigrants and the position of workers, however, the textbooks divert the reader's attention from the owners' activities and intentions, and from the otherwise obvious economic relationship between low wages and increased profits. Of the four textbooks that do include the profit motive as one of the causes of low wages during the period,[18] two suggest that it was an evil of industrialization and no longer causes problems,[19] and the other two argue that it was used in excess by only a few businessmen, "certain hard-driving manufacturers . . . [who] thought that wages . . . must be cut to the bone in order to raise profits."[20] More commonly, however, the relation between the activities of immigrants and the disadvantaged position of workers as presented in these textbooks disguises and rationalizes the relationship between increased owners' profits and decreased workers' wages.

The second point made by most textbooks (and also represented in the quotation above) is that poor working conditions stemmed from the inability of owners to care for workers because of the increased size of the firm.[21] The source of this argument can be traced to a popular belief expressed by businessmen at the turn of the century. Industrialists often lamented the loss of personal contact between worker and owner, and argued that such contact would benefit worker, society, and industry.[22] This argument motivated companies to sponsor educational activities for employees—lectures and classes in industrial efficiency, civil and moral responsibility, and family life. These activities, although allegedly for the benefit of the workers, have been described by some scholars as providing a mechanism by which employers could instill self-control in vast numbers of employees with whom they, as "bosses," no longer had intimate personal contact.

Critics have also argued that the machinelike quality of work that the textbooks attribute to mechanization was largely the result of business practices designed to make industrial production more efficient. Many measures (for example, the scientific management of work) increased worker alienation by delegating to managers all responsibility for planning and for decisions formerly made by the workers themselves, including decisions regarding the production processes to be used and the type and pace of the daily work to be done.[23]

These alternative arguments could have been used by the textbook authors to help explain the problems of workers. None is impartial, but together with those offered in the texts, they would ensure a more balanced discussion.

Radical Solutions to Economic Problems

All the textbooks support governmental reform as an appropriate mechanism for bringing about economic change by denying either subtly or overtly the legitimacy of more radical methods of change. Although socialism has been a popular response to industrialization in virtually every capitalist country in the world, and although the American Socialist party at the turn of the century was regarded as significant by dominant political and economic groups, twelve of the books do not describe the

American Socialist party or its platform, nor do they mention radical sympathies among various groups in the population.[24] Of the five books that discuss the Socialist party, all but one contain disparaging comments about the intentions of socialists, and minimize their influence. They argue, as do the twelve books that do not describe the party, that only a few people were attracted to radical ideas;[25] one implies that honest men were not.[26]

The emphasis in the textbooks on the insignificance of the socialist movement in the United States can be contrasted with accounts of the period more sympathetic to the goal of redistribution of economic power and ownership.[27] These treat socialism at the turn of the century as an important indication of social protest and dissent, citing as proof the popularity of socialist leaders such as Eugene Debs, Bill Haywood, and Elizabeth Gurley Flynn.

Labor Unions

The period of rapid industrialization between the Civil War and World War I was one of intense and often violent conflict between business interests and the new industrial work force. There are various ways in which this conflict might be presented. It might be described as a rebellion by workers against industrial exploitation and economic inequality. From this perspective, one would emphasize strikes and lockouts, focusing perhaps on those confrontations that were successful from labor's point of view. One might also describe problems common to all workers and provide details on the union activities that attempted to unite workers to counter the challenge of industrialists.

A second approach might present labor unions as illegitimate organizations that interfere with an owner's right to hire and fire, and workers' rights to work where and for whom they please. Adherents of this view might describe the strikes and labor-organizing efforts of the period as the result of "foreign" or anti-American influence, government regulation of industry as a violation of individual rights and the principles of free enterprise, and unions as making unreasonable and inflationary demands.

Still another view might describe labor unions as necessary for the protection of the rights of workers in a democracy. The interests of all parties are supposedly served by the peaceful resolution of conflict. Such a narrative might criticize confrontation, such as strikes, and sanction the use of political and social avenues for reaching consensus, emphasizing the activities of unions that respected the prevailing arrangements of power and recourse and were willing to operate within those constraints.

Despite the variety of possible descriptions, textbook characterizations of labor history are strikingly narrow and unsympathetic to the more radical segments of the union movement. The average length of the section in the texts on labor history is six pages. Although there were more than 30,000 strikes during the period,[28] fourteen of the seventeen books choose from among the same three strikes, ones that were especially violent and were failures from labor's point of view: the railroad strike of 1877, and Homestead strike of 1892, the Pullman strike of 1894.[29] Each of these strikes represented a severe setback for the labor movement, leading either to the demise of a particular union or to the withdrawal of support by the middle class.[30]

The authors of the textbooks may have chosen these particular strikes to demonstrate the difficulties faced by early unions; several imply that these strikes show what labor was up against. Whatever their intentions, however, the effect is to cast doubt on striking as a valid course of action. The historically inaccurate impression is given that strikes fail as a method of recourse. Nine books go further, stating that strikes only hurt labor's cause, are costly, and result in violence.[31]

One successful strike is discussed in fifteen of the books, although usually in accounts of Progressive reform rather than in the section on labor history.[32] This is the anthracite-coal strike of 1902, which was resolved in favor of the workers by the intervention of President Theodore Roosevelt. Thirteen of the textbooks state that this strike showed that President Roosevelt and the federal government treated workers fairly, suggesting that strikes are only successful if government intervenes, and that government mediation is a fruitful and more appropriate recourse in labor disputes.[33]

This suggestion is strengthened in textbook discussions of labor laws, which are also most often found in the sections on Progressive reform. State or federal laws passed to improve conditions for working men, women, and children are described in these terms: "State laws . . . prohibited the employment of children. . . . More than ½ of the states limited the work week . . . to 60 hours . . . The [third] type of . . . law established a minimum wage."[34] Some historians have argued that this legislation did not substantially alter the lives of most workers, citing the fact that much of it was declared unconstitutional. For example, the Supreme Court declared the laws against child labor unconstitutional in 1918, and again in 1919.[35]

Fourteen of the textbooks, however, present the labor laws either without noting that they were overturned, or as examples of social progress even though they were overturned.[36] None mentions that many businesses simply disregarded the laws, nor asks what the implications are when the Supreme Court decides that laws allegedly passed to con-strain business powers are unconstitutional. The omission of accounts of successful strikes and the implied success of political avenues for resolution of conflict suggest a desire to discourage conflict and to facilitate consensus.[37]

The only labor organization of the turn of the century to be emphasized in textbook discussions is the American Federation of Labor (AFL). Not coincidentally, this was also the only major labor group of the time to accept the new corporate order and advocate bargaining and union contracts rather than confrontation and changes in the social structure. As president of the AFL, Samuel Gompers argued against confrontation with business and in support of labor–management cooperation. The use of strikes by AFL locals was not sanctioned by union leadership. Gompers argued throughout his career that labor unions and business trusts were similar organizations and were necessary forms of social cooperation. They were "voluntary associations for production and distribution."[38]

While the AFL is almost always described in favorable terms by the textbooks, radical unions are usually either disparaged or simply ignored. A count of all paragraphs in the seventeen books in which labor unions active between 1865 and 1917 are discussed reveals ninety-two paragraphs in which the AFL is mentioned and ninety paragraphs in which all other labor unions are referred to, including the Knights of Labor, the National Labor Union, the American Railway Union, the Western Federation of Miners, the United Mine Workers, and the Industrial Workers of the World (IWW). In other words, the AFL receives as much discussion as all other unions combined.[39]

Most AFL local affiliates admitted only skilled workers. This generally eliminated blacks, recent immigrants, and women, most of whom were unskilled. Only two textbooks criticize these exclusionary practices.[40] Eleven argue that reliance by the AFL on the skilled workers was a major reason for its growth and success.[41] No textbook mentions Samuel Gompers's cooperation with industrialists in suppressing strikes by other unions or his frequent attempts to undermine radical labor groups.[42] The books praise Gompers's pragmatism and character, which they contrast with what they call the weak, belligerent, and intolerant leaders of the radical unions.[43] They thus implicitly define a successful and legitimate labor union as an organization of skilled workers who accept and cooperate with the prevailing corporate and political orderings.

The textbooks do not discuss several historical circumstances that contributed to the AFL's success. While reliance on the skilled and therefore better-paid and more continuously employed worker certainly provided stability, the AFL also had other advantages. It was not decimated by political trials, as was, for example, the major socialist union of the time, the IWW.[44] AFL leaders were not harassed or hanged between 1865 and 1917, as were a number of radical union members and leaders.[45] It can be argued, then, that the strength and legitimacy of the AFL was at least in part a result of its relative immunity from business violence and legal harassment. As one historian has pointed out, "Much of the business support that was given Gompers and the AFL was the result of a widespread agreement in business circles to uphold convervative union- ism as against the socialists, and, after 1905, as against the IWW. Gom- pers played on this constantly."[46] There is also evidence that, within the AFL, Gompers's view of the role and function of unions was often challenged by union members, many of whom argued that the union should "declare in favor of socialism."[47]

The IWW, whose leaders favored strikes and were opposed to con- tracts with employers and to the business values and power structure of capitalism, is ignored by all but five of the textbooks, despite the fact that it organized such well-known and successful strikes as Lawrence, Mas- sachusetts, Western Mining, and Northwest lumber camp strikes, and the well-known but unsuccessful Paterson, New Jersey, strike.[48] One of the books misnames the IWW the International Workers of the World;[49] one says that it and other radical groups took advantage of workers.[50] All of the books outline parts of the AFL platform: only two of the five do the same for the IWW.[51] One describes the IWW in some detail and seems respectful of it but, in contrast to some reports of the period, blames the IWW for the violence that occurred.[52]

No textbook suggests that the leaders of the IWW or other radical unions were supported by any other groups in American society. *The Rise of the American Nation* states that of all the radicals, Emma Goldman was "the most feared and hated," implying that she and other radicals were feared and hated by all Americans.[53] In fact, Emma Goldman was well liked by some groups of working people, as were other radicals, two of whom, Bill Haywood and Eugene Debs, were often idolized as folk heroes.[54] The claim that radical organizations were feared and hated in the United States can, of course, be used to rationalize government and business attempts to limit the activities of these groups.

The books in this study praise cooperation between labor unions and business owners; they do not, however, seem to value cooperation be- tween the various groups within the labor movement. The antagonisms between skilled and unskilled, between various immigrant groups, and between black and white are presented by thirteen of the books as natural and inevitable, a result of their belonging to separate interest groups with different problems. Textbooks suggest that skilled and unskilled workers had nothing in common, and that unskilled workers and immigrants were a threat to the labor movement:

> Laborers in different crafts and industries had little interest in working for common goals. Unskilled laborers were too often undisciplined and too willing to use violence.[55]

> Skilled workers especially disliked the [Knights of Labor's] policy of taking in unskilled workers, with whom they felt they had little or nothing in common. . . . Many immigrants had left Europe partly to be as free as possible from all sorts of restrictions. Thus they did not like labor unions, with their dues, their rules, and their insistence that no one work for less than a certain wage.[56]

There is no doubt that competition for jobs, cultural and language differences, and other factors did result in divisions in the workforce. Neither is there any doubt that business owners benefited from these divisions and often promoted them.[57] Historians point out that it was not uncommon for owners to import immigrants or Southern blacks to take the jobs of striking workers.[58] Owners also hired workers who could not communicate because of language differences, in order to impede the unionization of a shop. Ethnic segregation was the rule in factories after 1880; the various immigrant groups were placed in different areas of a shop to ensure that contact between them would be no more than minimal.[59] Thirteen of the textbooks either do not mention this, or do not relate it to divisions in the work force.[60] There is relatively little textbook discussion of the substantial contributions of immigrants to the labor movement during this period. No textbook, for example, discusses any of the strikes where the involvement of immigrants of many nationalities is well known, including those in Lawrence in 1912, Paterson in 1913, and the New York City garment-worker strikes between 1865 and 1917.

Not only are workers portrayed as naturally divided, but their numbers are underestimated: the emphasis on the AFL and skilled workers, to the exclusion of unskilled workers, immigrants, blacks, and women, contributes to this impression. Only one book discusses the several black unions of the time,[61] and only one describes the contribution of women as strikers, speakers, organizers, and union leaders.[62]

Industrialists and Labor Conflict

Historians are well aware that individual industrialists of the time actively attempted to prevent the formation of labor unions. As the United States Commission on Industrial Relations stated, in a report issued in 1916: "Freedom does not exist either politically, industrially or socially for workers trying to organize." The commission found that

> the use of thugs, spies and hired gunmen was general throughout the country in the employers' efforts to keep the open shop. . . . Almost without exception the employees of large corporations are unorganized as a result of the active and aggressive "non-union" policy of the corporation managements. . . . Our Rockefellers, Morgans, Fricks, Astors, Vanderbilts [and Carnegies] can do no industrial wrong because all effective action and direct responsibility is shifted from them to executive officials.[63]

One industrialist exclaimed of his power to put down a strike with armed guards, "I can hire one half of the working class to kill the other half."[64]

Newspapers, whether in collusion with other businesses or not, often attempted to discredit the labor movement by printing fallacious and inflammatory accounts of strikes: "Chicago in Possession of Communists" (headline, *New York Times*, July 25, 1877); "Pittsburgh Sacked: The City Completely in Power . . . of Devilish Spirit of Communism" (headline, *New York World*, July 22, 1877). Even though these antiunion activities are well documented, only eight of the books provide examples of such activities, and even these either omit discussion of corporate violence or rationalize it and other antiunion activity by pointing to nineteenth-century attitudes of individualism and laissez-faire.[65]

Fourteen of the textbooks provide a very different picture of the industrialists. Here is one example: "Carnegie, more than anyone else, made the U.S. a great steel-producing country . . . After Carnegie sold his company, he spent all his time helping other people with his money and writing. He helped build libraries, improve schools, and keep peace between the countries of the world. He gave away a lot of money."[66] Carnegie, of course, did give away a great deal of money, as did other industrialists, but to present this information while ignoring his vigorous and well-known antiunion activities is to omit evidence about the way Carnegie accumulated his fortune by exploiting labor.

The emphasis on "bread-and-butter unionism" with its focus on wages and conditions now dominates organized labor. Unions in the United States have until recently concentrated their attention on industrial workers. Although this has brought considerable power to these unions and economic wellbeing to their workers, it has also resulted in the exclusion of approximately 80 percent of the American work force from union representation. Large numbers of workers who are unskilled, who are of minority or immigrant status, or who are women, are still unrepresented by unions, though they constitute the majority of workers in low-wage sectors of the economy such as clerical, service, and sales, where the conditions of employment are often marginal.

The social philosophy regarding workers and unions transmitted by the textbooks benefits primarily those unions that have accepted the legitimacy of, and have been empowered by, the United States business establishment. Thus, the accounts benefit not only these powerful unions but also those who own and manage business, while failing to legitimize the needs, perspectives, and histories of those groups who benefit only marginally from the activities of organized labor, and those groups who would alter the distribution of economic and labor power.

Conclusion

An examination of school knowledge as a social product suggests a great deal about the society that produces and uses it. It reveals which groups have power, and demonstrates that the views of these groups are expressed and legitimized in the school curriculum. It can also identify social groups that are not empowered by the economic and social patterns in the society: they do not have their views, activities, and priorities represented in the school curriculum. The present analysis suggests that the United States working class is one such group;[67] the poor may be another. Omissions, stereotypes, and distortions that remain in "updated" social studies textbook accounts of Native Americans, blacks, and women reflect the relative powerlessness of these groups.[68]

Despite periodic changes in curriculum content, an underlying concern for the perspectives of dominant groups has remained. Recent references in textbooks to successful minority group members, deletions of Cold War aggressiveness, and revisions of Native American history are examples of changes that have not altered the basic ideology. Even in the most "radical" curriculum ever to penetrate United States schools, that of Professor Harold Rugg in the 1930s, ideological support was offered for the fundamental arrangements of political and economic power.[69] By identifying the ideology of power in curriculum content, we make apparent an underlying perspective that has provided continuity over generations of students.

The school curriculum has contributed to the formation of attitudes that make it easier for those powerful groups whose knowledge is legitimized by school studies to manage and control society. Textbooks not only express the dominant groups' ideologies, but also help to form attitudes in support of their social position. Indeed the importance of ideology to the power of dominant groups increases as the use of overt social coercion declines. In the twentieth century, the authority of tradition and the legitimacy of visible methods of control, such as force, have diminished. Government and other powerful groups increasingly justify their activities by appeals to "reason," to the logic of evidence, and to the consent of populations;[70] the public is ostensibly called upon to make intelligent social choices.

Inasmuch as social choices are likely to be made on the basis of the social knowledge and symbolic meanings that are available, what one knows about social groups and processes is of central importance. The perceived legitimacy of certain ideas increases their acceptance and use. Social agencies, such as the schools, the media, and government, whose functions include the dissemination of information, are major sources of knowledge that is both available and socially approved. If the views embedded in the information disseminated by these agencies predispose people to accept some values and not others, support some groups' activities and not others, and exclude some choices as unacceptable, then they provide invisible intellectual, internalized, and perhaps unconscious boundaries to social choice. These boundaries are a basis for social management and control.[71]

Textbook history illustrates one way of imposing beliefs and constraining choice. Textbooks offer concrete examples, and thus substantive instruction, in past "success" and "failure" in social, economic, and political matters. Governmental reform and labor–management cooperation are characterized as successful methods of social recourse, whereas confrontation and strikes are depicted as failures. Evidence of what constitutes success or failure, whether or not it coincides with actual fact, provides a compelling guide for making choices today.[72]

Alvin Gouldner has recently argued that ideological accounts of how society works, of what succeeds and what fails, have associated with them specific recommendations for action.[73] These "command implications," if internalized, direct social action. The command implications of the business and labor history in the textbooks analyzed in this study, for example, are actions that support or restrain—but do not seek to redistribute—social and economic power. The command implications of the textbook version of the methods appropriate for solving economic and labor problems are actions that maintain the balance of power in society; confrontations between contending groups that could increase the likelihood of changes in the power structure are not implied.[74]

The textbook reports of work, wealth, and the problems of industrial workers imply that we should regard the poor as responsible for their own poverty: poverty is a consequence of the failure of individuals, rather than of the failure of society to distribute economic resources universally. This ideology encourages education and other actions that attempt to change the individual, while leaving the unequal economic structures intact.

Finally, textbooks promote the idea that there is no working class in the United States, and contribute to the myth that workers are middle class. The schoolbooks provide no label with which to unify as one group with a set of distinct concerns all those wage and salaried persons who are industrial laborers, craftspersons, clerical workers, or service, sales, and technical workers.[75] Without such a label, workers are not easily called to mind as a group, and the objective fact of the working class has no subjective reality. In this way the textbooks predispose workers and others against actions on behalf of the interests working people have in common. Predictably, then, we will not find school textbooks that are written from the point of view of the working class. Textbook economics that discusses or promotes management techniques or ways of increasing profit and worker efficiency is socially legitimate; textbook economics that identifies or promotes working-class resistance to these activities is likely to be regarded as politicized or ideological.

Social meanings in school history can contribute to management and control by imposing ideological boundaries, by predisposing toward some choices and not others, by legitimating some ideas, activities, and groups, and not others. The conceptual legitimacy conferred by school knowledge on powerful social groups is metabolized into power that is real when members of society in their everyday decisions support—or fail to challenge—prevailing hierarchies. The idea that certain groups have legitimate social power leads to the belief that these groups deserve our support and that contending ones do not.

The textbooks' failure to promote a working-class identity may be advantageous to powerful business groups. A recent article in *Fortune*, a journal of corporate executive opinion, reminds its readers that capitalist groups in this country enjoy a legitimacy and political stability that their counterparts in Europe, threatened by "class-conscious labor unions" and Eurocommunism, do not. This article suggests why capitalism is less secure in Europe than it is in America: "Capitalism has never had the secure hold in European culture and in the popular imagination that it has had in the U.S. This may be partly true because the U.S. has never had a proletariat . . . that so regarded itself, while the European working class has never fully shared the American belief that the little man can make it big."[76] This article attributes the political stability of capitalism in part to a lack of working-class consciousness. Indeed, among all of the industrialized capitalist nations of the world, the United States working class is unique in not producing a labor movement that successfully promoted class consciousness.

A history curriculum that inhibits the formation of a "proletariat that so regards itself" increases the power of business owners, but may have less felicitous consequences for workers. A recent speech by John Lippert, an assemblyline worker at the Fleetwood Fisher Body Plant in Detroit, describes unsuccessful attempts to organize workers to challenge union and management policies they oppose. The speaker argued that the attitudes among working people in the plant were partly responsible for their inability to take united action. The description he provides is of factory workers, but it applies to other workers as well:

> People [in the plant are] basically cynical about the ability of workers to act collectively as a group. This is the single most concrete expression of how people perceive their powerlessness today . . . [Many people in the plant] simply do not challenge their work environment. They accept it as given and then try to find little nooks and crannies within which they can express themselves comfortably. Very few people actually like their work or take pride in it. Very few people believe that there is an equitable exchange going on between workers and management . . . [Some workers] do not challenge what goes on around them [because they] are just timid; they are people who are not accustomed to leaving an imprint . . . Most workers have been told from the day they were born that their perceptions of the world are not important to anybody. A lot of people actually believe they do not have anything important to say.[77]

Lippert also identifies pessimism among the workers stemming from the failure of past attempts to change union and management policy, and cites their fears of union and management reprisal. But he makes the point as well that how workers regard themselves as individuals and as a group may prevent them from acting in their own best interest.

The legitimation of powerful groups in the textbook version of economic and labor history may most adversely affect the inner-city poor. Many of the students using the books analyzed in this study are poor, including many blacks and Hispanics. A consequence for these students, should they believe the textbook interpretation of social reality, is the legitimation of the power of groups whose decisions, at best, often benefit them only marginally. The textbooks provide an invisible means of soliciting their support, thus preventing their potential disruption of an economic and social system that has not served them well. The transmission of these ideas by the schools imposes on them what Bourdieu would call cultural and symbolic violence.

This article has utilized a mode of inquiry that is suggested by the interest theory of ideology and has attempted to assess the social meaning of commonalities in United States history textbook content. This approach highlights the ideological characteristics of what schools teach, suggests that social groups with power have had their perspectives legitimized and indicates that school curricula can lay a subjective basis for social control. It does not, however, imply resignation in the face of persistent and unpalatable curriculum distortions. Perhaps the most important conclusion to be drawn from the point of view expressed here is that since the school curriculum is a major contributor to social attitudes, it can be used to change those attitudes. To argue that ideologies influence behavior is to accord real power to symbols and symbolic forms in education. Just as the public school curriculum has hitherto supported patterns of power and domination, so can it be used to foster autonomy and social change.

Social change is intimately connected with changes in available cultural symbols and meanings. Although it is probably true that ideological shifts in curriculum are ultimately a reflection of shifts in social power, it is also true that the availability of ideological alternatives increases the likelihood of power shifts and changes.

Diverse perspectives can provide genuine alternatives to standardized knowledge. The presentation and critical discussion in classrooms of many interpretations of economics, labor, minority, and other social histories provides conceptual and behavioral options. This kind of classroom work fosters in students an awareness of the possibilities of social change and facilitates constructive activity. Contributions to the professional literature can also make alternative analyses and information available, and thereby contribute to a climate of change in society, to different expectations of what counts as textbook knowledge, and to the use of United States schools for a more equal social structure.

Notes

A more extensive version of this analysis appears in *Harvard Educational Review* 49 (August, 1979): 361–86.

1. Pierre Bourdieu, "Cultural Reproduction and Social Reproduction," in *Knowledge, Education and Cultural Change*, ed. Richard Brown (London: Tavistock, 1973), pp. 71–112; also Pierre Bourdieu and Jean Claude Passeron, *Reproduction in Education, Society and Culture* (Beverly Hills, Calif.: Sage, 1977). These issues will be treated at greater length in Jean Anyon *Social Class and Gender in U.S. Education* (Boston: Routledge and Kegan Paul, forthcoming).

2. The present use of ideology is in the marxist and critical theorist tradition of ideology as an expression of group interest. See Karl Marx, *Contributions to a Critique of Political Economy* (New York: International Publishers, 1976); also Karl Marx and Fredrich Engels, *The German Ideology* (New York: International Publishers, 1976); Karl Mannheim, *Ideology and Utopia* (New York: Harcourt Brace Jovanovitch, 1936); Jurgen Habermas, *Theory and Practice* (Boston: Beacon Press, 1973); Jurgen Habermas, *Knowledge and Social Interest* (Boston: Beacon Press, 1971).

3. In 1967 only 22.7 percent of the total labor force was unionized; in 1974,

only 21.7 percent. *Handbook of Labor Statistics*, U.S. Bureau of Labor Statistics Bulletin (Washington, D.C.: U.S. Government Printing Office, 1966/1977).

4. By 1904 the top 4 percent of American concerns produced 57 percent of the total industrial output by value. James Weinstein, *The Corporate Ideal in the Liberal State: 1900–1918* (Boston: Beacon Press, 1968), p. 63. By 1929, 100 large companies had legal control of approximately 40 percent of the total assets of all manufacturing corporations, and 44 percent of their net capital assets (land, machines, and so on); the largest 200 corporations legally controlled 48 percent of the assets and 58 percent of the net capital assets reported by all corporations other than banks (Gardner Means, *Economic Concentration*, From Hearings Before the Subcommittee on Antitrust and Monopoly of the Committee on the Judiciary, 88th Cong., Senate, 2nd Sess., pursuant to Senate Resolution 262, Part I: Overall and Conglomerate Aspects [Washington, D.C.: U.S. Government Printing Office, 1964]. In *The Capitalistic System*, ed. R. C. Edwards, M. Reich, and T. E. Weisskopf (Englewood Cliffs, N.J.: Prentice Hall, 1972), pp. 147, 150.

5. See Henry Bragdon, Samuel McCutchen, and Charles Cole, *History of a Free People* (New York: Macmillan, 1973), in which 47 of 60 pages are devoted to aspects of industrialization considered salutary; or Bernard Weisberger, *The Impact of Our Past: A History of the United States* (Boston: Houghton Mifflin, 1972), in which 38 of 51 pages are so used, or Leonard Wood, Ralph Gabriel, and Edward Biller, *America: Its People and Values* (New York: Harcourt Brace Jovanovitch, 1975), in which 51 of 63 pages are so used.

6. See Jerome Reich, Arvarh Strickland, and Edward Biller, *Building the United States* (New York: Harcourt Brace Jovanovitch, 1971), p. 436; Henry Graff, *The Free and the Brave* (Chicago: Rand McNally, 1977), p. 556; also Weisberger, *Impact of our Past*, p. 488.

7. Margaret Branson, *American History for Today* (Lexington, Mass.: Ginn, 1977), pp. 295–360.

8. See Wood et al., *America: Its People and Values*, p. 847; also Richard Wade, Howard Wilder, and Louise Wade, *A History of the United States* (Boston: Houghton Mifflin, 1972). (This book states that "effective antitrust laws were adopted" [p. 568].)

9. See Graff, *Free and the Brave*, pp. 556–77; also Weisberger, *Impact of our Past*, pp. 488–93; and Reich et al., *Building the United States*, pp. 436–40.

10. See Mitchell Okun and Stephen Bronz, *The Challenge of America* (New York: Holt, Rinehart and Winston, 1973), pp. 549–52, 556–68. Also Lewis Todd and Merle Curti, *Rise of the American Nation* (New York: Holt, Rinehart and Winston, 1973), pp. 469, 474, 478, and 485; also Sidney Schwartz and John O'Connor, *Exploring our Nation's History* (New York, Globe, 1975), pp. 413–26.

11. See Okun and Bronz, *Challenge of America*, pp. 557–58; also Todd and Curti, *Rise of the American Nation*, pp. 472 and 483; also, Schwartz and O'Connor, *Exploring Our Nation's History*, p. 420.

12. See the chapter entitled "A New Day of Reform," in Graff, *Free and the Brave*, pp. 556–77; or Unit Eight, "The Arrival of Reform" and chaps. 5 and 6, in Todd and Curti, *Rise of the American Nation*, pp. 464–86. Only one textbook (Robert Madgic, Stanley Seaberg, Fred Stopsky, and Robin Winks, *The American Experience* [Reading, Mass.: Addison-Wesley, 1975]) does not characterize the laws as examples of progress or reform. Rather, this textbook calls the federal legislation a "conservative bulwark against more radical state laws" (p. 286).

13. There are several varieties of this argument. See William A. Williams, *Contours of American History* (Cleveland: World Publishing, 1961); Gabriel

Kolko, *Triumph of Conservatism* (New York: Free Press of Glencoe, 1963); James Weinstein, *The Corporate Ideal in the Liberal State: 1900–1918* (Boston: Beacon, 1968); and Joel Spring, *Education and the Rise of the Corporate State* (Boston: Beacon, 1972).

14. See Weinstein, *Corporate Ideal*, intro., p. ix, and chaps. 1, 2, 3, and 6.

15. See Okun and Bronz, *Challenge of America*, p. 463 (two paragraphs); and p. 473 (one paragraph); Weisberger, *Impact of our Past*, p. 495 (two paragraphs); and p. 494 (one paragraph); Bragdon et al., *History of a Free People*, p. 537 (one paragraph).

16. Madgic et al., *American Experience*, p. 275. All of the textbooks surveyed included at least one of these explanations.

17. See Gerd Korman, *Industrialization, Immigrants and Americanizers: A View from Milwaukee: 1866–1921* (Madison, Wisc.: State Historical Society of Wisconsin, 1967). Also Daniel B. Luria, "Trends in the Determinants Underlying the Process of Social Stratification: Boston, 1880–1920," *Review of Radical Political Economics* 6, no. 2 (1974): 98–109; and David Brody, *Steelworkers in America* (New York: Harper & Row, 1960), esp. chap. 5.

18. Okun and Bronz, *Challenge of America*, p. 463; Weisberger, *Impact of our Past*, p. 495; Graff, *Free and the Brave*, p. 518; and Leinwand, *Pageant of American History*, p. 325.

19. Leinwand, *Pageant of American History* and Okun and Bronz, *Challenge of America*.

20. Weisberger, *Impact of our Past*, p. 495; see also Graff, *Free and the Brave*.

21. In contrast to this argument are less flattering views of the intentions of business owners. See Stephen A. Marglin, "What Do Bosses Do? The Origins and Functions of Hierarchy in Capitalist Production," *The Review of Radical Political Economics* 6, no. 2 (1974): 38–60. See also Joseph Page and Mary O'Brien, *Bitter Wages* (New York: Grossman, 1973).

22. Joel Spring, *Education and the Rise of the Corporate State* (Boston: Beacon Press, 1972), p. 24. See also William H. Tolman's *Social Engineering* (New York: McGraw, 1909), p. 24; E. Wake Cook, *Betterment: Individual, Social and Industrial* (New York: F. A. Stokes, 1906), E. A. Filene, "The Social Improvement of Grammar School Graduates in Business Life," *Social Education Quarterly* 1 (1907): 146–55.

23. Harry Braverman, *Labor and Monopoly Capital: The Degradation of Work in the 20th Century* (New York: Monthly Review Press, 1974). See also Stephen A. Marglin, "What Do Bosses Do?" and Katherine Stone, "The Origins of Job Structures in the Steel Industry," *The Review of Radical Political Economics* 6, no. 2 (1974): 61–97.

24. Only five books describe the Socialist party. They are Madgic, et al., *American Experience*, pp. 279–80; Schwartz and O'Connor, *Exploring our Nation's History*, pp. 401–02; Bertha Davis, Dorothy Aranoff, and Charlotte Davis, *Background for Tomorrow* (New York: Macmillan, 1969), pp. 417–18; Bragdon et al., *History of a Free People*, p. 535; and Graff, *The Free and the Brave*, p. 564.

25. Schwartz and O'Connor, *Exploring Our Nation's History* and Bragdon et al., *History of a Free People*. Making a typical point, this last text argues that Socialism "gained only a small following, mostly among immigrant groups in big cities. Although these people talked about 'the revolution' as though it were just around the corner, and published violent little newspapers with titles like *The Volcano*, they were not much of a threat to American society" p. 444).

26. Graff, *Free and the Brave* states that "President Roosevelt was especially

afraid that honest people might be attacked and that such attacks might hurt the country" (p. 564).

27. The Socialist party was, in fact, very successful at the turn of the century. See James Weinstein, *The Decline of Socialism in America* (New York: Random House, Vintage, 1969); also Richard Boyer and Herbert Morais, *Labor's Untold Story*, 3rd ed. (New York: United Electrical, Radio and Machine Workers of America, 1970); Philip Foner, *From the Founding of the A.F. of L. to the Emergence of American Imperialism* (New York: International Publishers, 1955).

28. Estimates by labor historians place the figure higher than 30,000. Personal communication, Prof. Irving Richter, Fellow, Woodrow Wilson Center for Scholars, November 1976.

29. All books but Wood et al., *America: Its People and Values*, Todd and Curti, *Rise of American Nation*, and Reich et al., *Building the United States* discuss one or more of these three strikes. Two mention, in passing, the Lawrence, Massachusetts, strike of 1912, and what is known as the Coeur d'Alene Massacre. The Railroad Strike of 1885 was successful from a labor point of view, and while no book discusses it in any detail, five books mention it as having taken place. For representative reports of strikes, see Leinwand, *Pageant of American History*, pp. 324–25; Wilder et al., *America's Story*, pp. 486–91; and Bragdon et al., *History of a Free People*, pp. 435–38.

30. See, among others, Boyer and Morais, *Labor's Untold Story*.

31. See Shafer et al., *United States History for High School*, p. 405; Branson, *American History for Today*, p. 347; Bragdon, *History of a Free People*, p. 435.

32. See Leinwand, *Pageant of American History*, pp. 341–342. Okun and Bronz, *Challenge of America*, p. 554; and Reich et al., *Building the United States*, 438, 439.

33. Reich et al., *Building the United States*, p. 438. See also textbooks and pages cited in note 51.

34. Wade et al., History of the United States, p. 555. See also Todd and Curti, *Rise of the American Nation*, p. 493; and Shafer et al., *United States History for High Schools*, pp. 445–46.

35. See Milton Meltzer, *Bread and Roses: The Struggles of American Labor*, 1865–1915 (New York: Alfred A. Knopf, 1967); see also Boyer and Morais, *Labor's Untold Story*.

36. See Graff, *Free and the Brave*, p. 575; Wilder et al., *America's Story*, pp. 492–93; Shafer et al., *United States History for High Schools*, pp. 445–46; and the section entitled, "Improving Conditions for American Industrial Workers," in Todd and Curti, *Rise of American Nation*, pp. 493–94.

37. Other studies of social science materials have reported that the subject of social conflict either is absent from educational curriculum materials or, if present, is discussed within the framework of a search for resolution and social consensus. See Mary Turner, *Materials For Civics, Government and Problems and Democracy* (Boulder, Colo.: Social Science and Educational Consortium, 1971); Michael Apple, "The Hidden Curriculum and the Nature of Conflict," *Interchange* 2, no. 4 (1971): 27–40; Thomas Fox and Robert D. Hess, "An Analysis of Social Conflict in Social Studies Textbooks," Final Report, Project No. 1–1–116 (Washington, D.C.: U.S. Department of Health, Education and Welfare, 1972). See also Jean Anyon, "Elementary Social Studies Textbooks and Legitimating Knowledge," *Theory and Research in Social Education* 6, no. 3 (1978): 40–45.

38. Samuel Gompers, *Seventy Years of Life and Labor*, vol. 2 (New York: E.

P. Dutton, 1948), p. 110. Indeed Gompers held, as did many businessmen, that "trusts should not be suppressed, but regulated and helped to develop constructive control" (pp. 20–22).

39. The following are representative of the contrast in description of the AFL and radical labor unions. Weisberger, *Impact of Our Past* cites the Knights of Labor's goal of "cooperating in ownership and sharing the profits" as "ignoring economic realities" (p. 496); this is contrasted with "the AFL's careful planning" (p. 497). Okun and Bronz, *Challenge of America* characterizes a radical union (The American Railway Union of Eugene Debs) as having "leaders [who] were weak" (p. 463), and states that Gompers was "a shrewd and able man" (p. 465). The authors describe the "bloody and unsuccessful" Homestead and Pullman strikes, and say that "In both cases the AFL was careful not to get deeply involved" (p. 469).

40. Todd and Curti, *Rise of the American Nation*, p. 448; Davis et al., *Background for Tomorrow*, p. 574.

41. The following excerpts are representative: ". . . through its policy of organizing only skilled workers and through Gompers's leadership, the AFL steadily gained members" (Okun and Bronz, *Challenge of America*, p. 649); "The idea of bringing all workers together in one big union [such as the Knights of Labor] did not work well. The workmen did not have enough interests in common" (Wood et al., *America: Its People and Values*, p. 460). In contrast, the AFL's success is attributed to its being ". . . a craft union, in which the members have interests in common" (p. 649).

42. See Boyer and Morais, *Labor's Untold Story*, pp. 181–82, 204. See also Brody, *Steelworkers*, esp. chap. 5, and citations in fn. 45 below.

43. See the quotes in fn. 39 as examples. In *History of a Free People* "intolerant" is used to describe a leader of the IWW (p. 536).

44. See Boyer and Morais, *Labor's Untold Story*, p. 198, and citations in fn. 45 below.

45. See Joyce Kronbluh, *Rebel Voices: An IWW Anthology* (Ann Arbor, Mich.: University of Michigan Press, 1972), p. 162; Boyer and Morais, *Labor's Untold Story*; Philip Foner, *The Industrial Workers of the World* (New York: International Publishers, 1965); and Melvin Dubofsky, *We Shall Be All* (New York: Quadrangle, *New York Times* publication, 1969). See also the following autobiographies and biographies: William D. Haywood, *The Autobiography of Big Bill Haywood* (New York: International Publishers, 1969); Ray Ginger, *Eugene V. Debs: The Making of an American Radical* (New York: Macmillan, 1970); Emma Goldman, *Living My Life* (New York: Dover Publications, 1970); and Elizabeth Gurley Flynn, *The Rebel Girl: An Autobiography* (New York: New World Paperbacks, 1974).

46. Weinstein, *Corporate Ideal*, p. 21.

47. Ibid.

48. Madgic et al., *American Experience*, pp. 280–82; Weisberger, *Impact of Our Past*, p. 501; Okun and Bronz, *Challenge of America*, p. 563; Davis et al., *Background for Tomorrow*, p. 418; Wade et al., *History of the United States*, p. 551.

49. Okun and Bronz, *Challenge of America*, p. 563.

50. Wade et al., *History of the United States*, p. 551.

51. Madgic et al., *American Experience*, pp. 280–81; and Weisberger, *Impact of Our Past*, p. 501.

52. Madgic et al., *American Experience*, p. 281.

53. Todd and Curti, *Rise of the American Nation*, p. 449. This statement is representative of a textbook pattern in which it is sometimes stated that "Americans" or "the Public" as a unified group, hold various beliefs. For example, "The Public was afraid of labor unions" (Branson, *American History for Today*), p. 348.

54. Joseph Conlin, *Big Bill Haywood and the Radical Union Movement* (Syracuse, N.Y.: Syracuse University Press, 1968). p. viii. See also citations in note 45 above.

55. Bragdon et al., *History of a Free People*, p. 437.

56. Todd and Curti, *Rise of the American Nation*, pp. 445, 446. See also, Okun and Bronz, *Challenge of America*, p. 469; Graff, *Free and the Brave*, pp. 505, 509.

57. Meltzer, *Bread and Roses*, pp. 95–97; Gabriel Kolko, *Main Currents in Modern American History* (New York: Harper & Row, 1976), pp. 92–93. See also Brody, *Steelworkers*; Boyer and Morais, *Labor's Untold Story*.

58. See Luria, "Trends," for the use of immigrants. For the use of Blacks, see Philip Foner, *Organized Labor and the Black Worker, 1619–1973* (New York: International Publishers, 1974).

59. Meltzer, *Bread and Roses*, pp. 95–97; see also, Brody, *Steelworkers*, esp. chap. 5, and Kolko, *Main Currents*, p. 75.

60. While seven books mention the use by industry of strikebreakers, lockouts, and so on, and cite them as examples of owners' power, no book considers the divisive effects of these activities on the labor force. See Weisberger, *Impact of our Past*, p. 497; Leinwand, *Pageant of American History*, pp. 325–26; Current et al., *United States History*, p. 319. One book does argue, however, that the exclusion of blacks from the labor movement weakened it (Todd and Curti, *Rise of the American Nation*, pp. 447–48).

61. See Todd and Curti, *Rise of American Nation*, pp. 447–48.

62. Jack Abramowitz, *American History* (Chicago: Follett, 1979), p. 436. There are also two sentences in Todd and Curti, *Rise of the American Nation* about an upper-class women's group (p. 447); the following sentence appears in Graff, *Free and the Brave*: "Many women were among the strikers," pp. 506–07.

63. Final Report of the Commission on Industrial Relations (Washington, D.C., 1915), quoted in Boyer and Morais, *Labor's Untold Story*, pp. 184–86.

64. Boyer and Morais, *Labor's Untold Story*, p. 72.

65. See Davis et al., *Background for Tomorrow*, p. 418; Todd and Curti, *Rise of the American Nation*, p. 446; Graff, *Free and the Brave*, p. 505; Shafer et al., *United States History for High School*, p. 392; and Wade et al., *A History of the United States*, p. 481.

66. Graff, *Free and the Brave*, p. 476. See also Wilder et al., *This is America's Story*, pp. 474, 560; Weisberger, *Impact of our Past*, p. 439; and Wade et al., *United States History*, pp. 315, 370.

67. A recent study of basal readers suggests a bias against working-class jobs in these textbooks as well. See William Luker, Floyd Jenkins, and Lewis Abernathy, "Elementary School Basal Readers and Work Mode Bias," *Journal of Economic Education* 4 (Spring 1974): 92–96.

68. See Council on Interracial Books for Children, *Stereotypes, Distortions and Omissions in U.S. History Textbooks* (New York: Racism and Sexism Resource Center for Educators, 1977). Also, Baltimore Feminist Project, *Sexism and Racism in Popular Basal Readers: 1964–1976* (New York: Racism and Sexism Resource Center for Educators, 1976).

69. See Peter F. Carbone, Jr., *The Social and Educational Thought of Harold Rugg* (Curham, N.C.: Duke University Press, 1977); and Frances FitzGerald, "History Textbooks," parts 1–3, *New Yorker* 26 February 1979, 5 March 1979, and 12 March 1979.

70. See Alvin Gouldner, *The Coming Crisis of Western Sociology* (New York: Basic Books, 1970) for this argument. See also Bernstein, *Class, Codes and Control*, for a discussion of visible and invisible controls, and social agencies through which invisible control may be exercised.

71. See Allen Dawe, "The Two Sociologies," *British Journal of Sociology* 21, no. 2 (1970): 207–218; and Young, *Knowledge and Control*, for insightful discussions of control as the imposition of meaning.

72. Alan Blum, "The Corpus of Knowledge as a Normative Order," in Michael F. D. Young, ed., *Knowledge and Control* (London: Collier Macmillan, 1971), pp. 117–32.

73. Alvin Gouldner, *The Dialectic of Ideology and Technology* (New York: Seabury Press, 1976), p. 206.

74. In an analysis of elementary-school social-studies textbooks, Fox and Hess in "An Analysis of Social Conflict in Social Studies Textbooks," found that "it would seem from the social studies textbooks we analyzed that American youth are expected to believe that virtually every existing social problem is resolvable with established knowledge and practices" (p. 83).

75. Wage and salaried workers in the groups cited made up, in 1970, 69 percent of the nonagricultural labor force, or 55.3 million persons. (Braverman, *Labor and Monopoly Capital*, p. 379).

76. Robert Ball, "The Surprising New Optimism of Europe's C.O.E.'s [Chief Executive Officers]," *Fortune*, 14 Aug. 1978, p. 112.

77. John Lippert, "Shopfloor Politics at Fleetwood," *Radical America* 12, no. 4 (1978): 63–64.

Appendix

The United States history textbooks used in this study are those that appeared on the most recent board of education lists of "Books Approved for Use" as of July, 1978, in New York City (1975 with a supplement in 1976) and Newark, New Jersey (1977). The author analyzed the latest editions of these books that were available as of January 1, 1979.

Abramowitz, Jack. *American History*, 5th ed. Chicago: Follett, 1979.

Bragdon, Henry, Samuel McCutchen, and Charles Cole. *History of a Free People*. New York: Macmillan, 1973.

Branson, Margaret. *American History for Today*, Lexington, Mass.: Ginn, 1977.

Current, Richard, Alexander de Conde, and Harris Dante. *U.S. History: A Developing Nation*; *U.S. History: A World Power*. 2 volumes. Glenview, Ill.: Scott Foresman, 1974.

Davis, Bertha, Dorothy Aranoff, and Charlotte Davis. *Background for Tomorrow: An American History*. New York: Macmillan, 1969.

Graff, Henry. *The Free and the Brave*. Chicago: Rand McNally, 1977.

Leinwand, Gerald. *The Pageant of American History*. Boston: Allyn and Bacon, 1975.

Madgic, Robert, Stanley Seaberg, Fred Stopsky, and Robin Winks. *The American Experience*, 2nd ed. Reading, Mass.: Addison-Wesley, 1975.

Okun, Mitchell, and Stephen Bronz. *The Challenge of America*. New York: Holt, Rinehart and Winston, 1973.

Reich, Jerome, Arvarh Strickland, and Edward Biller. *Building the United States*. New York: Harcourt Brace Jovanovitch, 1971.

Schwartz, Sidney, and John O'Connor. *Exploring our Nation's History*. New York: Globe, 1975.

Shafer, Boyd, Everett Augsperger, and Richard McLemore. *United States History for High School*. River Forest, Ill.: Laidlaw, 1973.

Todd, Lewis, and Merle Curti. *Rise of the American Nation*. New York: Harcourt Brace Jovanovitch, 1977. (Heritage edition)

Wade, Richard, Howard Wilder, and Louise Wade. *A History of the United States*. New York: Houghton Mifflin, 1972.

Weisberger, Bernard. *The Impact of our Past: A History of the United States*. New York: McGraw-Hill, 1976.

Wilder, Howard, Robert Ludlum, and Harriet Brown. *This is America's Story*. Boston: Houghton Mifflin, 1975.

Wood, Leonard, Ralph Gabriel, and Edward Biller. *America: Its People and Values*. New York: Harcourt Brace Jovanovitch, 1975.

CHAPTER 3

The American Revolution in Children's Fiction: An Analysis of Literary Content, Form, and Ideology

JOEL TAXEL

A growing number of scholars influenced by Marxist thought have argued that culture does more than provide innocent, value-neutral entertainment and, in fact, serves important political functions that require understanding.[1] Bourdieu, for example, suggested that cultural artifacts such as literature reproduce in transfigured and therefore unrecognizable form the structure of prevalent socioeconomic relationships. Bourdieu's claim was that the form or structure of novels, films, and even classroom interactions, contains an implicit "symbolic representation of the social world adjusted to the structure of socioeconomic relationships." Because these relationships are perceived as "natural," Bourdieu argued that they contribute to the "symbolic buttressing of the existing balance of forces."[2] A similar point was made by Willis in his ethnographic account of life in a British working-class high school.

> It is in the passage through the cultural level that aspects of the real structural relationships of society are transformed into conceptual relationships and back again. The cultural is part of the dialectic of reproduction.[3]

Both Bourdieu and Willis suggest that cultural artifacts—be they novels, films, or the social relations of classrooms—embody the form or structure of the socioeconomic relationships that dominate society at the historical moment in which they are produced or occur. This chapter presents an overview of a larger study that made similar assumptions about the way cultural artifacts such as literature for children function in society and about how socioeconomic and historical forces contribute to the shaping of their ultimate content and form.[4] The analysis of the content of thirty-two recommended children's novels about the American Revolution published between 1899 and 1976 reconstructed the historiographic conception of that event. The analysis of the form or narrative structure (terms used synonymously in this chapter) of the novels was concerned with ascertaining whether common approaches to the depiction of characters, plot development, conflict, and the resolution of conflict were used by the various authors in their fictionalized recreations of the Revolution. Both form and content were considered in relation to the changing socioeconomic and historical milieu of the seventy-seven-year period during which the books were published.

The analysis documenting the evolutionary changes in the content and narrative structure of the novels is preceded by a discussion of the methods and procedures used to select and analyze the sample. The chapter concludes with a discussion and explanation of how particular socioeconomic and political developments may have contributed to the shaping and production of this body of fiction.

Methodological Background

In an insightful essay, R. Gordon Kelly criticized the dominant approach to literary study and analysis for considering literature solely in terms of its capacity to generate emotional and intellectual responses in its readers. He challenged the often-held view that literary works are autonomous or independent of social and historical forces. Central to Kelly's work was the belief that narrative forms like literature for children are cultural artifacts best understood within the historical context of the groups that produced and responded to them. His thesis was that the form of narratives such as children's fiction embodies a vision of the world that provides a model of behavior consistent with its author's perception of a desirable social order.[5]

Kelly's effort to situate historically the nineteenth-century children's periodical literature he examined was successful in articulating a theory of the social functions of children's literature. It fell short, however, of the "critical sociology of cultural forms" called for by Michael W. Apple and Philip Wexler, who emphasized the need to analyze novels, films, and magazines, as well as curricula, in terms of their connections to the specific collectivity and socioeconomic configuration to which they are dialectically linked.[6]

A critical inquiry of this sort is, however, available in Will Wright's analysis of the evolution of the narrative structure of Western films. Wright examined the development of the Western in light of the socioeconomic and political changes in American society and viewed it as a myth communicating a model of social action, a "paradigm for making sense of life."[7] His approach was similar to that of Kelly, who regarded the often-repeated sequence of character and plot elements of magazine fiction as "informed and sustained by a particular definition of social experience."[8] Wright presented some impressive evidence pointing to a "correspondence" between the structure of the Western and the "conceptual needs of self-understanding required by the dominant social institutions."[9]

Two interrelated procedures utilized by Wright to explicate the narrative structure of Western films were adapted in the study being reported in this chapter. The first involved "coding" the characters in terms of a series of binary oppositions, a procedure developed by Lévi-Strauss in his study of primitive mythodology. By analyzing how characters were defined according to oppositions such as "good versus bad" and "strong versus weak," the meaning of the characters and the social basis of their characteristics were ascertained. This is possible because understanding of what constitutes the qualities of, for example, "good" people, is highlighted by comparison to an opposite image, "bad" people.[10] Wright's "central interest" in using binary analysis, like my own in this chapter, was to show how a particular kind of narrative (the Western) is related to society's institutions or social actions.

Analysis of characters in terms of oppositions reveals their meaning; it does not, however, tell us about their actions. If one assumes that a narrative presents a model of social action, it is necessary to understand the actions of characters as well as their meaning. These actions are determined by reducing the stories to a descriptive set of "functions" describing the character's activities over the course of the novel. The novels under discussion were not reducible to a set of functions, although twenty-nine of the thirty-two books making up the sample did have important structural characteristics in common.

The analysis of content reconstructed the historiographic conception of the Revolution used by each author to frame the narrative. Here a phenomenological assessment of the author's perceptions of the issues, events, and personalities contributing to the rupture between England and her American colonies was sought. In making this assessment, I "bracketed" my own conceptions about the Revolution and recorded all references to it in the texts. By then comparing these statements with the various paradigms advanced by professional historians who have studied the Revolution, it was possible to determine which "theory" of the Revolution each author either consciously or unconsciously manifested.[11]

The sample contained the thirty-two novels that both appeared in selection guides such as Wilson's *Children's Catalogue* and Brodart's *Elementary School Library Collection*—sources frequently consulted by public and school librarians when they order books—and were available either through the publisher, or at one of the libraries I had at my disposal. In narrowing an initial list of books to those that were both recommended and available, the process of selection yielded a sample likely to contain the most common and culturally accepted views, the very things I sought to investigate.

The sample contains books that are distributed fairly equally throughout the years covered by sample (1899 to 1976). There was, however, some clustering around certain years, with gaps in between the clusters. For this reason, four periods—1899 to 1930, 1937 to 1953, 1959 to 1961, and 1967 to 1976—were established. These periods were initially viewed merely as a useful way to organize and discuss an unwieldy number of books. Ultimately, they proved to have considerable conceptual usefulness, since particular historiographic interpretations and narrative devices were characteristic of certain periods.

The Revolution in Periods 1 and 2

The content analysis revealed that the sample is dominated by a selective, simplistic, and conservative view of the Revolution that ignores the complexities and ambiguities evident in most historians' explanations of that event. While historical fiction for children neither can or should contain the detail and subtlety of an historical monograph, such fiction should not reduce a historical event to a caricature, as many of the novels do.

Historians like George Bancroft (1858) saw the Revolution as an epochal, divinely inspired struggle waged to wrest independence from Britain and to defend long-cherished political rights and liberties. This explanation, called the "Whig" interpretation, emphasizes the colonists' commitment to ideological principles such as representative government, individual liberty, and the sanctity of property. The Whig historians saw unanimity among the colonists on these matters, and felt that economic issues played little role in generating the conflict between England and her American colonies. This interpretation is present in all of the books written in periods 1 (1899–1930) and 2 (1937–1953). It is also implicit in all of the books, save three—written during periods 3 (1959–1961) and 4 (1967–1976)—that draw instead on the more refined, less pedantic "Consensus" interpretation. Like their Whig predecessors, Consensus historians emphasized the supposed consensus among the colonists about the aforementioned ideological principles and beliefs that were claimed to have motivated the Revolution.

The Whig and Consensus historians focused almost exclusively on the factors that led the colonists to seek independence, or "home rule," from Britain. These historians ignore matters that were of central concern to the "Progressive" historians, who wrote at the turn of the century, as well as to their contemporary descendents, the "Revisionist" historians. The last group emphasized instead the importance of ideas about the nature of the government to be established after home rule was secured. That is, the Progressive and Revisionist historians gave equal weight to the question of "who should rule home." They therefore focused on the role of economic factors, conflict between competing social classes, and issues relating to racial and sexual justice and equality as motivators of the Revolution.

Only one book in the sample makes economic and social issues central to its conception of the Revolution. A few mention them, while the overwhelming majority ignore them altogether. It is interesting, and not coincidental, that the only book to incorporate the Progressive/Revisionist interpretation is also the only one to have a black protagonist. Sally Edwards's *When the World's On Fire* (1972) is also alone in addressing what Morgan termed "the central paradox of American history" when he referred to the fact that the movement for American freedom developed at the very time that slavery was being institutionalized in many states.[12]

The Whig vision of the Revolution as a life-and-death struggle waged by valiant American colonists against a tyrannical king bent on the destruction of their rights and liberties is evident in Gertrude Crownfield's *Freedom's Daughter* (1930). The novel's heroine, Reba Stanhope, speaks repeatedly of risking war to gain independence for her "oppressed land" and of the determination of the colonists "to resist further oppression" (pp. 10, 19). Gilbert Westwood, the hero of this novel, explicitly articulates this viewpoint even when stating:

> I know what my lot must be . . . I would not choose it, were the cause less just, less noble than it is, but what right have I, or anyone . . . to dwell secure and protected, while others struggle and jeopardize their lives and all they own to preserve us as well as themselves from sinful oppression and wicked tyranny that violate the God-given right of humankind? [p. 21]

Several authors writing during the first two periods echo this theme of equating British violations of colonial rights with tyranny and trace the conflict to these British actions.[13] This theme is central to Esther Forbes's

Johnny Tremain (1943), undoubtedly the most widely read book in the sample, and one said to encapsulate the dominant view of the Revolution in American popular culture.[14]

Johnny Tremain provides extensive discussion of the causes and issues surrounding the Revolution, a marked contrast to the many books that only refer to these matters in passing. That Forbes conceives of the Revolution as an ideologically motivated struggle is made apparent when James Otis addresses a meeting of the Sons of Liberty in one of the novel's most dramatic scenes. To Otis, the Revolution was being fought

> For men and women and children all over the world . . . we are fighting for rights such as they will be enjoying a hundred years from now.
> There shall be no more tyranny. A handful of men cannot seize power over thousands. A man shall choose who it is shall rule over him.
> The peasants of France, the serfs of Russia. Hardly more than animals now. But because we fight, they shall see freedom like a new sun rising in the west. Those natural rights God has given to every man, no matter how humble. . . .
> We give all we have, lives, property, safety, skills . . . we fight, we die for a simple thing. Only that a man can stand up. [pp. 189–190, 192]

Johnny Tremain contains one of the sample's most passionate evocations of the Whig interpretation. Its themes are reiterated time and again in the books published during periods 1 and 2 and especially in those written during the era when European fascism threatened the freedoms and liberties of the entire globe. The post-World War II period witnessed a transference of American fears and insecurities from the fascists to the Russian communists. The effect of these two distinct threats is, however, indistinguishable, as writers during both of these periods perceive the Revolution as a struggle for abstract principle and identify no economic or materialistic basis for it.[15] This last point is apparent when Bill Barlow, the hero of Merritt Allen's, *Battle Lanterns* (1949), explains the tenacity and persistence of the American army in the face of the overwhelming superiority of the British forces:

> Money was a mean cheap thing . . . It was not what these men were fighting for. They were giving their lives for something that could not be wrapped up in a purse. It had neither weight nor shape, it was invisible, yet it burned forever before their eyes like a torch. It was the finest thing in the world . . . Liberty! (p. 28)

The disavowal of any mercenary motives on the part of the Americans is crucial to the assessment of an author's historiographic conception of the Revolution, because, as we have seen, the Whig historians deny that the Revolution had any materialistic basis. It assumed even greater significance because a character's reasons for acting helped to define his or her worth as a person. Determination of characteristics such as goodness or badness and strength or weakness was central to the analysis of the narrative structure of the novels and provides perhaps the best illustration of the interdependence of novel content and structure. Because changes in the conception of the Revolution as a historical event were accompanied by changes in coding of the characters, one must examine the latter factors before considering how the Revolution is presented in periods 3 and 4.

Character Coding in Periods 1 and 2

In the dominant configuration in the books written during periods 1 and 2, a good, relatively weak, and dependent protagonist lives in a home dominated by a male who is good, strong, and has the unquestioned loyalty and respect of the protagonist. This initial youthful weakness and dependence of the protagonists is a defining characteristic of the genre in that the action of virtually every novel results in the transformation and growth of these characters to stronger, more independent individuals. The basis of the characters' goodness or badness is extremely important and is invariably concerned with their political affiliation and especially their reasons for choosing sides. In the novels written during periods 1 and 2, for example, goodness is a function not only of the characters' intrinsic qualities (that is, their "niceness") but also their motivation for becoming either a Patriot or a Tory.

Reba Stanhope is typical of the characters who dominate the early novels. Resolutely committed to the Revolution, Reba works tirelessly for it and speaks of the sacrifices she willingly makes upon the "altar of freedom." *Freedom's Daughter* is, in fact, a chronicle of the heroism and sacrifice Reba and Gilbert Westwood make for the "life and death struggle for high principle" (p. 66). An essential component of Reba and Gil's goodness is their idealism, a quality apparent in virtually all period 1 and 2 heroes and heroines.[16]

Belief that the meaning of characters is magnified when their qualities are contrasted with those of individuals possessing the opposite characteristics is basic to the idea of binary analysis. Reba and Gil, for example, are a striking contrast to Richard Skinner, a man with a "cold and selfish nature" (p. 77) who hides his activities for the Crown behind a pretense of neutrality. Caring for neither the Tory or Whig side, but convinced that the Crown would prevail, this "ambitious and unscrupulous man" is "determined to wrest every iota from his country's crisis that it could be made to yield" (p. 35). Richard Skinner is evil, not simply because he sides with the British, but rather because he does so for materialistic reasons, a fact made clear by his father, Henry Skinner. Henry is also a Tory but is good, because his allegiance to the Crown stems from his loyalty to the King. Because the reasons for a character's affiliation—for example, idealism or materialism—constitutes the key to him or her being defined as good or bad, many of the period 1 and 2 books contain a configuration where good, idealistic Patriots, such as Reba and Gil, are opposed by calculating, avaricious Tories, such as Richard Skinner. The idealistic Tory, while not present in all of the novels, helps bring the nature of good and evil into sharper relief and highlights the fact that good and evil in these novels is usually coded in economic terms.

In periods 1 and 2, the contrast between good and evil characters is sharpened by an "idealistic/materialistic" refinement of the good/bad opposition that functions to remove ambiguity in the meaning of the characters. This refinement also brings a particular perspective on the Revolution into focus, as a character's reasons for action provide insight into the conflict itself. Interestingly, the books having the most clearly defined good and bad characters are those containing extreme statements of the Whig interpretation. This is logical, given the belief, shared by Whig historians, that the Revolution was a great step forward in the struggle for freedom and the rights of man. As a result of this belief, and the tendency of many authors during the first two periods to simplify and reduce the complex for their youthful audience, the protagonists of the first two periods are those driven by a fervent attachment to high ideals, while the villains are base and self-serving individuals who seek only to advance their narrow self-interest.

By the mid-1960s, however, there was an increased demand for greater realism in children's books. While it is difficult to determine the precise impact of this, the books written during Period 4 (1967–1976) do manifest a greater concern with the realistic portrayal of character, family relationships, and the war itself. During this period the individual psyches of the protagonists are explored in a manner and detail rarely evidenced in earlier works. The same can be said of family relationships where one now finds signs of conflict and division that contrast sharply with the familial harmony found in the earlier periods. Interestingly, these changes in narrative structure are more visible in books that move away from the Whig interpretation, a finding suggesting the interdependence of novel content and structure. Before examining the changes in historical interpretation underlying the novels in periods 3 and 4, it is necessary to consider how the actions, conflicts, and events making up the novels are structured.

The American Revolution as a Rite of Passage

The central concern of the novels is the way the hero or heroine becomes involved with, and contributes to, the Revolution. Regardless of the nature of this involvement, it has a transforming effect on the character in question. In essence, the individual, who is initially presented as physically and or emotionally weak and dependent, is tested and toughened by experiences constituting a rite of passage to the world of responsible adulthood. As a result of these experiences, the individual is stronger, wiser, more mature and is usually perceived and treated as such by his or her elders. At the very least, the character comes to view him or herself in a different light. This personalized rite of passage is an expression of the protagonists' movement from one end of the strong/weak opposition to the other. It also provides the basis of the unity of content and structure by serving as a metaphor for the experiences of the nation itself: a transformation, via the Revolution, from a state of weak, colonial dependence to independent nationhood.[17] Use of this rite-of-passage motif also reinforces the notion that the Revolution was concerned exclusively with the questions of independence and nationhood, as the Whig and Consensus historians claim, and not with altering social relationships among the colonial population (the Progressive/Revisionist interpretation). It is in this sense that one sees the structure and content of the novels informing and interpenetrating each other in ways that reinforce a particular perspective on the Revolution as a historical event.

There is considerable variation in the way individual authors construct their narratives, as well as two significant variants—the "conversion" and "fence-sitting variations"—in the rite-of-passage motif. These variants however, fit comfortably within the pattern already described. The overwhelming majority of the books in the sample are classified as "straight initiation." This pattern is clearly evident in *Johnny Tremain*, a novel Kammen described as "an epitome of the American Revolution as rite de passage."[18]

Johnny Tremain is an orphaned apprenctice to a Boston silversmith. Although he does not come from the Patriotic home that characterizes most "straight initiation" protagonists, his first, and only, political awareness is that of a revolutionist. Unlike the protagonists of the conversion and fence sitting variants who flirt with the Loyalist cause, Johnny's friendship with Rab Silsbee brings him directly into the Patriot camp. The question for Johnny is whether he can muster sufficient strength to overcome the personal crisis brought on by an unfortunate accident and find his place in the world. In this regard, as Kammen (1978) points out, "Johnny's time of troubles and his symbolic rebirth coincide exactly with that of the colonies" (p. 207). For Johnny Tremain and virtually all of the protagonists, the Revolution serves as the vehicle through which they are transformed from weak and dependent adolescents into men (and women) ready to fight and, if necessary, die for a country that is itself in the throes of a similar transformation.

The Oppositions in Periods 3 and 4

In periods 3 (1959–1961) and 4 (1967–1976) we continue to find weak, dependent protagonists being transformed into stronger, more independent adults as a result of their involvement in the Revolution. Other factors, however, have changed, some in rather significant ways. To begin with, there is a noticeable absence of the venal, avaricious Tory whose "badness" was so important in defining the "goodness" of the idealistic Patriots. Goodness and badness are now primarily a function of "niceness" and "nastiness"; books like Jean Fritz's *Early Thunder* (1967) and Ann Finlayson's *Redcoat in Boston* (1971) contain Patriots who are "bad" because they are mean and brutish. On the other hand, the protagonists in James Collier and Christopher Collier's *My Brother Sam Is Dead* (1974), John Beatty and Patricia Beatty's *Who Comes to King's Mountain?* (1975), and Richard Snow's *Freelon Starbird* (1976) explicitly reject Revolutionary ideology, but are good because they are kind and decent. Contributing to this development is the fact that many of the father figures, who in earlier works were models of strength and virtue, are now weak. Some are even Tories. This change in the father figure is also accompanied by a breakdown in parental authority as sons begin to either disagree with or defy their parents.

Because the father is no longer always strong and good, (that is, an idealistic Patriot), commitment becomes a problem for several of the latter-day heroes. Some, like Tim Meeker in *My Brother Sam Is Dead* and Alex MacLeod in *Who Comes to King's Mountain?*, "sit on the fence," and agonize over whether to cast their lot with the Patriot or Loyalist factions. Others, like Daniel West in *Early Thunder* and Harry Warrilow in *Redcoat in Boston* are initially pro-British and are "converted" in the course of the novels. In spite of this problem of commitment, the last period is marked by a de-emphasis in the role played by values and ideals in generating action. Thus, while the protagonists in the first two periods are fervently attached to Revolutionary ideology and desire only to contribute to its advancement, those in the last period often lack such commitment. Several end up rejecting Revolutionary ideals, a development that would have been unthinkable in the moral universe of periods 1 and 2.

The novels in the last period focus on the personalized, often highly introspective experiences of the protagonists that often become a substitute for values and ideals as reasons for acting. Despite these important changes, the fundamental outline of the Revolution as a rite of passage remains intact. Whether or not commitment is an issue, the protagonist's involvement with the Revolution continues to serve as a crucible that readies him or her for initiation into the adult world.

The Revolution in Periods 3 and 4

The novels in periods 1 and 2 emphasize the role played by ideas and ideology in generating opposition to British rule. The tyrannical attempts of King George to limit colonial rights and liberties are met with the almost unanimous opposition of characters who recognize that these policies threaten their way of life. Discussion of these matters is usually presented in a simplistic manner with heavy reliance on impassioned rhetoric and the repeated invocation of rarely defined slogans such as "freedom," "liberty," and "the rights of man." Another important characteristic of these novels is the fact that many of these champions of liberty who wax so eloquently about freedom are themselves slaveholders. What is most striking—aside from the shockingly vulgar manner in which black characters are stereotyped—is that the characters never perceive the contradiction between their rhetoric and their action. This issue is first, though fleetingly, addressed in Rebecca Caudill's, *Tree of Freedom* (1949). Thereafter blacks effectively disappear from the novels; authors, with the exception of Edwards, seem either unwilling or unable to confront this central paradox of American history.[19]

Although the novels in Period 3 (1959–1961) continue the essential outlines of the Whig interpretation, there is less of the overblown rhetoric that characterizes the earlier novels. One book, Wibberley's *John Treegate's Musket* (1959) contains considerable discussion of the economic issues that contributed to the Revolution, although it ultimately rests on a conception stressing the fact that British policies resulted in "the butchery of rights which seem . . . natural to every man" (p. 183).

Of the eight books written during Period 4 (1967–1976), five embody the Consensus interpretation, although the way the issues are discussed varies considerably. Jean Fritz's *Early Thunder* (1967) and Ann Finlayson's *Redcoat in Boston* (1971), for example, contain extensive discussion of issues in addition to manifesting the increased preoccupation with the psychological state of the protagonist alluded to previously. While in other instances this concern leads to a de-emphasis of discussion of the issues involved in the conflict, such discussion is central to *Early Thunder* and *Redcoat in Boston*. These novels exemplify the "conversion variant" of the rite-of-passage motif. Both envision the Revolution being fought for political rights and liberties—consistent with the Consensus interpretation—but do *not* see the American side having exclusive claim to virtue and decency. Because these books are more evenhanded in their presentation of the issues at hand, there is a noticeable absence of the sharply defined good/bad opposition present in the earlier novels. This is so because the protagonists themselves are, at first, actively pro-British, necessitating a less biased approach to the depiction of that side and its beliefs.

Perhaps the most significant changes in Period 4 (1967–1976) concern the fact that the values and ideals that the earlier protagonists were so willing to sacrifice and even to die for are no longer sufficient motivation for several of the contemporary protagonists. Even *My Brother Sam Is Dead*, however, a book whose protagonist chooses not to participate in the war, ends with an epilogue that speaks with certainty that the nation will have a "great history."

Although the novels written during periods 3 and 4 depart in important respects from those of the earlier periods, the differences have more to do with changes in tone, emphasis, and the coding of the oppositions than with differences in the underlying vision of the Revolution. Despite these important changes, the majority of the novels in Period 4 conceive of the Revolution in a manner consistent with the earlier periods. An exception is *My Brother Sam Is Dead*, a book that falls short of its claim to incorporate the Progressive interpretation. Another is Richard Snow's *Freelon Starbird*. While Snow succeeds in debunking the Whig interpretation, he fails to provide a sense of what the Revolution was really about. The one book to offer a truly alternative perspective on the Revolution is Sally Edwards's *When the World's On Fire* (1972). The book is unique for several reasons, including its explicit incorporation of the Progressive/Revisionist interpretation. *When the World's On Fire* contains the only black protagonist in the sample and is alone in confronting the paradox of a war for liberty and national freedom being conducted by a group including large numbers of slave-holders. Finally, the book is one of three that do not contain the rite-of-passage motif that is central to the others. That a single novel should vary in so many important respects from the rest of the sample is more than a coincidence: it follows from the text's unique perspective on the Revolution.

Set in Charleston, South Carolina, the novel is a fictionalized account of how a ten-year-old-slave, Annie McGee, blew up a British munitions arsenal. The author extensively discusses the economic grievances that drove artisans like Annie's master, Timothy McGee, to revolt against the British. Here, Edwards makes an explicit connection between economic interests and the much-discussed, though rarely defined, liberties threatened by British policies. Men like McGee, for example, saw that their "rights as full-fledged citizens were slipping away" and "wanted American manufactures for Americans" (p. 56). McGee and his leather-aproned cohorts were opposed by the aristocratic "Nabobs," who viewed them as vulgar and unfit to be "profound politicians or able statesmen" (p. 57).

Edwards's poignant picture of the tragic situation confronting blacks during the Revolution, is best summarized by Maum Kate:

> The Americans promise freedom, if only we will ride and fight with them in the swamps. The Americans babble about liberty—yet it is only their own liberty they dream of, not ours. And the British, the most civilized of men, promise freedom only to enslave the slaves. We lose either way.[p. 101]

Kate's greatest rage is voiced as she recalls the day when the Declaration of Independence reached Charleston. Her words are especially important given the extent to which other authors ignore, or deny, the very reality she so forthrightly confronts:

> What beautiful words the white men write—life, liberty and the pursuit of happiness. Four men from Charleston signed that declaration. Yet their slaves are still slaves, serving at tables, toiling in the fields. [p. 101]

Because Edwards presents such a different conception of the Revolution, it is not surprising that her book also differs structurally in terms of the rite-of-passage motif. The difference can be seen in the changes the Revolution works on Annie as well as in the attitude the author conveys toward the events she describes.

Annie McGee is one of the youngest heroines in the sample and so is particularly weak and vulnerable. Being a slave, she is completely dependent on her master. Despite undergoing some significant changes, Annie remains a frightened little girl at the novel's conclusion. What is perhaps most significant is her realization that her people *can* struggle successfully on their own behalf and that with courage and steadfastness even a terrified child can contribute to that struggle. Annie has also survived the tragic death of her brother, which contributes to the sense that she has become stronger, and more self-reliant. Nevertheless, she remains a slave at the conclusion of the novel, whose tone is one of tragic resignation. An epilogue to the novel states that even those slaves who fought for the American cause were, "with few exceptions, returned voluntarily, and otherwise, to their masters" (p. 124). Edwards leaves the reader with an impression of the Revolution that is quite different from the one presented in the other books, with a sense of rage mingled with despair.

Consequently, it is difficult to conceive of Edwards's Revolution as a rite of passage. In fact, her book contains the implicit understanding that for significant numbers of Americans, the Revolution had not been won and had actually just begun.

Historical Interpretation and the Selective Tradition

A major conclusion of the foregoing analysis is that the authors have drawn selectively from the range of interpretations of the Revolution. Despite changes in tone and emphasis, and several exceptions, the sample *as a whole* is dominated by a vision of the Revolution as a struggle to secure political rights and independence from Britain. Missing from the overwhelming majority of books is any discussion of the internal conflict over who should rule at home. This question, which preoccupied Progressive and Revisionist historians, is central only to Edwards's book.

A simplistic, selective, and conservative conception of the Revolutions also reinforced by the narrative structure of the novels. The coding of the characters along the good/bad opposition, for example, was said to reinforce an image of the Revolution as a conflict pitting virtue and progress against evil reaction. This was particularly true of the novels in periods 1 and 2, which are all informed by the Whig interpretation. Finally, the metaphoric use of the rite-of-passage motif reinforces the notion that the Revolution was exclusively concerned with the question of home rule and not with issues relating to social, economic, and political justice. In choosing to conceive of the Revolution in this manner, the novels ratify an image of America as a society free of deeply rooted social conflict.[20] Given the high degree of social stratification in contemporary America and the persistence of racism and sexism, the perspective on the Revolution and American history that dominates the sample clearly seems to favor those occupying positions of wealth and dominance.

In conclusion, the evidence presented in this chapter indicates that the overwhelming majority of books contain an interpretation of the Revolution that is both simplistic and conservative, because it omits significant dimensions of the conflict including the concerns of the black segment of the colonial population. The point is not to claim that "the struggle over 'who should rule at home' was as important as the conflict for home rule against Britain—although for some people it clearly was just that."[21] Instead the evidence suggests that within at least one body of children's historical fiction, a selective tradition exists that legitimates a conception of the Revolution that does not embody the interests of all Americans. That *When the World's On Fire*, the only book to address the contradictions raised by the black presence in revolutionary America, is already out of print only supports this contention.[22]

Social Sources of the Narrative Form

Wright argued that the model of action presented by the Classical Western corresponded to the requirements of a "market economy," while the model implicit in the more contemporary Professional Western provided a blueprint for behavior suited to the demands of life under a "corporate economy." He marshalled some impressive evidence suggesting that these changes were reflected both in the oppositions that define the meaning inherent in the characters and in the sequence of events, or functions, that describe their actions.

A reductive reading, or interpretation, of the meaning of the narrative structure of either the Western or the novels under discussion is fraught with dangers. It assumes, first, that one can specify what Eagleton termed "the dominant ideology of an age.[23] It is also predicated on the belief that such ideologies are reflected in a straightforward way into the art, literature, and myriad institutions (such as schools, for example) of a society. Assumptions such as these pose significant theoretical as well as practical problems. These include the difficult questions of how the highly idiosyncratic lives of authors, film directors, and others "mediate" these ideologies, as well as how the processes of literary (and motion picture) production, distribution, and consumption shape and or transform both the ideologies and the cultural artifact in question. The view that a monolithic series of ideological structures are inexorably imprinted on literature, films, and institutions such as schools also leads to the reduction of human agents to mere puppets in the face of overwhelming forces beyond their ability to control. It fails to address the question of whether the meanings imputed to these works are those the general public, whether consciously or not, gains from reading a novel or watching a film. Despite these words of caution, the parallels between Wright's study and my own in regard to matters such as the coding of oppositions demands that careful consideration be given to the possible impact that the general ideological climate of an era has on products of the culture, such as novels and films. In order to make this point clear it is necessary to discuss these similarities in greater detail.

In the Classical Western that dominates the period from 1930 to 1955 (such as *Shane* and *The Far Country*), one encounters strong and good heroes who give up their independent status when they decide to oppose the bad, materialistic villains who threaten society. The society itself is weak but represents such important social values as peace, equality, family, love, and morality. In giving up their independence to defend society and its values, the heroes are said to represent the autonomous market individual who symbolically works out the conceptual conflict between bourgeois values and the institutions of capitalism.

> Bourgeois values . . . are . . . founded on consensual norms that stress freedom, equality, peace, and the theoretical availability of meaningful human relationships—family, love, satisfying work—to everyone. The institutions of capitalism, however, structure actual human relationships according to the needs of the self-regulating market, which, of course, is not concerned with social values but with profit and production.[24]

The Classical Western seeks to resolve this institutional contradiction on a practical level by providing a paradigm of appropriate behavior to overcome it.[25] The solution occurs when the hero decides to oppose the villains, who, in their unrestrained drive for wealth and power, represent the unbridled market self-interest theoretically necessary for the self-regulating market to operate. Their defeat is an affirmation of the social values of bourgeois society, which the heroes uphold when they give up their independent status to oppose the villains.

A similar configuration exists in the books that dominate periods 1 and 2, although children's Revolutionary War fiction certainly does not directly seek to resolve the dilemma posed by the conflict between bourgeois social values and those demanded by the self-regulating market. The underlying dimensions of this conflict are, however, apparent in the coding of the good/bad opposition found in the overwhelming majority of books written during these two periods, which cover the years 1899 to 1953.

Books like *A Continental Dollar* (1923), *Freedom's Daughter* (1930), *The Green Cockade* (1942), *Rebel Siege* (1943), *Treason at the Point* (1944), and *Battle Lanterns* (1949) paint a clear and unambiguous picture of the world. Repeatedly, one encounters youthful heroes and heroines who are models of good behavior. They are obedient, respect authority, and accept their elders' perception of the crisis between England and her colonies. The protagonists' embrace of the values and ideology of the American cause is an important characteristic of the novels in periods 1 and 2 because these constitute the reason for their involvement in the conflict. Thus, the heroes and heroines of these early novels struggle to advance a set of values, in a manner similar to their counterparts in the Classical Western.

The families of these early protagonists are strong and harmonious and provide them a source of nurture and sustenance. They also serve as the locus of social values—a role played by the society in the Classical Western. The elders, be they fathers or "father figures," accept these values and as a result are invariably portrayed as models of strength and virtue. They fight on behalf of the ideology of the Revolution because it promises to bring about a just social order conducive to the maintenance of the institutions of home, family, church, and so on—which Classical Western heroes also seek to uphold. In their struggle to advance these aims, these good and strong adults are opposed by calculating, avaricious individuals whose efforts to advance their narrow self-interest threatens to undermine the success of the cause. This selfish materialism is the most significant characteristic of these early villains. In rejecting the values that their opposites espouse, the villains of periods 1 and 2—like counterparts in the Classical Western—may be seen as a manifestation of the "unbridled market self-interest" that poses so ominous a threat to those seeking to establish a just and humane society. Thus, two quite different narrative forms, created at approximately the same time, manifest significant parallels in the codings that define the most basic qualities of their central characters.

Determining the "source" of the good/bad opposition, especially its idealist/materialist coding, is particularly important in light of the insignificance of economic causation in the Whig interpretation that informs all of the books written during periods 1 and 2. Because·the era during which the Classical Western predominated overlaps periods 1 and 2, one can argue that the meanings embedded in characters in both the Western films and the Revolutionary fiction are, to some extent, products of the dominant ideological structures of this time. Wright argued that these structures are those of the "market economy." Being a fundamentally different genre intended for a different audience, children's Revolutionary War fiction does not, as was noted previously, seek to resolve the contradiction between bourgeois social values and the needs of the self-regulating market that is the "subject" of the Classical Western. Nevertheless, the underlying meaning of the coding of the characters of these novels does seem to embody the same tensions and contradictions that inform the Classical Western. It is, therefore, possible to conclude, if not prove in a strictly empirical sense, that a basic dimension of the novels in periods 1 and 2—the coding of the good/bad opposition—is consistent with that found in the Classical Western films. That is, they seem, in admittedly varying degrees, to bear the imprint of the contradictory ideologies of the market economy.

Coming of age for the characters in period 1 and 2 is primarily a question of demonstrating readiness and worthiness to enter the world of responsible adulthood. It is *not* concerned with finding a set of meanings and values to guide one's life. The Revolution functions as the vehicle by which the characters prove their readiness. On the most basic level, then, the model of social action presented in these books suggests that duty, commitment, persistence, and obedience will ultimately lead to success and acceptance into the adult world. There is, however, a significant shift in the manner in which characters are coded and the model of action presented in both the Western and the final periods of this study (1959–1961 and 1967–1976).

The coding of the Professional Western, which begins in the late fifties and dominates the sixties and seventies, is a radical departure from that of the Classical. The good/bad distinction, which had previously depended both on an individual's qualities as a person and on his or her commitment to social values, is now dependent solely on the viewer's feelings for the heroes as opposed to the villains. Consequently, the sympathy we feel for the likes of Butch Cassidy and the Sundance Kid—the heroes of perhaps the best known Professional Western—stems from their niceness and geniality in comparison to those they oppose. The fact that heroes of the Professional Westerns often act in a decidedly antisocial fashion (Butch and Sundance are outlaws) is a development that would have been unthinkable in the world of the Classical Western.

According to Wright, a change of this magnitude is possible because of the transformation of the image of society itself. No longer the seat of social values, the society of the Professional Western is characterized as "petty, self-righteous, dull, and mercenary."[26] Wright explained this change in society's image as being a result of the evolution of the basic economic matrix of society from one based on a self-regulating market to one managed, and directed, by corporate and government technocrats. Concomitant to this change is a commitment to the creation and utilization of large-scale technology. Consequently, "the values of the institutional framework of society—equality, community, freedom, and so forth—are replaced by the values of the . . . economy—economic growth, profits, and creation of markets."[27]

A result of this change in society's image is a change in how the strength of the heroes is defined. Strength is now solely a function of a character's technical proficiency as a gunfighter. Virtue and idealism are no longer significant in the assessment of a character. Furthermore, the fight that energizes the Professional heroes is fought for money rather than to advance social values—a development stemming from the fact that neither the heroes or society have any values.[28]

What *is* valued in the Professional Western is the elite group formed to "fight the fight." Membership in this group depends entirely upon technical skill (for example, fighting ability) and absolute acceptance of the goals of the group (for example, the fight for money), and the interactions of the group are characterized by loyalty, respect, and friendship. Thus, because the changes in social institutions preclude the formation of satisfying relationships within society itself, and because society has become something to be avoided, powerful elite groups are created to provide meaningful social interactions. Summing up the significance of this transformation, Wright observed that

> In the sixties and seventies, the traditional conceptual conflict between the idea of society and the idea of the individual has been transformed into a conflict between society and an elite group. This is perhaps one of the most significant consequences of the emergence of capitalist technology as a social and ideological force.[29]

As was the case with the parallels between the Classical Western and the novels in periods 1 and 2, the similarities between the Professional Western—the first of which appeared in 1959—and the books in periods 3 (1959–1961) and 4 (1967–1976) pertain to the coding of characters along the various oppositions. In addition, the novels written during periods 3 and 4 evidence a displacement of values as instigators of action. Finally, the contemporary novels also manifest a change in the image of the family, which in the earlier novels served a function similar to that of the society in the Classical Western.

Although the protagonists of periods 3 and 4 do not reject the values and ideology of the Revolution in the manner that the Professional Western heroes disdain society and its values, a comparison of the role of values in the novels and the Westerns does reveal some striking similarities. We have seen, for example, that both the protagonists and adults in periods 1 and 2 wholeheartedly embrace the ideals of the Revolution and that this idealistic stance is crucial to their definition as individuals who are "good." The first crack in this consensus occurs in *Tree of Freedom* (1949) where Jonathan Venable and his son Noel argue over the proper course of action to take in regard to the Revolution. Their disagreement, however, does not concern the efficacy of the cause but rather whether or not it is necessary to get involved in it. Nevertheless, this initial "falling out" between a father and son constitutes a fissure in the previously unbroken solidarity of family relationships and foreshadows a significant disintegration in family relationships in the novels of periods 3 and 4.

Disagreement and dissension between fathers and sons is visible in *John Treegate's Musket* (1950), *April Morning* (1961), *Early Thunder* (1967), *My Brother Sam Is Dead* (1974), *Who Comes to King's Mountain?* (1975), and *Freelon Starbird* (1976). With the exception of the split between the Coopers in *April Morning*, all of these disputes are concerned with differing perceptions of the correct course of action to take in the war. However, while books like *John Treegate's Musket* and *Early*

Thunder depict a disagreement between father and son over the question of allegiance and end up affirming the values espoused by the Patriots, *My Brother Sam Is Dead*, *Who Comes to King's Mountain?* and *Freelon Starbird* end up rejecting Revolutionary ideology as sufficient cause to go to war. Furthermore, two other novels written in Period 4, *Rebecca's War* (1972) and *Ruffles and Drums* (1975), have little to say about principles and values, being more concerned with the highly personalized, introspective reactions of an individual to crisis and conflict. Finally, while *When the World's On Fire* (1972) affirms the need for individuals, both black and white, to live with dignity and freedom, it exposes the hypocrisy and contradictions inherent in Revolutionary ideology and therefore constitutes a particular kind of rejection of these values.

The last two periods are thus marked by a decline in the role of values in determining the actions of characters in regard to the Revolution. Period 4 (1967–1976) novels in particular also parallel the Professional Western in the way that reader sympathy and identification is established. Since belief in the ideology of the Revolution no longer contributes to this identification, the reader's sympathy for the contemporary protagonists becomes an exclusive function of his or her empathy with the existential dilemma faced by these characters. Thus, the significance of a Tim Meeker's (*My Brother Sam Is Dead*) decision to sit out the war, an Alec MacLeod (*Who Comes to King's Mountain?*) deciding to join the American army because of his affection for Francis Marion (instead of belief in the efficacy of the American cause), and Freelon Starbird's (*Freelon Starbird*) "accidental" enlistment into the Continental Army, can only be grasped when measured against the explanations of allegiance offered by the likes of Reba Stanhope (*Freedom's Daughter*), Rab Silesbee (*Johnny Tremain*), and Bill Barlow (*Battle Lanterns*). The protagonists of periods 1 and 2 display heroism, fortitude, and courage that justifies their being called heroes or heroines. In contrast, most of the central figures in periods 3 and 4 are often less than heroic. This evolution of the central character from hero or heroine to simple protagonist parallels the change from the hero of the Classical Western to the antihero in the Professional Western. Both tendencies seem to be related to the fact that neither the protagonists of the contemporary novels nor the antiheroes of the Professional Western champion an explicitly articulated set of values.

This decline in the importance of values also coincides with and reinforces the fracture of the family and family relationships. Not only do fathers and sons have ideological disagreements not visible in the earlier novels, but the image of the father himself has, in many instances, been transformed. While fathers had previously been depicted as paragons of strength and virtue, several of the fathers of the contemporary period are portrayed as weak and indecisive. One father, Lachan MacLeod (*Who

Comes to King's Mountain?) is even shown to be driven by the same selfish materialism that had defined the villains of periods 1 and 2. Thus, two of the defining characteristics of periods 1 and 2 have been markedly altered in the last two periods. The first of these changes, that in the role of values in determining the allegiance of the protagonist, directly parallels a change Wright documented in the Professional Western. The second, the disruption of the solidarity of the family, is paralleled, in a more general way, by the changed image of the society in the contemporary Western. While the family in the later books is not depicted as bad, unlike the society of the Professional Western, the divisions within it and the altered appearance of some of the fathers do constitute a shift in the perception of an institution basic to the structure of the novels.

A possible explanation for this altered perception of the family and family relationships is available in Christopher Lasch's account of the changing nature of the relations between the family and society. Lasch argues that capitalism's "late stages" have reduced the conflict between society and the family to a minimum while intensifying "almost every-other form of conflict." In a world grown "more menacing and insecure," the family is no longer able to "offer protection from external dangers," a fact which results in the attenuation of "all forms of loyalty." As a consequence, the work ethic, as well as the drive for achievement once nurtured by the family, "gives way to an ethic of survival and immediate gratification." An important result of this development is the replacement of the seeker of status and success by what Lasch terms "the narcissist."[30]

The developments described by Lasch are visible when one compares the families in periods 1 and 2 to those in periods 3 and 4. We have seen how an overwhelming majority of the families in the earlier periods provide their sons and daughters with a strong sense of security and duty as well as a devotion to the values represented by the Revolution. In contrast, many novels published in periods 3 and 4—several of which contain the fence-sitting and conversion variants of the rite-of-passage motif—present families that do not function in this fashion. Most of the protagonists in the latter periods no longer seek, above all, to contribute to the Revolution (and in so doing become a hero or heroine) but desire only to survive the conflict that has disturbed their previously tranquil world. Thus, in novels like *Early Thunder*, *My Brother Sam Is Dead*, *Who Comes to King's Mountain?*, and *Freelon Starbird* the focus turns to an intense, at times almost narcissistic, attempt by the protagonists to chart a course in a world that has, in effect, lost its compass points.

Wright argued that the change from the Classical to the Professional Western corresponded to the transition from a "market" to a "corporate" economy. This change is reflected in the replacement of the lone gunman of the Classical Western, who gives up his independent status to fight for social values, by the elite group of gunfighters who undertake a fight for the sake of money alone. Of course the protagonists of the contemporary novels, even those who reject Revolutionary ideology, do not join the cause to make money, nor do they form elite groups comparable to those found in contemporary Westerns. Nevertheless, it is suggested that this congruent displacement of values as motivators of action in both the novels and the films is traceable to a shift in the basic pattern of institutional organization. This change has undercut, and in some instances negated, values that had previously been important. The differences between the two kinds of narratives (for example, the absence in the novels of the elite group) are not nearly so significant as this similarity in their underlying "deep structure." The differences can simply be explained by the inherent dissimilarity between the forms themselves. In this regard, Eagleton's suggestion that each literary form has a "relatively autonomous" history that needs to be scrutinized in its own right is significant. Eagleton does, however, point out that literary forms crystallize out of "certain dominant ideological structures" present at specific junctures in history.[31] A possible implication of the foregoing analysis is that the changes in the narrative structure of children's Revolutionary War fiction are, at least in part, products of the structural changes Wright advanced to explain the changes in the form of Western films.

This thesis is also helpful in explaining another important development found in Period 4: the preoccupation with highly personalized, introspective accounts of the Revolution. In *Rebecca's War* and *Ruffles and Drums*, concern with individual characters leads to the virtual exclusion of discussion of the war and its issues. In *My Brother Sam Is Dead*, *Who Comes to King's Mountain?* and *Freelon Starbird*, this preoccupation with subjective feelings and reactions leads to outright rejection of Revolutionary ideology. While the novel itself is a literary form whose history reflects a growing preoccupation with the individual, and individual experience, that preoccupation accompanied social and economic transformations concomitant to the growth of industrial capitalism.[32] The intense focus on individual experience manifested in the later books carries these tendencies to extremes not evidenced in earlier works. This tendency, taken in conjunction with the lessening importance of values and beliefs as instigators of action, yields an intensely subjective picture of the Revolution not present in earlier works, where there is, at least, agreement on what the war is about.

The model of social action suggested by many of the contemporary novels differs significantly from that of earlier works, where virtue, selflessness, duty, and commitment to clearly defined values led to success and acceptance in the world of responsible adulthood. Although passage to adulthood is still the central concern of these latter-day novels, there is now a preoccupation with each individual's perception of reality and a rejection of the notion that the initiates must accept the dictates of their elders. Many no longer do so, and as a consequence they struggle to decide precisely what is, and what is not, worth fighting for. Thus, one of the implicit "messages" of many of the Period 4 novels is that values and ideals are suspect and to be viewed with suspicion—a development that means that each individual must chart his or her own way through the confusion and tumult of life. Further, one cannot always expect guidance from others, since even parents are shown to fail occasionally to provide proper guidance and sound judgment. Personal experience and feeling are thus the keys to knowledge and can be said to have been elevated to the status previously held by Revolutionary ideology and the values associated with the family. Indeed the frequency of the fence-sitting and conversion plot variations during this period points to the uncertainty and confusion resulting from the eclipse of the values that were previously accepted without question. It is only through an often painful testing of the waters—often involving serious disagreements with their family— that some of the contemporary protagonists decide on a suitable course of action.

Several other social theorists provide additional support for this attempt to understand the changes in structure and character coding in light of changes in socioeconomic institutions and values. Sennett, for example, explained contemporary America's preoccupation with the self as follows:

> The value American society places on individual experience might seem to lead its citizens to measure all social life in terms of personal feeling. However, it is not rugged individualism which is now experienced; rather, it is anxiety about individual feeling which individuals write large in terms of the way the world works. The source of this anxiety lies in broad changes in capitalism and in religious belief.[33]

Basil Bernstein's discussion of the relationship between class, several forms of pedagogy, and historical developments within the middle class provides an additional explanation of the decline in the role that a coherent set of values plays in instigating the action in the novels published in periods 3 and 4. Bernstein noted that the relatively recent development of a "new" middle class has resulted in the displacement of the "old" middle class. Born in the nineteenth century, the old middle class was based on an ideology of "radical individualism" that presupposed "explicit and unambiguous values." The new middle class, a product of the "middle/late twentieth century formation," is characterized by "ambiguity in its values and purpose,"[34] a quality we have seen to be typical of many of the important protagonists of the last two periods of the sample.

The analysis outlined here lends credence to the claims of Bourdieu and Willis presented at the outset of this chapter. We have seen that the novels discussed in this chapter and the films scrutinized by Wright do, in fact, contain "symbolic representation(s) of the social world adjusted to the structure of socioeconomic relationships." These cultural artifacts can thus be said to legitimate these relationships, which then assume a "natural appearance."[35] Such "symbolic buttressing" also tends to obscure what Williams termed "the indissoluable connections between material production, political and cultural institutions and activity and consciousness."[36] The connection between the specific behavioral models ratified by the novels (and those discussed by Wright) and the historical epoch in which they were written is an illustration of this crucial theoretical point.

Conclusion

A basic thesis of this chapter is that an adequate analysis of curricular materials such as textbooks or literature for children must consider the form or structure of these materials, as well as their content. Although researchers have increasingly focused attention on the form of classroom interactions, they have only recently begun to understand that the form of curricular materials is also a significant bearer of meaning and ideology.

Discussions about the "determinations" of social, cultural, and political phenomena are today the subject of considerable controversy, as is illustrated by the debate surrounding Bowles and Gintis's correspondence theory.[37] While the present chapter cannot, of course, resolve these issues, several points seem clear. The first pertains to the need for those who would understand the processes of schooling and cultural creation to remain sensitive to the profound ways in which historically specific organizations and institutions shape human activity. Life in an advanced industrial, capitalist society *does* cause us to enter into specific kinds of relationships with each other and with our social environment. It influences our thinking, work, art, and politics—in short, all areas of human endeavor. We think, organize, and perceive our world as we do, at least in part, because of the basic ways in which our society is organized. The remarkable similarities between the children's novels and Western films clearly suggests that there are parallels between the ways that historically rooted attitudes, social values, and ideologies make their way into and are reflected in imaginative works of different genres. Precisely how, and to what degree, the basic institutional matrix "determines" the content and form of specific products for culture, and our existence in general, is difficult to say, although it seems apparent that these matters cannot be simplistically reduced to a reflection of a given mode of production.

What is clear is that our understanding of the processes of schooling, as well as of the various forms of culture that are so central to the shaping of our lives and consciousness, has been greatly enhanced by the work of those who have taken the kind of approach to the study of these phenomena outlined in this chapter. The challenge confronting those who would enliven educational discourse and the study of culture with the insights of critical social theories—like those of Marx—is to use and go beyond analyses of the kind presented here and to maintain a sensitivity to the historic specificity of culture and classroom life without reducing them to mere reflections of inexorable, uncontrollable, impersonal "forces of production" that would ultimately deny us the power to shape and influence our world.

Notes

1. See Pierre Bourdieu, "The Thinkable and the Unthinkable," *Times Literary Supplement*, 15 October 1971, 1255–56; Terry Eagleton, *Marxism and Literary Criticism* (Berkeley: Univeristy of California Press, 1976); and Raymond Williams, *Marxism and Literature* (New York: Oxford University Press, 1977).

2. Bourdieu, "The Thinkable and the Unthinkable," p. 1255.

3. Paul Willis, *Learning to Labour* (Lexington: D.C. Heath, 1977), p. 74.

4. Joel Taxel, "The Depiction of the American Revolution in Children's Fiction: A Study in the Sociology of School Knowledge" (Ph.D. diss.; University of Wisconsin-Madison, 1980).

5. R. Gordon Kelly, "Mother Was a Lady: Strategy and Order in Selected American Children's Periodicals, 1865–1890" (Ph.D. Diss.; University of Iowa, 1970). See also R. Gordon Kelly "Literature and the Historian," *American Quarterly* 26 (1974): 141–159.

6. Michael W. Apple and Philip Wexler, "Cultural Capital and Educational Transmissions," *Educational Theory* 28 (Winter 1978): 40.

7. Will Wright, *Sixguns and Society* (Berkeley: University of California Press, 1975), p. 193.

8. Kelly, "Mother Was a Lady," p. 91.

9. Wright, *Sixguns and Society*, p. 14. There are, of course, serious conceptual problems with mechanistic correspondence theories. For discussions of this see Williams, *Marxism and Literature*, and Michael W. Apple, *Education and Power* (Boston: Routledge and Kegan Paul, 1982).

10. Wright, *Sixguns and Society*, pp. 20–21.

11. See Taxel, "Depiction of the American Revolution" for a more thorough review of the historiography of the Revolution.

12. Edmund S. Morgan, "Slavery and Freedom: The American Paradox," in Allen Davis and Harold Woodman, eds., *Conflict and Consensus in Early American History* (Lexington: D.C. Heath, 1976), pp. 5–17.

13. See, for example, Maribelle Cormack and William Alexander, *Land for My Sons*; M. P. Allen, *The Green Cockade*; and Enid Meadowcroft, *Silver for General Washington*.

14. Michael Kammen, *A Season of Youth: The American Revolution and the Historical Imagination* (New York: Alfred A. Knopf, 1978), p. 206.

15. See, for example, Lorna Beers, *The Crystal Cornerstone*; Rebecca Caudill, Tree of Freedom; and Jim Kjelgaard, *Rebel Siege*.

16. This is also true of the characters in M. P. Allen, *Battle Lanterns*; Esther Forbes, *Johnny Tremain*; E. B. and A. A. Knipe, *A Continental Dollar*; and J. C. Nolan *Treason at the Point*.

17. See also the discussion of the rite-of-passage motif in Revolutionary War fiction written for adults in Kammen, *A Season of Youth*, p. 206.

18. Ibid.

19. For a fuller discussion of the treatment of blacks in the sample, see Joel Taxel, "The Outsiders of the American Revolution: The Selective Tradition in Children's Fiction," *Interchange* 12, no. 2–3 (1981): 206–28.

20. These conclusions are consistent with those of Kammen, who found that authors of Revolutionary War fiction intended for adults also emphasized the political aspects of the Revolution while ignoring its internal, social dimensions. See Kammen, *A Season of Youth*.

21. Alfred F. Young, ed., *The American Revolution: Explorations in the History of American Radicalism* (DeKalb: Northern Illinois University Press, 1976), p. 450.

22. Of the twenty-one books published in periods 1 (1899–1930) and 2 (1937–1953), only Esther Forbes, *Johnny Tremain*; Enid Meadowcroft, *Silver for General Washington*; and Lorna Beers, *The Crystal Cornerstone* remain in print. Two of three books in Period 3 (1959–1961), Leonard Wibberly, *John Treegate's Musket*, and Howard Fast, *April Morning*, are still available. Of the eight books published in Period 4 (1967–1976) only Ann Finlayson, *Redcoat in Boston*, and Sally Edwards *When the World's On Fire*, are out of print. Finlayson's *Redcoat in Boston* offers a British soldier's view of the Revolution, the only book in the sample to contain this perspective. Thus the two books in Period 4 presently not available are those that present relatively unconventional views of the Revolution.

23. Eagleton, *Marxism and Literary Criticism*, p. 6.

24. Wright, *Sixguns and Society*, p. 135.

25. Ibid., p. 150.

26. Ibid., p. 183.

27. Ibid., p. 177.

28. Ibid., pp. 182–83.

29. Ibid., p. 184.

30. Christopher Lasch, *Haven in a Heartless World* (New York: Basic Books, 1979), pp. *xxiii–xxiv*.

31. Eagleton, *Marxism and Literary Criticism*, p. 26.

32. See Raymond Williams, *The Long Revolution* (London: Chatto and Windus, 1961), pp. 276–316 and Eagleton, *Marxism and Literary Criticism*.

33. Richard Sennett, *The Fall of Public Man* (New York: Vintage Books, 1978), p. 5.

34. Basil Bernstein, *Class, Codes and Control*, vol. 3 (Boston: Routledge and Kegan Paul, 1977), p. 20.

35. Bourdieu, "The Thinkable and the Unthinkable," p. 1255.

36. Williams, *Marxism and Literature*, p. 80.

37. Samuel Bowles and Herbert Gintis, *Schooling in Capitalist America* (New York: Basic Books, 1976). For an analysis of these debates, as well as for theories that go beyond such correspondence principles, see Michael W. Apple, ed., *Cultural and Economic Reproduction in Education: Essays on Class, Ideology and the State* (Boston: Routledge and Kegan Paul, 1982).

Appendix: Books Used in This Study

Period 1

Ford, P. L. *Janice Meredith*. New York: Dodd, Mead & Co., 1899.

Altsheler, Joseph. *The Scouts of the Valley*. New York: Appleton-Century Crofts, 1911.

Knipe, E. B., and Knipe, A. A. *A Continental Dollar*. The Century Co., 1923.

Boyd, James. *Drums*. New York: Charles Scribner's, 1925.

Skinner, C. L. *Silent Scot, Frontier Scout*. New York: MacMillan, 1923.

Perkins, L. F. *American Twins of the Revolution*. Boston: Houghton-Mifflin, 1926.

Crownfield, Gertrude. *Freedom's Daughter*. New York: E. P. Dutton, 1930.

Gray, Elizabeth. *Meggy MacIntosh*. New York: Viking, 1930.

Period 2

Hawthorne, Hildegarde. *Rising Thunder*. New York: Longmans, Green and Co., 1937.

Singmaster, Elsie. *Rifles for Washington*. Boston: Houghton-Mifflin, 1938.

Cormack, Maribelle, and Alexander, William. *Land For My Sons*. New York: D. Appleton-Century Co., 1939.

Allen, M. P. *The Green Cockade*. New York: Longmans, Green & Co., 1942.

Forbes, Esther. *Johnny Tremain*. New York: Dell, 1943.

Kjelgaard, Jim. *Rebel Siege*. New York: Random House, 1943.

Edmonds, W. D. *Wilderness Clearing*. New York: Dodd, Mead, & Co., 1944.

Meadowcroft, Enid. *Silver For General Washington*. New York: Thomas Crowell, 1944.

Nolan, J. C. *Treason at the Point*. New York: Julian Messner Inc., 1944.

Allen, M. P. *Battle Lanterns*. New York: Longmans, Green & Co., 1949.

Caudill, Rebecca. *Tree of Freedom*. New York: Viking, 1949.

Beers, Lorna. *The Crystal Cornerstone*. New York: Harper & Row, 1953.

Lawson, Robert. *Mr. Revere and I*. New York: Dell, 1953.

Period 3

Wibberly, Leonard. *John Treegate's Musket*. New York: Ariel Books, 1959.

Fast, Howard. *April Morning*. New York: Bantam Books, 1961.

Savery, Constance. *The Reb and the Redcoats*. London: Longmans, Green & Co., 1961.

Period 4

Fritz, Jean. *Early Thunder*. New York: Coward, McCann & Geoghegan, 1967.

Finlayson, Ann. *Redcoat in Boston*. London: Frederick Warne & Co., 1971.

Finlayson, Ann. *Rebecca's War*. London: Frederick Warne & Co., 1972.

Edwards, Sally. *When the World's On Fire*. New York: Coward, McCann & Geoghegan, 1972.

Collier, J. L., and Collier, C. *My Brother Sam Is Dead*. New York: Scholastic Book Co., 1974.

Cavanna, Betty. *Ruffles and Drums*. New York: William Morrow and Co., 1975.

Beatty, Jim, and Beatty, Patricia. *Who Comes to King's Mountain?* New York: William Morrow and Co., 1975.

Snow, Richard. *Freelon Starbird*. Boston: Houghton Mifflin, 1976.

CHAPTER 4

Aesthetic Curriculum and Cultural Reproduction

LANDON E. BEYER

While efforts to expose the social parameters of schooling have contributed a good deal to our understanding of the political, economic, and ideological dimensions of curriculum, several shortcomings of these efforts have become apparent which require a more extended analysis. First, the notion that schools and curricula serve as agents of economic reproduction is overly simplistic and reductionist. At the same time, even the more culturally oriented analysis of schools is frequently too deterministic as well. Further, we have tended to provide ideological critiques that are conceptualized and understood at a fairly abstract, macro-theoretical level. Such critiques provide little useful information with regard to how day-to-day activities and curricular offerings contribute to this process. Comparatively little attention has been paid, moreover, to the more particular question of how ideological and aesthetic form may become fused in school practice.

This chapter, while building on extant theories of economic and cultural reproduction, will address some of the important conceptual inadequacies of these theories. By examining a set of curriculum materials in aesthetic education, we will see how ideological analyses of school practice need to break with causal or impositional models of reproduction; how ideology, at the level of theory and practice, is a constitutive element of curriculum materials in aesthetics; and how aesthetic curricula, in spite of the connections that exist among aesthetics, ideology, and educational practice, are inherently contradictory, and therefore may be instrumental in creating possibilities for educational intervention that is nonreproductive. Two factors will be of special import in understanding these contradictory tendencies: the inherent capacity of aesthetic experiences to affect our thoughts, involvements, and actions outside the experience itself; and the intrinsic potential for change that modifications in curriculum form possess. Both these factors will prove helpful in understanding the contradictory nature of ideological domination—how possibilities for transformation exist within the process of domination itself.

One final introductory note is in order. This essay focuses in part on a specific curricular offering—the Aesthetic Education Program developed by the Central Midwestern Regional Education Laboratory (CEMREL). Yet the CEMREL undertaking is representative of a larger body of writing and theorizing in curriculum and aesthetics. In one sense this program is insightful in that it encapsulates both historical and contemporary theories in philosophical aesthetics and curriculum making that have attained a significant degree of popularity. It is the most thorough, systematic, and protracted attempt to date to bring aesthetic experience within the purview of general classroom instruction in this country.

Foundations for the CEMREL Program

The program in aesthetic education developed by CEMREL was directly inspired by a series of conferences and seminars held during the late 1960s and sponsored by the Arts and Humanities Program of the U. S. Office of Education. Between October 1964 and November 1966, seventeen such meetings were held in this country, thirteen of which were directly supported by the Arts and Humanities Program.

The Educators and scholars in the program divided their work into two phases. The initial phase was concerned with establishing philosophical and curricular foundations upon which a program of aesthetic education might rest, with "particular attention to substantive and methodological problems" in aesthetics and curriculum development.[1] Phase 2 of the program was to deal with the actual production, testing, and evaluation of aesthetic education materials. Those involved in phase 2 were to design materials that would embody the concepts outlined in the previous phase. It is crucial to see the conceptual foundations and the associated curriculum materials as essentially conjoined.

The selection of a curriculum development model within the Aesthetic Education Program was influenced by several complementary factors. First, in following the dominant tradition in curriculum making as outlined by Ralph Tyler,[2] those involved in this aspect of the program concluded that there was no substantive agreement among curriculum theorists about the relative importance of the learner, contemporary society, and subject matter specialists, and that "curriculum development should begin with decisions about the referents."[3]

Second, an important consideration was that any set of materials had to be constructed for national, rather than local or regional, distribution. Because of this concern it was felt that curriculum sources that involved studies of the learner or of the society would be restrictive. That is, it was felt that because the United States is a diversified country, generalizations about the society or about learners would not have a high degree of validity. Moreover, traditional disciplines, particularly the arts, were selected as the main source for curriculum development because "intellectual discourse is relatively unaffected by ethnic background, geographical location, community values, etc."[4]

Third, the program was housed in an already existing educational laboratory, with definite commitments and perspectives. A certain amount of prestige or status attends the work of such federally funded research laboratories which "necessitates adoption of organizational values consonant with their assumed responsibilities in education."[5] Educational agencies of this kind "make curriculum decisions not only in light of the arguments posed by the curriculum theorists, but also in light of the social and educational responsibilities as defined by their mission and prestige."[6] More specifically, CEMREL felt that "instructional materials similar to those that already existed in science, mathematics, and language arts were also needed to assist in curriculum development" in aesthetic education.[7]

Fourth, community and school acceptance were perhaps the key to determining a specific curriculum development model. Those involved in design and production were sensitive to the fact that some curriculum materials involving aesthetic experiences might alienate schools and communities to the extent that aesthetic education would be rejected by that school system, and so the materials had to be designed so that they would not be found objectionable by individuals and local groups, even though they were designed for national distribution. Part of this concern can be seen in the commitment to produce materials in aesthetic education similar to those found in other subject areas. In addition, it was felt that "a curriculum which incorporates the values of the society to use it will have greater chance of acceptance."[8]

For all these reasons, the curriculum workers at CEMREL decided on a system of instructional packages. Such a system, it was felt, would be able to utilize the expertise of specialists in the arts; would offer a system conducive to national distribution and implementation, in that it would be consistent with curriculum development efforts in other subject areas; would be sensitive to the "status and prestige" consideration noted above; and would allow enough flexibility to help assure school and community acceptance. A concern for educational respectability and acceptability thus dominated the thinking of those involved in this aspect of the program: a system of instructional packages was selected "to provide maximum flexibility for arrangement. The series of packages will be used by a school system as if it were a deck of cards; that is, shuffling order or sequence of units adaptable to variation in school settings and organizational patterns.'"[9]

The materials were to be designed along typical curricular lines involving scope and sequence, with different activities at different grade levels. Individual lessons were to be similarly divided into smaller components, with descriptions of the "concept," "objective," and "procedure" that would be pursued and used during the lesson. The materials were to be organized and sequenced along the lines of many curriculum kits to be, in effect, "teacher proof." Instructions in the teacher guides were to be specific, systematic, and detailed, with little room for "error." In short, "all packages [were] designed with *the general classroom teacher* in mind. Each teacher package includes a guide to general and specific objectives, evaluation, classroom management, and step-by-step lesson plans as well as all necessary media materials."[10] The individual instructional units in the program form a self-contained, autonomous system, to which little or no experience or expertise need be brought by the classroom teacher or students.

In terms of the philosophical or conceptual positions in aesthetics upon which a curriculum program might be constructed, several considerations seem important. Those involved in this program saw aesthetic education as a broader, more encompassing area of study than art education or appreciation. Rather than the construction of artifacts being emphasized, both the arts and the environment were to be used to supply examples of objects or events of aesthetic interest. In other words, the Aesthetic Education Program sought to complement instruction in the arts rather than so supplant it.[11]

In some respects an eclectic approach was taken and input into the conceptual foundations for this part of the program came from numerous sources. On the other hand, many of the theoretical positions and assumptions that were incorporated into the program were grounded in issues about which there was substantial agreement. In particular, within the writings of those who were influential in this phase of the program, there seems to be a high degree of consensus on the nature, function, and value of the aesthetic experience. Let us look briefly, then, at how these specific areas were conceptualized.[12]

Central to any program of aesthetic education is some conception of the nature of aesthetic experience. Within the work of CEMREL, it has been alleged by Stanley S. Madeja, formerly director of the program, and by Sheila Onuska, that "aesthetic education in its simplest form is learning how to perceive, judge, and value aesthetically what we come to know through our senses."[13] Further, Evan J. Kern has suggested that there "appears to be some support for the thesis that it [aesthetic education] should strive to provide a deeper understanding and appreciation for the aesthetic qualities of natural and man-made objects and events in the environment."[14]

Yet what precisely are the aesthetic qualities of our experiences with man-made and natural objects? What does it mean to learn how to perceive the aesthetic in our lives and, in appreciating this, enhance our aesthetic sensibilities? Here Madeja and Onuska illuminate a central understanding shared by virtually all the scholars, administrators, and educators who had a hand in shaping the CEMREL undertaking:

> . . . the aesthetic perception of a painting requires us to view its shapes, textures, colors, and other inherent visual elements and to interpret them into a whole conceptualization in which visual stimuli are converted into other sensory images. . . . This kind of perception has nothing to do with values extrinsic to the painting as it exists on its own, such values as how much it is worth, how large it is, how it fits into the history of art, or whether it will go with the draperies.[15]

This position is reinforced by the view that, although a definitive version of what constitutes the aesthetic experience—in terms of necessary and sufficient conditions—may never be forthcoming, "there is enough consensus among theorists to propose a functional concept of its nature: AESTHETIC EXPERIENCE IS AN EXPERIENCE WHICH IS VALUED INTRINSICALLY, an experience which is valued for itself."[16] That is, aesthetic experience is self-enclosed, not a means to any ulterior end. As Harry S. Broudy, a former member of CEMREL's National Advisory Committee, puts it, "whenever we concentrate attention on the appearance of houses, dress, sea shells, faces, automobiles, or on the dramatic structure of events and actions, we are responding aesthetically. . . . We can think of the aesthetic domain as including our experience with the appearances of natural objects and contrived ones. . . ."[17] The appearance of objects and events is here viewed as the embodiment of the aesthetic, and it is in such appearances that aesthetic value resides.

A further insight into this characterization of aesthetic experience is provided by Eugene F. Kaelin, also a former member of the National Advisory Committee of CEMREL. In considering the response of perceivers to an aesthetic object, Kaelin says, "In order to insure relevance from the outset, we may start with effectuating 'the phenomenological epoch,' i.e., attend only to the object as it conditions our present experience. Husserl referred to this practice as 'putting the world into brackets'; more accurately . . . one could say 'outside the brackets' which enclose our present state of consciousness as it is directed to its object"; and, in the process, Kaelin continues, "we consider the experience of the object for what it is, rather than as a sign for an occurrent phenomenon of nature. . . . [This bracketing of consciousness] may be the only practicable means available to the person who would come to an understanding of the data of an immediate experience. And only in those can intrinsic values be found."[18] In aesthetic experience we are instructed to bracket off from attention all but the phenomenal properties of the object under attention. In this way we may come to perceive and appreciate the object in and of itself, and to value it intrinsically.

The consequences of such phenomenologically oriented perspectives are important. In focusing on the presentational qualities of aesthetic experience, Broudy is led to suggest that, "whatever meaning or import the aesthetic object has it displays on its surface."[19] It follows that, "insofar as the realm of the aesthetic is the realm of appearance enjoyed for its own sake, it demands no commitment to action."[20] Aesthetic experience is, in this way, essentially apolitical and nonideological. Even more dramatically, Broudy instructs us that, "it is naive to believe that art cannot endanger morals. It can if the viewer is unable to perceive art objects aesthetically, *and the untrained perceiver is likely to have this infirmity* "[21] Given this characterization of aesthetic experience, any commitment to action does seem a rather distant, remote possibility, belonging more properly to other domains; moral considerations seem patently irrelevant, to be dismissed as an "infirmity" if they intrude within the brackets of our perceptual apparatus.

What emerges from the work of CEMREL, hence, is the view that aesthetic experience is essentially related to the sensual appearance of objects; is intrinsically valuable, to be judged for its own sake; is not importantly connected to external actions and experiences; and is fundamentally concerned, in sum, with the phenomenal properties of objects, and that, as a result, it is amoral, apolitical, and nonideological.

The materials that make up the Aesthetic Education Program represent a blending of these theoretical positions with the curriculum development model outlined earlier. Several aspects from each of these areas reinforce and help give legitimacy to each other. Recall that a central concern of those involved in the formulation of curriculum materials was that such materials should not jeopardize school and community acceptance of aesthetic education; there was a conscious effort to remain as neutral as possible in regard to educational values and ideas. This emphasis seems furthered by the apolitical, nonideological depiction of aesthetic experience discussed above. Both impulses seek to avoid valuational and ideological conflicts within materials designed to foster aesthetic education.

This avoidance of conflict can be seen as furthering a consensus orientation within schools generally. Even when curricular programs are intended to foster critical inquiry, they usually avoid discussion of deep, long-lasting conflicts and instead present a consensus-oriented perspective that avoids politicization. Issues and ideas are, then, frequently presented and discussed in a somewhat denuded form, abstracted from the larger social and political climates that give them life.[22] Thus the aesthetic is given, to a large extent, a life of its own. With these theoretical considerations in mind, let us look at portions of a specific curriculum unit within the program, to see how such ideas became part of the actual materials which make up the Aesthetic Education Program.

The Content of the Aesthetic Education Program

Those engaged in producing the CEMREL materials—phase II of the project—designed the program around a series of six levels or "centers of attention." In all, forty-four instructional packages were developed by the CEMREL staff. Though all these units were field tested in classroom settings, to date only ten have been published. These ten units make up the Aesthetic Education Program as it has been made available to schools and teachers across the country.

To give the flavor of this program, we will look briefly at selections from the "Relating Sound and Movement" unit designed to be used with second grade students. This curricular package forms part of the material for level three, "Aesthetics and the Creative Process." While a more detailed examination of this and other curriculum units is available elsewhere,[23] a representative slice will serve to exemplify the content of Cemrel's program.

As the title for this curriculum unit intimates, the package is designed to help students explore and experience "continuums within pitch, tempo and amount of intensity in sound; within amount of space, amount of time, and amount of force in movement."[24] This unit contains seven lessons that are aimed at helping the student explore various relationships between sound and movement: "matching sound with movement, contrasting the two, and, finally, interpreting his experiences with sound and movement and sharing with other students and the teacher the evaluation of his progress."[25]

In centering on the relationship between movement and sound, three sets of categories are specifically selected as guides: high–low, fast–slow, and loud–soft/strong–weak continuums. The general concept for this unit is that, "in a music-dance event, there is a fusion of sound and movement, and the resulting relationship produces an integrated expressive effect on the spectator."[26] The underlying goal of these materials is, thus, that "the student should increase his capacity to experience a dance-music event by perceiving several relationships between sound and movement."[27] How these goals are met can be made clear by examining lesson six.

Lesson six integrates previous lessons. The concept underlying it is that particular, intentional combinations of sound and movement will produce a "rudimentary form of a dance-music work of art."[28] The objective is to encourage the students to develop "sound-movement statements" that will include samples of both matching and contrasting sounds and movements. As well, students are to evaluate their own work along with the teacher.

The lesson begins with a review of previously discussed concepts, with the teacher asking five specific questions, as enunciated in the teacher's guide:

1. In the first lesson, we listened to a record and watched a film to see if we could hear sounds that were _____, _____, _____, _____, _____, and _____. Can you tell me what the sounds were like? We tried to see which movements showed _____, _____, _____, _____, _____, and _____. Can you remember what the movements were like?
2. Then in lesson 2 we tried to find our own sounds that did these six things. Did we find out anything about making these sounds?
3. In lesson 3 we worked with our own movements. What did we find out in doing this?
4. Lessons 4 and 5 had us put sounds and movements together. We did this in two ways. What was the first way? What does 'matching' mean? Can you give an example?
5. What was the other way we related sound and movement? What does 'contrasting' mean? What is an example?[29]

Possible answers to these review questions are also provided in the teacher's guide.

After the review, students are divided into groups of four or five, with each group going to a different area of the classroom. Students in each group are to create at least five movements and five sounds, some of which match and some of which contrast, and to decide how their combination of sounds and movements should fit together, practicing this arrangement. After sufficient rehearsal, each group sits together to present its sound/movement exercise and evaluate the activities of the other groups. To aid in the process of evaluation, each group is numbered and given an "observation sheet" from the materials included with the kit.

The seventh and concluding lesson in this unit involves perceiving and appreciating the sound and movement aspects of an actual music-dance event. The students watch a film, "Fogarty Park," included with the other materials, and discuss the relationship between sound and movement contained in it.

The film itself, approximately four minutes in length, contains a variety of scenes with musical accompaniment. About fifteen different scenes are depicted, with music ranging from a slow, melancholy flute solo at the beginning, to a faster, lighter ensemble involving a flute, a guitar, and a reed instrument in the middle, to a brisk guitar solo at the end that becomes increasingly loud as the film concludes. Scenes show the sun shining through a stand of trees, children playing on various pieces of outdoor playground equipment, a boy catching a ball, children playing tag, and children going down a slide. In all, the film and music exhibit most if not all of the sound and movement qualities that were discussed in the lessons.

Class discussion of "Fogarty Park" is initiated by the teacher asking questions such as:

> Can you remember any point in the film where the music seemed to match the movement? When?
>
> Can you remember times where the music contrasted with the movement?
>
> When did you think the music and movement went together very well?
>
> Did you think there were times when the music was not right for the movement? When?
>
> Did you think there were moments when the sound and movement fitted together and made one beautiful thing? When?[30]

Based on these kinds of inquiries by the teacher, students discuss their reactions to the film, focusing on how sound and movement patterns work together in this production. This, then, is the culminating activity for the "Relating Sound and Movement" unit, wherein students are to apply what they have learned about the relationships between sound and movement to make their appreciation or understanding of a specific work deeper and more sophisticated.

Cultural Reproduction and Aesthetic Education

The assumptions that guided the development of curricular and aesthetic meanings in CEMREL's Aesthetic Education Program are ideologically laden in many ways. Perhaps most striking in this connection is the extent to which people involved in this effort succeeded in obtaining the kind of curricular program they wanted. The units of instruction developed by CEMREL—as exemplified in the "Relating Sound and Movement" package—bear a striking resemblance to those developed in other subject areas. Yet there are consequences attending an emphasis on wide school and community acceptance—which was in large part responsible for this attempt at imitation—that adversely affect how aesthetic forms are understood by both teachers and students who come into contact with these materials. There is, in other words, a price to be paid for regarding the current set of educational and community sentiments as givens, to be capitulated to by any set of curriculum materials that we may wish to proliferate.

The phenomenon of "commodification" has been widely discussed in relation to the arts, and is of special importance in the present context.[31] For the CEMREL program, existing within a large, multifaceted educational laboratory, was clearly intended for mass distribution, to be used in a wide variety of classroom situations and locations. Indeed this desire for widespread usage was one of the central features of the curricular foundation discussed earlier: the view that "instructional packages" should permit the sort of flexibility that would ensure large-scale community and school acceptance, purchase, and use. This desire for large-scale distribution results, among other things, in aesthetic experience being packaged, purchased, and consumed as one type of commodity.

The commodification of aesthetic meanings is thus inherent in the very packaging of curriculum materials in the CEMREL program. Indeed the very notion of a "curriculum package" or "kit" denotes such a process of commodification. The way the materials contained in this curriculum program are packaged lends credibility to the view that aesthetic meanings, contained as they are within a prepackaged format with specific instructions for their use and evaluation, can be purchased in the same way that we purchase clothing and furniture. The actual meanings that are derived from these particular materials may be less salutary, as a result, than we might like. What is possible and valuable aesthetically becomes transformed through the process of commodification. Let us look at this issue more closely.

In an exceptionally incisive and intriguing work, John Berger argues that in the process of bringing mechanical reproduction to bear on the arts, something of crucial importance happened to the aesthetic meaning of paintings. While paintings were originally placed in structures that suggested or accentuated part of their meaning, the possibility of mechanically reproducing visual images meant they could be perceived in a wide variety of settings, each of which then contributed something to their total meaning. However, within this process it was no longer what the image expressed that was important, but rather what, in one particular respect, it was—that is, what became important was the fact of something's being a reproduction, rather than what the object itself expressed or conveyed to the viewer. Thus the meaning and significance of works of art was changed by the very fact that massively reproducing them for massive distribution became technically feasible. Because of this technical advance it became easier (as they became less costly, more available, and so on) to purchase reproductions of even the most highly acclaimed works of art.

At the same time, Berger points out, we need to be sensitive to the connotations embedded in the word "purchase" in this context. Since the meaning of a painting is transmittable through a process of replication that takes the painting out of its otherwise important context, it becomes itself a commodity, to be bought and sold on a market like other objects and services. The "information" contained within the work can, on this view, then be perceived, consumed, or ignored by individual "customers," just as are other kinds of information and services. Aesthetic meanings thus become one kind of information and medium of exchange among many others, all of which share an important feature: their status as commodities on a market. In the process of transformation into consumable objects or "things," with the consequent alteration of their potential impact and significance, the value of aesthetic experiences becomes delimited by being placed within a stream of other commodities, materials, and information to be used and then discarded.

In the case of the CEMREL materials, sound and movement (or, more generally, "music" and "dance") activities and displays are presented as part of a consumable "package of aesthetic experiences." Students and teachers are to work their way through the step-by-step instructions, performing the activities required in each lesson. Then the materials (packages) are to be put aside, presumably to await the next set of "customers." Dance is thus something you engage in because it is prescribed by a set of material objects that form their own discrete "universe" or domain. Aesthetic meanings tied to this process are instigated, carried out, and evaluated in terms of the internal logic of this self-contained system—a system that is bought, used, and set aside or passed on to others.

The activities and exercises contained in the curriculum unit described above also share a basic utilitarian perspective: specific activities are to lead to particular, prespecified ends. The reason for attending to musical recordings, relating sound and movement characteristics and activities, and so on, is to reach some pregiven endpoint thought desirable by those who, working outside the individual classroom in which the materials are to be utilized, conceptualized this program. Aesthetic experience thus conceived becomes a means to some external end, undertaken for specific objectives. Moreover, the way in which the materials are designed and employed serves to separate conception from execution. Those responsible for developing the goals and objectives to which the exercises contribute are not involved in the actual use of the program in classrooms, and conversely, teachers and students are divorced from the process of actually constructing materials that could embody specific, personal meanings and values.

Within these lessons aesthetic response is also highly standardized and routinized, with all the students expected to reach the same general goal or endpoint in more or less the same way, using more or less the same amount of time and procedures.

This tendency toward standardization of experience is further emphasized by the kinds of evaluation instruments and activities included in the curriculum package. This becomes fairly clear, for example, in pretest activities involved in lesson one of the sound and movement series. Choices are circumscribed by the answers provided on included answer sheets, with little or no room for other interpretations or identifications. The movement toward standardization of response may also be seen in other, less obvious ways, however. In watching "Fogarty Park" as the culminating activity for this unit, students are directed to focus their attention on specific sound/movement combinations, to the exclusion of other possible activities, interpretations, and meanings. Indeed it seems that the only "content" embedded in the film, seen under these circumstances, is in the sound/movement relationships that it allegedly exemplifies; what the actions and scenes may mean in other terms—either literal or symbolic—is left totally unexplored. The film's only permissible meaning is that uncovered by situating it within the confines of antecedent exercises and objectives. Furthermore, the specific discussion questions following the film serve to orient students toward the categories established in previous lessons. Students are judged by how well they integrate sound and movement relationships in terms based on previous discussions and understandings. These practices discourage any personal interpretations and meanings.

An interlocking effect of the curriculum form and aesthetic content of the unit is the highly segmented, isolated nature of the resulting aesthetic experiences. This unit utilizes only a comparatively small portion of two aesthetic categories. Only a few aspects of musical forms (their pitch, tempo, and intensity) and movement patterns (their space, time, and force) are used to illustrate the desired outcomes. Musical and movement understandings become centered on these aspects, and isolated from others as well as from other art forms and activities. "Music" and "movement" as aesthetic categories become abstracted from other experiences. Aesthetic forms are seen not from any larger perspective, but rather as self-contained, fragmented areas that are valued apart from other categories and meanings. The result is a sense of unreality about the activities undertaken, since they have little or no connection with other human concerns, values, and commitments. To put this point another way, students who experience and investigate the unit dealing with sound and movement relationships might learn something about the formal qualities of these aesthetic forms, and the surface features of each, but it seems unlikely that they will understand the value or importance of using these mediums as vehicles for personal or social expression. They are impoverished as a result.

An important part of the valuational aspect of aesthetic forms within the CEMREL program results from the fact that it is not only the ends of instruction that are prespecified, but the means as well. Frequently throughout the units examined here, as noted above, specific questions and inquiries are detailed in the relevant teacher's manual to aid in shaping the discussion which takes place among students. "Discovery" or "creativity" on the students' part is frequently prefigured or circumscribed, leaving the students merely to figure out the correct response as determined by the teacher, in consultation with the curriculum materials.

Aesthetic meanings, hence, are seen as something to be achieved by the proper sequence of rationalized steps or processes, completed in the proper manner, so that answers or activities match a predetermined correct response. Aesthetic meanings exist "out there," and if we but follow the proper directions carefully, we will be able to discover them. Instead of actively constructing aesthetic meanings in concert with others, students in the CEMREL program have a passive role. Aesthetic meanings are external to the person experiencing them, to be uncovered via the proper application or replication of activities that revolve around the use of our senses.

In sum, the aesthetic meanings implicit in CEMREL's Aesthetic Education Program show the following characteristics: 1) aesthetic experience is "packaged" in such a way that its meaning and value become transformed into objects to be purchased, consumed, and discarded; 2) aesthetic experiences are useful insofar as they lead to some external objective or end point; 3) the specific activities undertaken to reach these ends are relatively standardized or routinized; 4) the evaluation instruments and activities that assess how well these ends have been achieved show a correlative degree of standardization; 5) aesthetic meanings are rationalized, segmented, and isolated from each other and from other concerns and areas of inquiry; 6) this results in a degree of abstraction from day-to-day experiences such that the aesthetic is seen as, in a sense, artificial and unreal (or, perhaps, merely decorative); and 7) in acquiring aesthetic knowledge the student has a passive role wherein the senses are used to discover the proper set of such meanings. These practices and patterns reinforce and legitimate ways of thinking and perceiving that have considerable ideological significance.

The tendency toward commodification—the translation of ideas and meanings into objects to be bought and sold—can be seen as responding to the emphasis on production, salesmanship, and consumerism that typifies contemporary society. In a culture where a wide variety of experiences, activities, and ideas become objects to be purchased on some sort of market, the trend toward commodification is fully understandable if not inevitable. Packaging curriculum materials in this way reaffirms our culture's emphasis on production and marketing, making it appear that even those experiences that might plausibly be most resistant to commodification—artistic creations and aesthetic meanings—can become ensnarled in this process. Dispensing such experiences to elementary-school students begins the commodification process at an early age, encouraging the perspective that experiences and objects exist to be purchased, used, and discarded, that an idea's or an object's meaning and value are tied to market conditions of one sort or another, in a seemingly never-ending process of consumption. Fostering these attitudes promotes the development of ways of thinking about and orienting oneself to experiences that are ideologically beneficial in a society where concerns for market conditions and economic values prevail.

Further, the utilitarian perspective of the CEMREL materials contributes to a way of thinking dominated by pragmatic concerns for ends and goals, rather than a concentration on how these are to be achieved and what their interrelationships are. This way of thinking seems comforting in a society that stresses the production and consumption of material goods, rather than focusing, say, on the process and consequences of producing and acquiring them. When maximizing the number of goods and services is crucial for the perpetuation of the economic system, an emphasis on activities and objects as ends, and a corresponding de-emphasis on the results and side effects of the process, seems central.

The tendency toward standardization and routinization of activities and evaluation serves also to promote ways of thinking that complement current social practices. With the increased use of technology of a certain sort, standardization of tasks and assignments takes on a greater sense of being natural and desirable. The use of computerized forms within both private corporations and state bureaucracies is but one example of how activities and communication patterns have become increasingly stylized and routinized. By designing educational experiences and pedagogical practices that foster a sense of routinization in interpersonal response and communication, we are preparing young people to accept forms of social interaction that have legitimacy in the larger society.

The tendency to segment, isolate, and depersonalize experience can be seen in a variety of settings. Consider as examples the segmented tasks of blue-collar factory workers and the "chain of command" communication patterns followed by large state institutions. Such processes of segmentation and isolation have, in many cases, become a part of our collective consciousness, an unstated assumption in many kinds of activities. Through the tendency toward task analysis and the specialized division of labor, experience becomes increasingly fragmented. Some of the qualities associated with the Aesthetic Education Program further these modes of thought and conduct.

This segmentation can be seen to some extent in the fact that the activities and exercises in this program were conceived apart from the arenas where they are put into practice. In this separation of conception from execution at least two processes can be seen operating. First, teachers and teaching are being "deskilled," so that the craft of teaching becomes more closely aligned with managerial and administrative duties; this leads to further emphasis on the individual as a consuming and possessive being, rather than a reflective, constructive one.[32] Second, students are tacitly led to view themselves as removed from important decision-making responsibilities and mechanisms; they come to think of themselves as responding and conforming to external values, meanings, and commitments rather than as helping to create them.

Abstracting aesthetic experience from other life situations and regarding the role of aesthetic participants as passive serve other ideological purposes. Both perpetuate an individualistic perspective in which the respondent is seen as separated from collectivities while at the same time relatively inactive within the experience itself. The increased atomization and abstraction of individuals that coincided with the shift to a market economy, has been well documented.[33] The point I wish to emphasize here is that many of the activities that make up the Aesthetic Education Program help to accentuate this sense of individualism. It is true that some activities in the unit dealing with sound and movement involve students working in small groups on cooperative exercises. Yet the emphasis on individual interpretation and response, especially in the evaluation instruments and activities, may at the same time serve to differentiate important "work" from unimportant "exercise" or "play."[34] Pre-tests and discussion-centered review sessions are predominantly individualistic. For students who miss more than three questions on a test, for example, there is a remedial activity wherein students independently review pictured movements in an accompanying *Continuum Book*. Such emphases, occurring as they do in the higher-status evaluation activities of classrooms, may tacitly serve to perpetuate the idea that collective activities are less important than individual ones.

In sum, the program of aesthetic education developed by CEMREL serves in the following ways to perpetuate ways of thinking and seeing that are ideologically useful to the current social order. First, it helps instill perspectives on the process of commodification that are important in a society where production and consumption are basic. Second, it furthers a utilitarian perspective that systematically de-emphasizes the importance of the quality of processes and consequences, while accentuating the importance of goals and ends. Third, it provides activities that help to segment, fragment, and isolate experience, reinforcing the disjointedness of much of contemporary social life. Fourth, it depersonalizes experiences: students and teachers are separated from the conceptual part of their activities, and left only a relatively passive role. Fifth, experiences within the program are, in important ways, individualistic, emphasizing personal separateness and the importance of individual participation over collective action. Such emphases reveal how specific curricular and pedagogical practices contribute to the establishment of world views, to ways of thinking, feeling, and seeing, that both respond to and help legitimate the social order in its present forms.

Beyond Ideological Imposition

The previous sections of this essay clarify how ideological elements may permeate curriculum materials and programs so that they appear to be "natural" or commonsensical components of the day-to-day activities and exchanges that make up school life. Yet it is dangerously easy, as noted at the outset, to assume a kind of simplistic functionalism with respect to ideological domination and social reproduction. Several considerations militate against this sort of assumption.

First, nothing is always and uniformly reproductive. That is, even though some practice or idea may, in fact, serve certain ideological interests, we cannot *assume* that this is the case, still less that this is its only function. This is another way of saying that the concept of ideological domination is itself historical. While certain actions may serve specific ideological interests at a particular historical moment, other interests may be served given a changed set of social and material circumstances. It is also true, of course, that we cannot assume that any given practice will prove to be progressive or emancipatory. Whether that practice turns out to be reproductive, progressive, or some combination of the two, will depend on the historical circumstances within which it unfolds; we cannot know, a priori, whether it will enhance reproduction or emancipation.

This is especially relevant in the context of our analysis of aesthetic education. For even though the CEMREL program has embedded within it ways of seeing and acting that are ideologically compelling and culturally reproductive, we cannot assume that the effect of using such materials with students will be similarly reproductive. The latent messages, meanings, and patterns of interaction of such programs cannot completely foretell their actual use and interpretation by students and teachers. Since this analysis is in no sense meant to delimit or even characterize the actual experiences that will ultimately develop out of an interaction with such materials, any assumption about their actual effect on students is premature. While I have begun to expose the ideological implications of the theories in aesthetics and curriculum that went into the design and production of these materials, more empirical field study is required before we offer reasoned conclusions about the actual experiences that result.

We must also be sensitive to the contradictions within the materials and processes themselves—to the ways in which ideological constructs even within CEMREL's organized practices are essentially contradictory. Within the framework of the current investigation two areas of contradiction are important. The first has to do with the peculiar potential of aesthetic meaning.

Numerous attempts have been made by aestheticians and others to specify how aesthetic experiences are different from, or related to, more common, day-to-day encounters. Some writers have speculated that the essential difference between aesthetic and nonaesthetic experiences lies in the fact that with the latter we often feel compelled by ethical considerations to act in certain ways. However, when aesthetic experience is characterized as involving sustained, concentrated attention to the formal qualities of objects—as it is within the CEMREL program—the realm of moral judgment seems foreign and distant.

We say we act out of moral considerations in situations where we believe there is a correct or proper course of action to follow; that is, where it is required of us as moral agents to act in such and such a way. We have some sort of (usually unwritten) "moral code" that helps us decide what to do in particular circumstances. From time to time, of course, this code may change if we come to see that we have not fully considered, whether from a theoretical or empirical perspective, all the relevant facets of a given situation. In short, our moral considerations are to some extent fluid, subject to reconsideration and refinement.

Some such process of reconsideration can occur in our moral deliberations when we reflect upon our aesthetic experiences as well. When an art work affects our thoughts and feelings in a profound and significant way, it also affects the way we feel about and analyze the issues raised or the subject matter presented in the piece. Consider as an example here the award-winning documentary, *Harlan County, U.S.A.* At one level of appreciation—representative of the approach taken by those involved in the CEMREL program—we may consider the formal, surface features of this film; elements such as camera angle, the sequence and interrelationships of scenes, lighting techniques, musical elements and their relationship to these other features, and so on, become important within this approach. But the meaning of aesthetic objects goes beyond a delineation of formal qualities. Films such as *Harlan County* also say something that is of some personal significance to their audience. Specifically, in this case viewers may come to understand something of the nature of workers' struggles to organize againt mining companies in this country; this film may add another dimension to our attitude toward these and related events. Such changes in attitude, in ways of seeing and feeling, can also influence what we consider to be appropriate or desirable conduct. As a result of rethinking the relationship between worker and owner within the context of U.S. mining industries, the aesthetic participant may well be led to think and act differently toward people caught in such situations of economic and social exploitation. This process of rethinking and re-evaluating moral questions and issues reconnects aesthetic experiences with those more general human concerns and dilemmas.

Art and the aesthetic have the power to make us see our world differently, to view our individual and collective situations from new perspectives and change how we will respond to the events in our lives. When a work of art makes us see some object, person, or event in a new way, to consider it from a fresh perspective, it can inform and reform our perception of that object or event: "That nature imitates art is too timid a dictum. Nature is a product of art and discourse."[35]

Our perception of aesthetic forms can make a genuine contribution to our knowledge of the world in which we live and work, and can provide us with alternative conceptions of different, divergent worlds. Aesthetic forms can, in brief, move us to enlightened social action. As D. W. Gotshalk has put it, "we act largely on the basis of what we value and cherish. And if the fine arts at their best refine these bases of behavior, making our capacities more able and our values more wide and discriminate, they constitute a discipline in decency and a modification of character from which decent social action can spring."[36] Ultimately, the best aesthetic forms have meaning because they tell us something about our world and allow us to see both it and possible alternatives to it in a way that fosters social action that is informed, responsive, and ethical. Consequently, they may well encapsulate experiences that serve to liberate, emancipate, and work against social reproduction.

Yet this is only a potential value of the aesthetic experience, of course—one that may or may not be realized within specific contexts. In the case of the CEMREL program, recall the views of Harry S. Broudy, Eugene Kaelin, Stanley S. Madeja, and others discussed earlier. The perspective outlined there is one that places art and aesthetic experience in a domain abstracted from the demands and concerns of everyday life. As a result, art and moral conduct seem to demarcate mutually exclusive categories. The perception and appreciation of works of art is not mingled with moral questions or ethical debate. Thus Broudy insists that the ability of a viewer to be morally affected by a work of art rests on an "infirmity." At the same time, the phenomenologically oriented perspective which dominates in the theoretical portion of the Aesthetic Education Program helps ensure the fracturing of ethics from aesthetics. We are instructed to pay attention to, and value intrinsically, only components of works of art that are immediately present in the artifact.[37]

When the surface elements of aesthetic phenomena are treated as authoritative, and aesthetic perception, value, and appreciation are isolated from other interests and concerns, aesthetic and ethical considerations become antagonistic. Indeed ethical irrelevance seems a prerequisite for something's being a proper aesthetic experience.

In essence, then, there is a fundamental contradiction between the potential impact, value, or significance of aesthetic experience as characterized above, and the theoretical assumptions and perspectives on which the CEMREL program is founded. Thus the program embodies contradictions that cannot be avoided in an ideological investigation of the sort this essay represents. Indeed it may well be the case—though proving it would require a more extended analysis and presentation than is possible here—that at least some of the very symbols, images, and exercises which are a part of the Aesthetic Education Program might be used in other than reproductive ways. By acknowledging and using alternative conceptions of aesthetics, that is to say, we may move some way toward exposing the contradictions of programs like CEMREL's and reorienting the kinds of aesthetic experiences we utilize with students. We may call this a "content contradiction" inherent in the Aesthetic Education Program.

A second contradiction emerges when we consider the program within the theoretical framework postulated by Basil Bernstein to examine changes in curriculum form.[38] Bernstein's analysis deals with the ways in which changes in curriculum form can be correlated with social and historical changes in our conception of authority and property; these latter changes, in his view, accompany modifications in the division of labor, and serve as a basis for social integration and control. By using the categories of "classification" and "framing," Bernstein develops a typology with which we can investigate curricular changes and tie them to changes in the wider society. Classification refers to the degree of insulation of subject areas—strong classification meaning that subject matter is increasingly rigidified and isolated, weak classification indicating a relative fluidity of curricular boundaries. Framing refers to the degree of control that teacher and student have over what is taught—strong framing indicating that they have little control, weak framing indicating a more substantial input. Bernstein develops the idea of educational "codes" by combining classification and framing. In "collection codes" the subject matter is the basis of personal identification for students and teachers; acquiring subject matter is the mark of competency. In "integrated codes," the authority of subject matter is lessened, and is replaced by some more general principle or idea.

Bernstein argues that, at the societal level, the changing demands for particular types of labor specialization have resulted in a shift from "mechanical solidarity" to "organic solidarity." The former refers to a condition where people share a common belief system; the latter refers to a situation where individuals relate to each other through a necessary interdependence of functions in society. According to Bernstein, changes in curriculum form—from collected to integrated codes, from strong classification to weak, and so on—paralleled the change from mechanical to organic solidarity, and the accompanying changes in the conception of property and relations of power. Changes in curriculum, by making subject matter less authoritative, and moving toward an integrated educational code, changed perceptions of property and power and reinforced the changing patterns of work in the wider society. The decrease in the importance of subject matter, by making the boundaries between curricular areas less distinct, facilitated social control and integration.

The Aesthetic Education Program evidences the sort of changing curricular form that Bernstein refers to in several ways. Even though subject-matter specialists were used in the development of CEMREL's program, no unit is based on only one individual art form. This is partly a consequence of how aesthetic education was itself defined by those in the program. As Stanley Madeja and Sheila Onuska indicated, for example, "aesthetic education deals with broader concepts and topics than any one of the arts disciplines . . . it goes beyond the limits of any single discipline and relates to the full range of human experiences, [and] is a necessary part of the general education of every child."[39] The notion of integrated codes seems to permeate the conception of aesthetic education endorsed by those involved in the CEMREL program. The lack of rigid boundaries within the Aesthetic Education Program is further indicated by an additional justification for this program: "linkages through concepts, activities, and through content of all disciplines, not just the arts . . . make the case for the inclusion of an aesthetic education curriculum based in the arts as a part of the program in the elementary school."[40] Aesthetic education was not just concerned with a variety of artistic mediums: its importance was in part related to its connection with other domains.

In many respects the Aesthetic Education Program is an example of an integrated code. At the same time, since outcomes, activities and evaluation procedures are pre-specified, with neither student nor teacher having much substantial input into activities and exercises, the program is an example of strong framing. Combining the two then, the Aesthetic Education Program is an example of an integrated code that allows for little input from its users beyond the actual timing of the units themselves.

The program exemplifies the sort of change in curriculum form that is the subject of Bernstein's analysis. Rather than treating the subject matter in aesthetics as authoritative, and insulated from other content areas, the Aesthetic Education Program fosters a broadly based approach to aesthetics, which is itself conceived as essentially multidisciplinary. Instead of the mastery of subject matter being the source of personal identity, a more generalized principle or set of ideas becomes relevant: the view that students ought to learn how to "experience, judge, and value the aesthetic in their lives."[41] In more traditional arts courses ownership or property relations are conceived in terms of specific knowledge about, for example, art history or techniques of artistic production. The student of aesthetic education is led to see aesthetic experience as a more integrated, less individualistic activity.

This integrated educational code also exemplifies the shift from mechanical to organic solidarity that is central to Bernstein's analysis. Although some individual activities and exercises are included in the program, the emphasis is on cooperative, interdependent activities. Many of the exercises involve students working in pairs or in groups of four or five, with the results of each group's activity being shared and integrated into the activities of other groups. We can see here how the curriculum form, with its particular interpretation of private property and authority, and its subordination of the mastery of subject matter to more general principles and ideas, fits the pattern that Bernstein advanced as being a consequence of the shift in the division of labor and changes in social control.

In exposing the contradictions of educational codes, Bernstein's analysis of the "message systems" of curriculum and pedagogy transmitted through classification and framing, respectively, is especially relevant to this study. Although Bernstein seems to indicate that integrated codes most often combine weak classification with weak framing, it is also possible for strong framing to accompany weak classification in content areas. Bernstein further indicates that integrated codes stand a better chance of becoming institutionalized where "(1) there were strong and effective constraints upon the development of a range of ideologies and (2) where the educational system was a major agency of political socialization."[42] Both of these conditions, I would suggest, are present in the social structure of the United States, and at least partly explain the movement toward integrated codes that the CEMREL program represents. Bernstein goes on to say, however, that integrated codes "carry a potential for change in power structures and principles of control. I would therefore guess that in such societies [as those outlined above] integrated codes would possess weak classification, but the frames for teacher and taught would be strong.[43]

The CEMREL program shows precisely this condition of weak classification and strong framing. What Bernstein is saying is not just that the integrated code assists in the movement toward organic solidarity, but that the particular combination of weak classification and strong framing is a way of generating such solidarity while at the same time delimiting the potential of integrated codes for social change. We need to see the Aesthetic Education Program, thus, as effecting, through its classification and framing, a kind of social control that cuts short the transformative potential of integrated codes. This is important not only because it exposes the social implications of the message systems of curriculum and pedagogy, within the context of ideological domination and cultural reproduction, but, even more so, because it points to contradictions within educational codes, and provides a clue as to how curricular programs such as CEMREL's may be reconstituted so as to serve less reproductive, more progressive or emancipatory ends. In essence, in Bernstein's view, if we are serious about changing patterns of inequality and social control, we should attempt to lessen frame strength, to better enable integrated codes to change existing power relations and property relationships.

To summarize, two important contradictions stand out when the ideological implications of CEMREL's Aesthetic Education Program are considered. These indicate the extent to which functional theories of cultural reproduction fail to account for ideological domination. First, aesthetic experiences can affect our thoughts, ideas, and actions outside the actual aesthetic encounter. One basic "datum" of aesthetic experience is its ability to puzzle, provide, and inspire its audience, to propel discussion of issues and situations long after we have finished perceiving it. Aesthetic objects possess the ability to affect not only our perceptual apparatus during the aesthetic experience, but our moral judgment and conduct outside of it as well. In affecting our patterns of thought and derivative conduct, works of art offer a potential for social change which contradicts assertions that their function is merely decorative. Second, Bernstein's analysis of changes in curriculum form demonstrates the transformative potential of programs such as CEMREL's. These programs, which change the interpersonal relationships within classrooms, thus affecting their power structures and principles of control, may be used to redirect and reorient classrooms in ways that subvert present patterns of dominance. In promoting a curriculum with weak classification, therefore, the Aesthetic Education Program is both constraining (in disallowing input from teachers and students) and transforming (in affecting principles of power and control). To exploit this contradiction, we would, to use Bernstein's terminology, need to weaken the frames of such curricular programs. It is important, however, to go beyond Bernstein's depiction of cultural reproduction and see aesthetic forms as other than reflections of material productions. We need, in other words, a materialistic aesthetic theory that underscores both the ideological and productive nature of aesthetic forms.[44] Such a theory could exploit the power of symbolic structures to change, rather than reflect, diverse material conditions and productive forces.

What we might plausibly work toward, then in a program for aesthetic education, is a politicization of aesthetic experience such that aesthetic meaning and ethical conduct are seen as coextensive rather than mutually exclusive; the adoption of a curriculum form that will include students and teachers in the actual construction of aesthetic experiences—a form, that is, that will possess an integrated educational code in which both framing and classification will be weak. This will require the development of a materialist theory of aesthetics that, in addition to validating the linkages between aesthetics and ethics, will move away from reflection theory toward a view of aesthetic forms as part of the productive apparatus of society. The theoretical, ideological, and educational effort needed for a truly emancipatory aesthetic program has only just begun.

Notes

1. Manual Barkan, Laura H. Chapman, and Evan J. Kern, *Guidelines: Curriculum Development for Aesthetic Education* (St. Louis: CEMREL, 1970), p. ii.

2. Ralph M. Tyler, *Basic Principles of Curriculum and Instruction* (Chicago: University of Chicago Press, 1950).

3. Stanley S. Madeja and Harry T. Kelley, "A Curriculum Development Model for Aesthetic Education," *The Journal of Aesthetic Education* 4, no. 2 (April 1970): 54.

4. Ibid., p.55.

5. Ibid.

6. Ibid.

7. Stanley S. Madeja, "The CEMREL Aesthetic Education Program: A Report," *The Journal of Aesthetic Education* 10, no. 3–4 (July–October, 1976): 210.

8. Madeja and Kelley, "A Curriculum Development Model," p. 55.

9. Ibid., 60.

10. *The Five Sense Store: The Aesthetic Education Program*, CEMREL, Inc., p. 3.

11. See Madeja, "The CEMREL Aesthetic Education Program: A Report," pp. 209–216.

12. In a telephone conversation on December 3, 1979, Madeja indicated that the following people had been especially influential in helping develop the theoretical foundations in aesthetics for the CEMREL program: Harry S. Broudy, David Ecker, Eugene F. Kaelin, Arthur Foshay, Nathaniel Champlin, and Morris Weitz. In reading through the literature on this aspect of the program, it became clear that the first three people, and Madeja himself, represent dominant points of view that became incorporated into the Aesthetic Education Program.

13. Stanley S. Madeja and Sheila Onuska, *Through the Arts to the Aesthetic* (St. Louis: CEMREL, 1977) p. 3.

14. Evan J. Kern, "The Aesthetic Education Program: Past, Present and Future," *Theory into Practice*, 10, no. 3 (June 1971): 185.

15. Madeja and Onuska, *Through the Arts*, p. 4.

16. Barkan, et al., *Guidelines*, p. 7.

17. Harry S. Broudy, "The Whys and Hows of Aesthetic Education" (St. Louis: CEMREL, 1977), pp. 1–2.

18. Eugene F. Kaelin, "Aesthetic Education: A Role for Aesthetics Proper," in Ralph A. Smith, ed., *Aesthetics and Problems of Education* (Urbana: University of Illinois Press, 1971).

19. Harry S. Broudy, "Preparing Teachers of Aesthetic Education," *Teacher Education for Aesthetic Education: A Progress Report* (St. Louis: CEMREL, 1972), p. 10.

20. Broudy, "The Whys and Hows of Aesthetic Education," p. 71.

21. Harry S. Broudy, *Enlightened Cherishing: An Essay on Aesthetic Education* (Urbana: University of Illinois Press, 1972), p. 48.

22. See Michael W. Apple, *Ideology and Curriculum* (Boston: Routledge & Kegan Paul, 1979), especially Chap. 5.

23. Landon E. Beyer, "Aesthetics and the Curriculum: Ideological and Cultural Form in School Practice" (Ph.D. diss.: University of Wisconsin—Madison, 1981).

24. *Teacher's Guide*, "Relating Sound and Movement," p. 6.

25. Ibid., p. 6.

26. Ibid.

27. Ibid.

28. Ibid., p. 32.

29. Ibid.

30. Ibid., p. 38.

31. See especially "The Work of Art in the Age of Mechanical Reproduction," in Walter Benjamin, *Illuminations* (New York: Schocken Paperback Edition, 1969); and John Berger, *Ways of Seeing* (New York: Penguin Books, 1972).

32. See Michael W. Apple, "Curricular Form and the Logic of Technical Control," in *Cultural and Economic Reproduction in Education: Essays on Class,*

Ideology, and the State, Michael W. Apple, ed. (Boston: Routledge and Kegan Paul, 1982).

33. See in this regard Steven Lukes, *Individualism* (New York: Harper & Row, 1973); and Lucien Goldman, *The Philosophy of the Enlightenment* (London: Routledge and Kegan Paul, 1973).

34. Michael W. Apple and Nancy R. King, "What Do Schools Teach?" *Curriculum Inquiry* 6, no. 4 (Fall, 1977): 341–58.

35. Nelson Goodman, *Languages of Art* (Indianapolis: Bobbs–Merrill, 1968), p. 33.

36. D. W. Gotshalk, *Art and the Social Order*, 2nd ed. (New York: Dover Publications, 1962), p. 213.

37. See Eugene F. Kaelin, "Aesthetic Education: A Role for Aesthetics Proper," in Smith, ed., *Aesthetics and Problems of Education*, pp. 152—53.

38. Basil Bernstein, *Class, Codes, and Control, Volume 3: Towards a Theory of Educational Transmissions* (London: Routledge and Kegan Paul, 1975).

39. Stanley S. Madeja and Sheila Onuska, *Through the Arts to the Aesthetic*, p. 5.

40. Ibid., p. 97.

41. Ibid., p. 3.

42. Bernstein, *Class, Codes, and Control*, p. 114.

43. Ibid.

44. The direction such theorizing might take is suggested by Raymond Williams, *Marxism and Literature* (New York: Oxford University Press, 1977); and John Berger, *Ways of Seeing*.

CHAPTER 5

Defensive Teaching and Classroom Control

LINDA M. McNEIL

Our image of the one-room schoolteacher, or the master of a Latin-grammar school, is of a teacher wielding the hickory stick to make students learn. Student discipline—sitting on hard benches, standing to recite, maintaining absolute silence unless spoken to—was instrumental to mastering the content. A study of four Wisconsin high schools reveals that today many teachers reverse those ends and means. They maintain discipline by the ways they present course content. They choose to simplify content and reduce demands on students in return for classroom order and minimal student compliance on assignments. Feeling less authority than their Latin-grammar school counterpart, they teach "defensively," choosing methods of presentation and evaluation that they hope will make their workload more efficient and create as little student resistance as possible. These findings are interesting because they shed light on the daily processes by which schools mediate cultural knowledge to students. They are important because they demonstrate some of the specific dynamics that lie behind the much-publicized lowered expectations that students and teachers are bringing to the classroom. In addition, they are significant because the teachers who teach defensively do not fit any one ideological or demographic category, and they use these techniques of classroom control with students of all ability levels and perceived "differences."

This report of "defensive teaching" is one detail in a series of research projects on the nature of high-school social-studies curricula. Before elaborating the techniques the teachers used, and their expressed rationale for selecting them, it will be necessary to explain these findings in relation to the larger research projects that brought them to light.

Concentric Circles of Curriculum Analysis

When Dwayne Heubner described curriculum as "the accessibility of knowledge," he was making the point that the curriculum was not merely the content or curriculum guide, but the totality of the learning environment within which that content became accessible to students.[1] Although he meant to call attention to many of the physical attributes of the educative setting, his conception of the curriculum as the means of making knowledge accessible has provided an apt phrase for shifting curriculum analysis away from formal definitions of course content and student achievement, toward the origins and nature of the content itself. The question of the role of the school in making knowledge accessible to students became the central research question of a series of three studies of high-school social-studies curricula conducted between 1975 and 1981. Beginning at the classroom, and expanding into the institutional and societal contexts of the classroom, these studies focused on the role of the school in conveying information to students: What kinds of knowledge do schools make accessible? How is school knowledge a product of the ways of knowing students encounter in school?

The first study in this series was an intensive ethnographic analysis of the nature of the economics information to which high school students are exposed in their required social studies classes.[2] The research began at the classroom level, where students encounter school knowledge. The intent of the study was to contrast the treatment of such historical topics as social, political and military history, with that given to economics, a subject which teachers are usually presumed to be less comfortable with, or less well-trained in. Daily observations in three teachers' classes for a semester were supplemented with interviews of the students and teachers and investigation into the history of the school and its policies. The purpose of the daily observations, rather than mere analysis of course outlines and texts, was to try to ascertain not only what information about the American economy was made accessible to students, but in what ways students encountered the information.

The findings on these two questions can be summarized as follows: While the teachers in most cases gave a great deal of time to economics topics within their history classes, and one was trained in economics and interested in it, unit titles were not necessarily indicative of course content. Contrary to the expectation that economics information would be treated more superficially than other historical topics, all topics in this southern Wisconsin high school's observed classes were reduced to simplistic, teacher-controlled information that required no reading or writing by the students little or no student discussion, and very little use of the school's extensive resources. This pattern distorted, or truncated, even those economics topics that were included. The teachers at this school, whose lectures provide many of the examples of defensive teaching to be discussed below, offered conscious reasons for wishing to control student access to information. Interviews with the teachers revealed that they had a much broader knowledge of the economy, both academically and experientially, than they admitted in class. Their stated goal of making sure students understood "how things work" was tempered by their expressed fear that students might find out about the injustices and inadequacies of their economic and political institutions. For these teachers, knowledge access—a goal consistent with the good reputation of their middle-class school and of their status in it—was proscribed by their deliberate selections of lecture topics that would distance the students from the content. *Their patterns of knowledge control were, according to their own statements in taped interviews, rooted in their desire for classroom control.* Their memories of the Vietnam war era made them wish to avoid topics on which the students were likely to disagree with their views or that would make the students "cynical" about American institutions. Administrative policies, which had redrawn the school's boundary to include more working-class families and which had done away with ability-group (I.Q.) tracking, had caused the teachers to feel that their school was not "as good as it used to be." The intangible rewards of teaching the "best" students in the "best" high school had been taken away, over their protests, and no incentives to deal with the new groups of students or newly heterogeneous classes had taken their place. Their expectations of their students and of their own ability to affect student learning skills had in their mind, been progressively lowered over the recent past. They saw student ability levels as endpoints that limited what they could do in their classes, not as beginning points for teacher help and instruction.

In addition, they felt burdened by an administration that expected them to enforce rules of discipline, but that rarely backed them on that enforcement. As a result, they wanted to avoid as many inefficient exchanges as possible in order to get through the day. I have described their control of classroom knowledge as their "negotiation of efficiencies": they calculated how much of their personal knowledge of the economy and other aspects of the society under study to put at risk in the classroom, given the smallness of their financial rewards and professional incentives in relation to the potential for classroom disorder, dissent and conflict. The economics information they made available to their students, then, reflected not their level of training or interest in the subject, nor their particular political position on a topic, but their skill at maintaining classroom control. Ironically, their very attempt to minimize student cynicism by simplifying content and avoiding class discussion only heightened student disbelief of school knowledge and fostered in students greater disengagement from the learning process. As discussed at length elsewhere, interviews with the students revealed how suspect they found school knowledge, especially if any teacher-supplied information was contradicted by an independent source.[3] Just as the teachers masked their more complex personal knowledge of the topics because of their desire for classroom order and efficiency, the students appeared to acquiesce to the pattern of classroom knowledge, only to silently resist believing it.

Because the teachers attributed so much of their need for classroom efficiency to an administrative context that placed constraints without compensating supports (as in the addition of lower-income neighborhoods to the school's boundary, or in de-tracking), a second study broadened the circle of analysis from the classroom to the institution itself.[4] Three other high schools, also in Wisconsin and having similar student populations, were chosen for their variation from the goals of the school. Whenever administrative personnel expend most of the staff's time, meetings, and resources on discussions of hall order, discipline, and numbers of course credits earned, teachers respond with overt but usually reluctant compliance on those goals, but reduce effort and aim for only minimal standards in their actual teaching. Students do not always understand where teacher motivations originate, nor even that the teachers know that the course is watered down or undemanding, but they do sense when the teachers take the work seriously.[5] When students see minimal teaching, they respond with minimal classroom effort (which is not the same as minimal learning; many students, like the teachers, are far more articulate and informed on a given topic than the classroom processes make admissible to the classroom). Much of the student apathy, and even occasional resistance, which administrators see as a motivation problem requiring more discipline procedures, arises in these schools precisely because goals of order have already undermined the ability of staff to deal with educative goals.

The third study in this set of concentric circles does not provide any of the examples of defensive teaching that will be explored here. But it does illuminate the context within which teachers are making curricular decisions. The two previous ethnographic studies revealed through teacher and student interviews come of the effects student part-time employment has on high school classrooms. Teachers reduce the number or complexity of assignments, or choose to lecture rather than hold a discussion based on an assignment, because so many students work long hours, many more than 30 hours per week. The students work for many reasons, but they are more likely to be buying cars than saving for college or helping to support their families. The third phase of the research is a survey of employment among students and their perceptions of its effects on their school work.[6] In interviews, many have expressed frustration that so little "happens" at school; having so little significant studying or homework, they decide to add five hours to their work week. The teachers express anger at the students' priorities and often resent the students' spending power. In silent retaliation, or in frustration after trying to involve sleepy students in a discussion, they water down the content even further. The cycle of resentment and low expectations that this pattern of student employment fuels is talked about by school personnel at all four high schools. But, so far, they only talk about it, talk about how it includes "even the bright kids now," talk about how inflation only makes it more likely to continue; but none have taken into account what it means to their program, whether there are ways to creatively respond and incorporate new economic realities into the learning process. So, even though the third phase of the research on the origins and effects of social-studies content is not completed, and does not offer us new examples of defensive teaching strategies, it is mentioned here because it helps explain the context within which teachers are making curricular decisions.

Conceptions of School Knowledge

In making school knowledge itself the subject of inquiry, one goes against the long-standing tradition of social-studies curriculum research. A careful reading of the comprehensive survey of social-studies education research sponsored by the National Science Foundation and the Social Science Education Consortium reveals that most education researchers accept the course titles and educationist instructional jargon at face value.[7] Every study cited in the sections on the "effectiveness" of social-studies instructional methods and materials left unexamined the assumption that schools exist to convey information, to increase learning, to increase achievements. Content and instructional method were discussed separately in the survey, reflecting their traditional theoretical separation in the ends–means conceptualization that underlies most education research. This attention to goal attainment ("effectiveness") omits two considerations. The first is the interrelation of instructional process and instructional content, irrespective of the effectiveness standard; that is, how the methods and forms of conveying knowledge affect the knowledge itself, and consequently, student perceptions of it. The second is the possibility that producing "effects" in terms of student learning or achievements might not be a primary goal of the classroom interaction. There was no analytical category for what might be left out of the information exchange. Our attention has been so focused on what teachers and curriculum planners want students to learn, that we have no empirical precedent for looking at what teachers do not want them to learn, or at reasons for the limits that teachers impose.

While a research procedure for analyzing the inaccessibility of knowledge seems on the surface absurd, it should not, given the history of cultural biases in content selection and testing practices that has been brought to light by special-interest groups. Frances Fitzgerald and Jean Anyon have documented the selective omission of economic history unflattering to the myth of corporate and technological "progress" and free enterprise.[8] Blacks, women's groups, Hispano-Americans and others have forced at least symbolic revisions of textbooks so that their contributions to American history will be acknowledged.[9]

The remedy of the 1960s and early 1970s was to revise texts in order to try to "put in" whatever was being "left out." While this ameliorative approach was probably better than nothing, it left curriculum analysis largely at the planning level, the level of curriculum development, to the exclusion of such considerations as the institutional forces at work in those cultural selections and the impact of curricula on students. The distinctness of these three aspects of curricula as subjects of different professionals' research should not mask their interrelation in the real world of schools. Where school knowledge comes from is part and parcel of what it looks like, what values it embodies, what forms it takes, and what impact it has on students.

Before demonstrating this interrelationship through examples selected from current curricula, it will be helpful to ground these examples in the context of the broader question of the role the school serves in society. Although most curriculum developers would stand by their assumption that schools serve to increase achievements, we have the benefit of many insights to the contrary. Bowles and Gintis, among others, have argued that the foremost role of the school is economic rather than educative, in the strictest sense.[10] The primary purpose of free public education in an industrial society is to sort students for positions of labor and management, and to stratify their access to knowledge to make them into docile and productive workers in an economy where they can expect to see the products of their labor appropriated into the profit structure of others. The structure of schooling into a credentialing system that supersedes instruction conforms to the individualized, alienating workplace with its external rewards. This view of the school as a tool ,that elites use to socialize the masses has different configurations in different societies. Bourdieu[11] has described the higher education system of France as a sophisticated system of stratified knowledge, wherein the high culture of aristocratic elites is promulgated as more worthy and more universal than the vernacular cultures of nonelites. "Real knowledge" and "true culture" are those historically characteristic of the aristocracy. Institutions of learning not only define what socially desirable knowledge is, but do so in ways that engender a "habitus," or disposition toward dominant values, that goes beyond holding specific pieces of information. The school serves to shape the consciousness of a nation by disposing individuals to define their world through the definitions of those in power.[12]

Before World War II, British education accorded highest status to the cultural forms of the classical education of the gentleman class, and kept the technical knowledge of working people at lowest status. This legacy persists in subtle forms; one's perceived job future, inferred from one's class background, helps determine which kinds of knowledge one has access to.[13] By contrast, in the United States, where economic power has been more associated with corporate growth than with centuries of inherited wealth, technological language, especially in the sciences, has displaced the traditional Latin-school culture as high-status knowledge. Post-sputnik investments in education were aimed originally at those students who showed through standardized testing, aptitude for physics, or higher mathematics, or who had proficiency in practical (nonliterary foreign language skills valued by the military and industrial complex). While valuing scientific inquiry among intellectual elites (to the point of applying scientific, or scientistic, modes of inquiry to almost every field of study), schools presented a very sanitized view of science to ordinary students in survey courses. There, science has been portrayed not as an arena of competing discoveries, but as an incremental series of progressing experiments whose results add up to "science."

This emerging critique of the social roles of school curricula forces us out of the habit of accepting the curricula as given, out of a research paradigm that manipulates all manner of instructional variables in search of the key to "effectiveness." However, this view of schools also seems to take too seriously the planning, or rational, component of school curricula. In talking about the role of school knowledge in cultural reproduction, writers frequently use terms that seem to imply that someone is deliberately pulling the strings of knowledge access, knowledge stratification, and knowledge control: "the state encodes . . . ," or "the school stratifies." I have argued elsewhere that both of the dominant models of curriculum theory—management and cultural reproduction—see the student as too passive, too acted upon, and that there is no interactive model for seeing whether the student is, in fact, resisting the processing of the school.[14] Similarly, cultural reproduction models of curriculum analysis seem to accept too readily the implication of planning—that someone out there is stratifying school knowledge, that the interests vested in school knowledge necessarily reflect manipulation by elites in a way that can be explained as the direct exercise of power. In fact, schools' mediation of dominant culture can be far more subtle.

What cultural reproduction models give us is a view of the curriculum as problematic, as reflective of human interests. From this perspective, we are no longer bound by the pretense that school knowledge is the product of neutral, experimental inquiry, resulting in an objective selection of the information most conducive to "effective learning." We can begin to see that school knowledge, in some vague way, seems to correspond to the interests of powerful groups in the society. But it is dangerous to carry this model of correspondence too far, especially in the American setting. The French have had their academies and elite schools established by the aristocracy and the church, and the British have had their tradition of aristocratic and, later, nationally centralized schooling, but schooling in the United States is much more decentralized, much more chaotic. The mechanisms by which certain forms of knowledge are transmitted in schools, and others are omitted, necessarily have local as well as national characteristics.

In a broad sense, there are some national pressures, such as university entrance requirements and national tests, such as those offered by Education Testing Service, that dominate some course offerings in American high schools. Demands by business people that public schools prepare their future lower-level employees have also resulted in direct interventions in the curriculum such as Career Education and a proliferation of office and trade courses. But the content of these courses, even where stipulated by state legislatures, does not reflect explicit centralized policy.

Because they have been of fairly low status since the post-sputnik promotion of science and mathematics, the social studies courses (sometimes called social science courses, in deference to technological trends) in most schools reflect little concern for national standardized tests or centralized curriculum planning. Authority for course titles usually rests with state departments of public instruction or local school boards, but the content of courses remains significantly at the discretion of the local school's individual teachers or social studies department. Social studies, then, is an interesting area in which to bring generalizations about the nature of school knowledge down to the level where selected knowledge about the society's institutions is encountered by the student. It is at the classroom level that we can best see the tension between making information accessible and making information inaccessible. By examining close up the ways the teachers offer and withhold information, we can test our generalizations about the rationalities of curriculum planning, and the school's role in cultural reproduction, against the actual presentation of cultural selections.

Knowledge Forms as Knowledge Control

The examples of classroom knowledge cited below are drawn from an early ethnographic study of economics information in the U.S. history classes of a southern Wisconsin high school, and from similar observations in three Wisconsin high schools selected for a later study of the administrative context within which teachers make curriculum decisions. The teachers are all middle-aged white men, except for one woman; all have at least a master's degree, and many have additional university training beyond that. All have taught for at least ten years. Although the academic reputation of the schools varies somewhat, the student populations are remarkably similar: predominantly white, middle-class children of professionals, state employees, small-business owners or well-paid laborers. Both the students and the teachers can be characterized by a wide range of political and philosophical values. Across these diversities, the techniques the teachers chose for controlling classroom behavior through approaches to course content are unexpectedly similar. After examining these techniques, we can better understand their relation to teacher and student diversities, and to the role schools play in the dissemination of cultural knowledge and knowledge forms.

According to the teachers themselves, the techniques they used to convey course content to their students had to fulfill two goals: they had to give the students information about American history and economics, and, at the same time, they had to impose firm limits on the complexity and topicality of class discussions, and on the efficiency of presentation. Most of the teachers resolved this tension by maintaining tight control over course content, eliminating almost all reading assignments or written work. Information related to the course came to students through lectures and teacher-selected films. As discussed in "Negotiating Classroom Knowledge," students rarely spoke (as infrequently as twelve student comments all semester in one class of thirty juniors), and when they did, it was to ask the teacher a question rather than discuss the topic with each other. Therefore, one may limit analysis to teacher comments and lectures and still gain a fairly full picture of the knowledge, and, most importantly, the ways of knowing that the students encountered.

Educators usually see "lecture" as a negative term, to be contrasted with inquiry, discussion, or other more enlightened forms of instruction. "Lecture" can actually bring to mind a wide range of verbal activities, from the dull half-reading of a prepared text to brilliant discourse, within which the lecturer can argue, dramatize, compare, or question. Lectures themselves need not be a limitation on knowledge forms and content. With these particular teachers, however, lectures provided the best means toward the contradictory goals of giving the students information about the required subject in a way that maintained the teachers' professional role, while withholding from them ideas and information that might disrupt class efficiency. Within each lecture technique, we will see that control of knowledge really has as its objective the control of the students.

Fragmentation

The simplest, and probably most notorious lecture technique among social studies teachers, is the reduction of any topic to fragments, or disjointed pieces of information—lists. A list lets a teacher avoid having to elaborate or show linkages, and it keeps students, especially those weak at reading and writing, from having to express "learnings" in complete sentences or paragraphs. No one is called upon to synthesize or give a picture of interrelationships.

At all of these schools, fragmentation was most commonly used when the teacher considered the information vital to the students' knowledge. The list as a lecture device has the benefit of reducing all information to "facts," as though each term in the list represents a consensus among historians or the general public about an event, a personage or an issue. In fact, lists usually take the issue-ness out of issues by collapsing contradictory opinions into a single enumeration of fragments of the story.

Several examples will illustrate the transformation a segment of history undergoes when confined to a list. The characteristics of political parties, economic policies or major institutions; the causes, results, or effects of various events or activities; and the people and dates central to historical events are all likely to be presented as lists or as points in a formal outline. Almost every teacher observed in the four schools described labor history in terms of the names of various unions and their founders or primary leaders. They printed on the blackboard lists of the "tools" or "weapons" labor and management had at their disposal during grievances (strike, lockout, injunction, and so on). The only exception was a seasoned labor leader, an organizer of teacher unions, who showed a film of the Triangle fire and told old stories about labor conditions. Otherwise, as Anyon has noted, the conditions giving rise to the labor movement are almost never discussed, or even put into a list. In this instance, as in many others, the list is not an aid to remembering the details from a complicated study of a topic, it *is* the study of the topic. Suddenly, with little background, the course chronology arrives at industrialization; the teacher reads a list of new labor unions. The same strategy was used to convey information about the benefits of TVA ("soil conservation, an energy yardstick, advanced farming techniques"), without any background information about the energy needs or policies of the period. The names of New Deal agencies, again with little background information about the economic conditions and political compromises involved, is a favorite subject for lists.

The teachers at the first high school observed were very articulate in explaining their view of their job and their rationale for their instructional techniques. They expressed the sentiment that their job as history teachers was to tell students the "true story" of American history. By presenting that story in fragments, they made efficient use of time, avoided arousing discussion, and presented information in a manner that facilitated quantifiable testing. When filled with lists, the course content appears to be rigorous and factual. It makes the teacher appear knowledgeable and gives students a sense of fairness in the grading: they know they have to memorize the lists. Lists and unelaborated terms reduce the uncertainty for both students and teachers. For this reason, it is clearly the dominant mode of conveying information.

The effects of lists on students were twofold: of all the strategies for controlling classroom knowledge, this one seemed to have the most pay-off for students. Depending on their abilities and diligence, they could turn the fragments of information in their notebooks into test points. Grades of B or C were easily earned because so little was expected in these classes; that softened the fact that the course was required for graduation.

But this fragmentation of information, without the opportunity for in-depth consideration of a topic, also carried within it a vulnerability of which the teachers seemed unaware. Interviews with the students revealed that their overt acquiescence to the lectures masked covert suspicions or rejection of much of the course content. One reason was that many of these students had had experiences (or had heard those of their parents) that contradicted teacher-supplied information. Many students mentioned that when the teacher presented as fact *one item* that the student believed to be untrue or misleading, the entire course became suspect for that student. Their information came from stories their grandparents told, from their parents' professions or travels, from their own jobs, from television documentaries, or, occasionally, from books or newspapers. These students, whom the teachers dismissed as needing to have everything "spoon fed" to them, were silently comparing the classroom version of the "facts" with whatever other source was available to them. Any discrepancy discredited the teacher in their eyes. The brisk pace of the lectures and the consistency of the course format in preventing discussion also prevented elaboration of items in lists and prevented comparison with varied interpretations. No doubt such comparisons, if they had taken place, would not always have validated the students' personal information. In their absence, the students' personal sources of information were often more credible to them. Thus the teachers successfully used fragments and lists to efficiently convey a vast number of facts and to proscribe discussion and disagreement by this appearance of factuality. The irony is that this technique created so much distance between the student and the content that it caused a backlash of the kind of cynicism the teachers were trying to avoid.

Mystification

Another treatment of information I have termed mystification. Teachers often tried to surround a controversial or complex topic with mystery in order to close off discussion of it. When the teachers mystified a topic, they made it appear very important but unknowable. When they mentioned the Federal Reserve or the gold standard or the International Monetary Fund, they asked students to copy the term into their notes. Then a comment would follow to the effect that students should know about this and remember the term for their next test, but that nonexperts really could not go into depth on this subject. Sometimes this seemed to be a ruse to hide the teacher's lack of knowledge of the subject, as when one teacher said the students should write down that Nixon took us off the gold standard, but that he did not know what that meant and was not going to go into it with an "economics major" (referring to me, though I am not an economics major) present. This point had been on the transparency outline from which he lectured every day for years, so one doubts whether he had ever "gone into it" beyond this brief mention.

Capitalism, the importance of political parties, free enterprise, and progress are all aspects of our system that were mentioned with an aura of respect or reverence, then left as slogans. The intent seemed to be to have students internalize the affective component of the term so that their trust of the system would be enhanced. This attention to affiliative language best conforms to Bourdieu's concept of creating "habitus" rather than mechanistic reproduction of the dominant culture. Certainly this was the intent of the teachers. The woman teacher told me that she wished more than anything that students would appreciate their institutions, because the people who came before them had worked hard to create them, especially during the New Deal reforms. A male teacher at her school added, "you have to sell the system." Both attributed student cynicism toward business institutions and school rules to the partial information that students during the Vietnam war era had come across. This partial information combined with student enthusiasm to make students disruptive in class, arrogant about their own opinions, and generally hard to control. These two teachers reflected on their manner of presenting information and deliberately wove a story that reinforced simple themes and minimized differences.

The effect of mystification was that students did for the most part internalize some of the emotional quality of the term, while remaining unable to explain it. When asked to explain free enterprise, students would answer with affiliative language based on little factual knowledge: "it means you can own your own business without government controls," or "we have labor unions here but I don't know what they do." They seemed to know that the mystified term was meant to be comparative, showing the superiority of the U.S. economic system, but they could not elaborate that system or the meaning of the term. For students suspicious of course content, and for some who were not suspicious but were frustrated that the course did not have more "meat" to it, this mystification created unease because they felt they should have a chance to have capitalism, or free enterprise, or fiscal and monetary policy, really explained to them until they understood it. Their common response sounded something like, "I hear that term every year, but I still don't know what it means."

Mystification also helped engender a client mentality: since students were not invited to pursue information on their own, to dig deeper into subjects that were mentioned and then closed off, they developed a feeling of dependence on externally supplied information. Frequently when asked what they thought they should learn about a certain topic, the answer shifted to the third person. " 'They' never tell us"; "they should tell us"; or "pollution must not be a problem because *they* don't mention it anymore" (emphasis added). Since many of these same students felt they could not trust teacher-supplied information, their "they" remained without antecedent.

Omission

The lecture strategy that produced the most suspicion, and the only one to which resistance was voiced in class, was omission. The students were less concerned about the omission of specific topics than about whole time periods omitted from the lecture. Several students did express concern that variant points of view were omitted from class, and most said they wished that students could discuss the topics that were mentioned. But their chief and almost unanimous concern was that their United States history courses dealing, according to the course title, with the most recent period of history, ended with Eisenhower or Kennedy. Especially at the first school observed, where the course was titled "Contemporary United States History," each teacher crammed the most recent twenty years, of the fifty or so to be covered by the course, into the last three to eight days of the semester.

There were several reasons for this. Most obvious was that to the teachers, events that had happened in their adulthood were "current events" to them, even though to the students "current events" usually meant this year's happenings. The Vietnam war (which ended several years prior to the observation) got from zero to four and a half minutes' treatment in the three classes in the original ethnography. Current presidential campaigns and economic turmoil (inflation, unemployment, energy, near-bankrupt cities), which were of great interest to the students, were "lightweight" topics on which "historians do not yet agree," in the teachers' conception of the "story" of history. The teacher who lectured daily from transparencies did not want to relate current events to historical topics, because he preferred to use the same transparency outline year after year. He said that he spent the greater part of the course discussing the New Deal and the Depression because no one could hope to understand current situations without a thorough grounding in these periods, which so shaped our current institutions. Aside from this pedagogical reason, the teachers also stated emphatically that they intended never to return to the days of Vietnam and student rights protests, when students shouted teachers down and when class discussion thereby became "unbalanced."

One teacher said that he had cut out research papers because the weaker students could not think of a topic on their own, and although the brighter students had, during the antiwar movement, "written terrific papers . . . they were *self-indoctrinated.*" They learned something that contradicted the teacher's analysis of the events. This teacher told the class being observed that he was not going to discuss the Vienam war (although his chronological coverage of American history had come to that period) because he had "heard Vietnam for the past ten years." He similarly dismissed poverty by saying that no one starves to death in this country; a black student tried to challenge this statement but had only intuition to go on and so was not believed. This teacher was a very friendly and caring person who usually tried to get students to realize how well-off Americans are compared to most other people. But one day he refused to accept a student's definition of "exploitation" as "rip-off." He said that the investment of American capital in other countries always had a beneficial effect on both the United States and the recipient economy. Again, a few students tried to object on the basis of news reports they had heard, but were unsuccessful, except that they did press the teacher to admit that United Fruit had given multinational corporations a "bad name." The concept of "exploitation" had come up in a one-day survey of U.S. policies toward Latin America. The framework of the course, built around lists of treaties, technical terms like exploitation, and similarly abbreviated facts, did not permit students or teacher to explore the emerging differences of interpretation. The students shrugged, wrote down the requisite terms, and resumed silence.

Omission also extended beyond current topics to include the controversial sides of topics that were mentioned. For example, no mention was made of protests against U.S. entry into World War II, of people who disliked Roosevelt's New Deal policies or of people who disagreed with Truman's decision to bomb Hiroshima. Variation across region, ethnic group, social class, or gender was also notably absent. "We Americans . . . " was usually the subject of any sentence describing an era or momentous event. Most of the students interviewed volunteered a concern that they felt was omitted from the course, whether it was a specific topic ("why is so much money spent on the space program") or a perspective ("what if your grandparents *liked* Huey Long?"). The girls were not too concerned that women were excluded from history, but the one black student, and many whites, wondered aloud why few issues related to blacks were included. Several noted the lack of mention of other countries, or the comparison of American institutions or events with related ones in other countries. In short, the teachers actually stimulated interest in the contemporary period by omitting it, although omitting it allowed them to avoid dealing with it.

Any course involves selections. Omissions described by Anyon and Fitzgerald are those systematically characteristic of commercial textbook publishers. There were instances at each of these schools of a teacher's choosing not to deal with a topic that was included in the text or in the school's resources or even in the course outline. While obvious constraints of time and student ability would account for some omissions any teacher makes, these teachers took pains to explain at some length the reasons for certain of their omissions. They wished to omit material, or perspectives on material, that would foster contradictory opinions and make students want to engage in discussion. The teachers felt they could cover more material more efficiently if controversial topics were omitted. The pace of the lecture was critical to covering the course adequately. To maintain that pace, student talk had to be kept to a minimum.

Defensive Simplification

The fourth strategy that will be mentioned here cuts across ideological lines and institutional contexts more than any of the others. Teachers use this strategy to circumvent what they perceive to be a lack of strong student interest or the weakness of student abilities. Rather than relying on that old standard, "motivation," the teachers will win the students' compliance on a lesson by promising that it will not be difficult and will not go into any depth.

While fragmentation, mystification and omission strategies may all be seen as efforts to simplify content, this last is distinguished by the term *defensive*. Unlike the old wielder of the hickory stick, the teacher announces the topic of study, which may sound very complicated, then apologizes for it and promises it will not demand much work. Examples might be supply and demand, or the industrialization–urbanization syndrome. Any real treatment of the topic would require time, comparison of varied interpretations, investigations of varied information resources and the effort of making repeated explanations or of offering distinct encounters with the topic (through small group discussion, film, research, reading, or whatever) until everyone in the class understood it at some reasonable level. Although the topic is formally listed in the course outline, and the teacher will present something about it for later use on a test, he or she may not intend for the students to go beyond this superficial treatment. Yet just announcing the topic makes students think they will have to do some work. The teacher gets them to cooperate without resisting by promising that, in fact, the study of this topic will require no commitment of effort, or little time, on their part. This strategy of making knowledge inaccessible makes twenty-plus years of research of "effectiveness" look incredibly naive. Equally naive was the research hypothesis that guided the classroom observations in search of the kinds of economics information made available in these classes. The specific topics became almost irrelevant when they were subjected to a defensive presentation.

Topics introduced "defensively" were less likely to be politically sensitive and controversial than those that were mystified. Rather, they tended to be topics that needed a great deal of unpacking to be grasped, topics not amenable to reduction to items in a list. Whereas the labor movement could be reduced to names, dates, famous strikes and weapons of labor-management dispute, fiscal and monetary policy could hardly be treated at all without explanation of the interrelationship of private- and public-sector economic decision-making, the concept of money supply and circulation, and other aspects such as public works programs, the tension between unemployment and inflation, and the nature of credit economies. Political trade-offs are a vital component, also. Sometimes such complicated topics were omitted altogether although in the interview the teacher said they were essential to a student's education. At other times, the teacher contrived a set of lists of factual terms that lay out key components of the topic. Yet other times, either because the topic was mentioned in a text or curriculum guide, or because a later unit built upon it, some treatment of the topic became unavoidable. When this became evident, the teacher very quickly followed the announcement of the topic with the caveat that "it won't be as bad as it sounds."

The simplification may take the form of a very brief sketch of the topic in the lecture, a worksheet with blanks to be filled in with fragments of fact, a filmstrip that reduces the topic to its simplest possible form, or a handout such as a one-page magazine article that talks around the topic without ever really explaining it. Most important is the ritual of seeming to deal with the topic. The teacher makes a few remarks, the students groan, the activity (lecture, filmstrip, or whatever) proceeds and is briefly concluded, the teacher asks if there are any questions, and there are none.

The observations and interviews turned up several possible explanations behind this strategy of controlling students by simplifying the lessons. The first that teachers express is fatigue. Having reached middle age or seen their paychecks long ago outstripped by inflation, the teachers say that they no longer feel the energy and drive to do whatever is necessary to make students understand. They feel that neither the support nor the financial reward is commensurate with the out-of-class time needed to adequately prepare learning activities, or to read and comment on the student essay tests or written assignments that a real treatment of such topics would require. The energy they recall being willing to expend during their earlier days of teaching has dwindled now to minimal effort.

A second factor is the minimal effort students seem willing to put forth. In two of the four schools, over half the juniors and seniors interviewed worked more than twenty hours per week in addition to going to school full-time.[15] Other teachers noted that the 1960's enthusiasm for social studies courses had given way to higher priorities for math and science in the 1970s and 1980s. Whatever school effort students were willing to spend, they saved for these courses, which they saw as more instrumental to job futures. There is no objective way to know if students today are less willing to work at learning than were students of ten or twenty years ago, but teachers who have been around that long swear this is the case. One mentioned that he can no longer plan to center a class period around a completed homework assignment; many assignments eventually trickle in, but not on time. Another mentioned that there seem to be fewer "slow" students who learn by consistently pushing themselves to "over-achieve"—in other words, to stretch beyond what is normally expected of them. Tired, bored, and rushed to cover content, teachers and students meet in a path of least resistance. Expected student resistance to taxing assignments is circumvented by making the assignments less taxing.

Thus, again, the teachers maintain classroom control and control of information at the same time.

A third explanation teachers give for simplifying content in order to gain student cooperation is the lack of a supportive administration. In the second phase of research, the administrative context was analyzed for its effect on the ways teachers make knowledge and ways of knowing accessible to students.[16] The basic finding was that there is a parallel between administrators' attempts to gain minimal compliance from teachers and teachers' settling for minimal compliance from students. In those schools where administrators devoted most of the schools' staff time and resources to maintaining order and to attending to such details as course credits, the administrators paid less attention to the academic quality of teaching. The content of the curriculum was clearly secondary to the maintenance of order. Teachers in these schools tended to expend minimal effort in the classroom; frequently this was deliberate and was explained by the teacher as retaliation for or reluctant accommodation to administrative pressure for precision in paperwork, extra hall monitoring, or extended meetings related to such matters as graduation requirements.

In the school where the administration most supported the teaching function, gave most attention to the quality of instruction, teachers responded by demanding more of themselves in the presentation and preparation of lessons. They felt, and demonstrated, less of a wall between their personal knowledge and the "official" knowledge of the classroom. They used fewer lists, and provided more extended descriptions, more opportunities for student discussion, more varieties of learning experiences (including the willingness to bring speakers in from the community). Not even in this school, however, were teachers free of the kind of "defensive simplification" that was prevalent at the other schools.

One teacher whose classes were extremely rich in ideas and in materials he had collected or developed, explained that he did not have high expectations that the students would really deal with those ideas. Although he did require more reading than teachers at the first school observed, he had students fill in the blanks on daily worksheets. He stated that he did not like the worksheets, but that he began using them after a year or two of teaching, when he discovered that students were not reading. He acknowledged that the worksheets did show that students had read, but did not necessarily mean they could discuss or integrate the ideas. The worksheet assignment allowed the teacher to deal with history in a way that kept his own interest because ideas were involved, but also in a way that let students know they were not responsible for more than the most basic components of the lesson. This same teacher was known for asking tough, analytical questions. He built his history courses around such themes as the relation of violence to human history and the obligation of the individual to the state. Yet he said that he had eliminated student research papers because "these students are too young to even ask a question, much less look for answers." Except for a very few students, who in interviews talked about having wrestled with his "questions that catch you off guard," most of these questions became rhetorical, with the teacher and students knowing that the real grade was based on the worksheets and short-answer tests.

The full impact of the administrative context is beyond the scope of this discussion. It is mentioned here because it is large in the minds of many teachers who reflect on their teaching strategies, and who acknowledge their willingness to settle for thin curricular substance if students will cooperate and help the class go smoothly. The institutional rewards for order do not entirely shape classroom knowledge; but they set up a dynamic that often places added burdens of time and energy, and added personal risk, on those teachers who would hope to teach beyond minimal standards.

Variations and Differences

Educators are accustomed to think in terms of student differences. Curriculum analysts speak of ideological differences among teachers. The examples of defensive teaching witnessed in these schools cut across differences in teachers' individual political and pedagogical philosophies and across formal definitions of variations in student ability. If we understand its pervasiveness in spite of expected variations and exceptions, we may better grasp what is at work when schools mediate social knowledge.

Most published educational research begins with the premise that differences in student ability and achievement matter and, in fact, lie at the heart of educational exchanges. This became clear to me as I presented these examples of knowledge simplification to various groups of researchers. Even those critical theorists most skeptical of formal educationist categories would ask, "what about the bright students? how was it different for weak students?" Our experiences with knowledge stratified by student acheivement or social-class levels make the questions reasonable. But none of the observed teachers followed the truism by teaching to the brighter or upper-class students, or by watering down content only for the non-college-bound or lower-income student. The way these teachers dealt with student differences is much more complex and demonstrates how the contradictory goals inherent in institutional roles can be rationalized.

The teachers at all four schools talked about differences in student ability. Many mentioned that it was difficult to try to teach classes in which many students were "very bright" and other students "could not read." Only one teacher ever named specific students as belonging in either category, even though several were pressed in interviews to elaborate their distinctions. The teachers at the first school observed felt that having to teach heterogeneous classes was a constraint, even a punishment. They felt that their ability to affect students' learning had diminished with the elimination of I.Q.-based tracking. Teachers at the other schools preferred the mixed-ability classes.

In both cases, teachers frequently made comments that demonstrated their knowledge of and consideration of traditional ability classifications for students. Yet the teaching strategies in their classes belied these differences. One teacher who had fairly weak students made his lectures simple and demanded no effort beyond answering a few questions each week on dittoed sheets. A teacher of an honors history class assigned roles for the students to play in a trial of Harry Truman for the Hiroshima bombings. He gave them no instructions on role-playing, did not check the extent of their background reading before the enactment, and interrupted the poor performances after only a few minutes and gradually resumed lecturing. Later he told me, "I knew they couldn't do it; I knew it would turn out like this." By abandoning the assignment, instead of continuing it and giving the instructions the students needed to prepare properly, he in effect apologized for having expected something of them. It was easier for him to diffuse the expectations than to act on them.

His treatment of the honors students was very little different from the strategy of the teacher of a mixed-ability class who assigned only one book per semester and then accepted nominal book reports, some of which were openly copied from book jackets.

The most telling concern about student differences came from the teachers who had fought de-tracking. They were convinced that differences in student ability greatly affected student learning and called for vastly different teaching techniques. They fondly recalled being able to have panel discussions and research papers with the bright students, but had "spoon fed" the "masses" and had let the lowest level of students read the morning paper with the football coach for their U.S. history course. These same teachers applied their spoon-feeding techniques to all levels once the levels were mixed. Although the rationale of the school system had been to further democratize classrooms by eliminating tracking, making each individual the focus of instruction apart from group labels, the effect of de-tracking was that teachers treated all the individuals as they had formerly treated their "masses." They began to define all students as belonging in the middle-level categories, as having to have everything done for them. They saw these students as having to be controlled in behavior and learning. They structured the lessons accordingly.

The result was that they began to teach as though the differences were no longer there. Rather than teach to the brightest students, they simplified the content and assignments for everyone. To stratify assignments is time-consuming; it means dividing the class for discussion or directions occasionally; it means having to grade more than one kind of assignment. And it means adapting a standard grading code, set by the school, in a way that will fairly reflect the difficulty levels of the assignments. It is easier, say the teachers, not to have the bright students write papers. Writing papers calls for many procedural directions and much paper reading by the teacher. It also puts students into contact with resources that make them vulnerable to "self-indoctrination." If some of the students in the same class can barely read, the differential assignments will bring this to attention. When teachers are aware of the problem, they feel obligated to help these students find suitable reading material or help them learn how to read the regular text. If one ignores these differences, or structures the class in a way that hides them, one can remove oneself from the obligation of dealing with the inefficiencies these differences pose.

Thus these defensive teaching strategies do not deal with differences between students with the instructional stratification that one might expect. One of the purposes of the fragmentation was to reduce content to pieces that could be managed by students of many levels of ability. One of the purposes of systematically omitting current topics was to prevent the intrusion of verbal students' ideas into the pace of the lecture. One of the purposes of mystification was to avoid having to go into a whole series of presentations of a complex topic until everyone understood. The teachers who chafed at de-tracking were in a minority. All but two of the fourteen observed teachers preferred teaching mixed-ability classes. Teachers in both groups talked about differences between students outside the classroom, yet taught as though there were no differences. When asked which students' needs were not being met by their department's offerings, most felt that the weakest students were receiving some help from dropout prevention programs and the like; one or two mentioned that the brightest students were probably bored, but that that "was inevitable." The others felt that if brighter students were not challenged, they should do something about it themselves. "They can always do more if they want to. Not many go that extra effort any more." In no school were any of the "defensive" teaching strategies limited to students of one ability group. In fact, according to their own explanations, teachers selected these strategies in order to deal with "all these different students."

Equally striking is the prevalence of these teaching strategies across differences in teacher ideology. My recent dialogue with Henry Giroux on the ability of teachers to foster emancipatory citizenship education through their resistance to technocratic rationale in schools centered on the failure of teacher practice to reflect teacher ideology.[17] The selection of teaching strategies that maximize efficiencies and control of student behavior can be observed among teachers who otherwise would appear to have very different political values. Miss L. teaches American history as a chronology of presidents and congresses, and tends to reify the view that citizens must support whoever is in power, because history is made at the top. Her lists consist of presidential plans and congressional enactments. Mr. S. frequently says that "We are all Progressives . . . " and claims ideological links to Jefferson, while making lists of Hamiltonian-like policies. Mr. R. is a labor organizer and teller of stories. He is clearly to the left of most of the other teachers observed; he assigns the reading of public-issues pamphlets designed to raise issues beyond the normal confines of consensus information, then turns them into seatwork by making students answer the questions at the end of the sections rather than discuss the issues, as the materials intend.[18] He himself loves political debate and has participated actively in state and national politics. He spoke openly with his students about the contrast between his own leftist leanings and the community's conservatism. Yet his treatment of course topics differed little from that of Miss L. and her presidential lists or Mr. S. and his transparencies.

Miss L. reduced content to fragments but never apologized for assignments. One teacher who innovated consumer-economics courses and was well-versed on consumer rights and regulatory policies, presented even these issues close to the lives of students in list form and made assignments without expecting any real interest or commitment from the students. Mr. I., the most intellectual of the teachers observed, is determined to stretch the minds of students. He says that he deliberately uses difficult words to force students to learn them, and requires students to watch *Washington Week in Review* and difficult films on such topics as futurology. Yet he permits students to carry on conversations during class, accepts the briefest of outlines as an "independent project," and in general demands little of students. His pleasure comes from his own intense involvement with the subject without the expectation of much student reciprocity; in the classes observed, he got little.

One last example serves to demonstrate the power of simplification strategies to obscure differences among teachers and reduce content to its most trivial, least controversial level. Mr. G. describes himself as a Marxist and at other times as a social democrat. He is as politically different from the man with the transparency lectures as could be expected within a range of high-school teachers. Mr. G. would *like* his students to understand the very inequities and injustices of capitalist economies that the teachers at the first school wish to hide from their students. He would like his students to see the validity of Marxian analysis of their economic system and to see that people may have honest disagreements about economic goals and political means. On the surface, the content of his lectures appears somewhat radical. Yet, when seen in the context of its method of presentation, it mirrors the defensive simplications of the more conservative teachers. While he is much less likely to deliberately mystify a subject, Mr. G. lectures in a very casual, low-key way, making minimal assignments in an apologetic tone, and expecting little student involvement in the topic. He told me that by the time the students become juniors and seniors they are "adults" and should learn on their own. He contradicts this by not requiring them to work on their own, and in fact does not even require them to listen attentively to his lectures. He occasionally presents reading material that contains two opposing perspectives on an issue, but he has little means of checking whether students read or understand the differences. His motivations are very different from the teachers reacting against de-tracking and Vietnam war era protests. He was one of the protesters; his reactions within his school are against what he sees as capricious and unsupportive administrators who overemphasize rules rather than instruction and faculty support. He openly admits that he has lowered the standards of his own efforts in recent years and is unwilling to exert effort on preparations or paper grading or forcing student compliance with demanding assignments. Points in his lectures that could have earned him censure in the 1950s come across as just another boring set of social-studies facts to his students. Their test scores are very low, and a constant hum of side chatter accompanies each lecture. He is liked for his rapport with students and his willingness to discuss the headlines at the beginning of class. But once the lecture starts, his ideas become "social studies" and are taken less seriously.

Institutional Goals and Personal Knowledge

One must not draw from this study the conclusion that all teachers deny students access to information critical to their functioning in society, or that all teachers use the techniques outlined here under the guise of lecturing just to limit student access to information. We have seen that when teachers do wish to control knowledge access, they often do so consciously. Their chief criteria for selecting strategies of knowledge control seem to be based on maintaining their own authority and efficiencies. The desire to control knowledge is as much a desire for classroom control as for selective distribution of information. This finding is crucial for our understanding of the ways schools legitimate certain kinds of information and delegitimate others. An appreciation of the processes and rationale of legitimation, and the legitimation of processes, or ways of knowing, is central to any understanding of the role of the school in transmitting fairly narrow selections from the infinite range of human knowledge.

Although cultural reproduction is generally discussed on a societal level, as the product of a complex of systemic forces, the mediation of cultural forms in these schools is highly conditioned by the individual's attempt to deal with institutional constraints. The constraints are not the same in each school. The philosophical values the individual brings to the classroom are not in all cases the same. Yet the strategies for instruction are quite similar: control students by making school work easy. The result is content that neither the teachers nor the students take very seriously. It is frequently distinct from their personal knowledge.

This has two important implications for our understanding of the nature of secondary schools. First, their role in reproducing dominant cultural forms is far more complex than any direct correspondence theory would capture. Second, the resulting "official knowledge" is often too impersonal to be appropriated, but its effects are nevertheless damaging.

In every case, these teachers can be said to have resisted the dominant technological forms of knowledge in their conceptualization of social-studies curricula. Two of the teachers participated in a strike, in which one issue was the imposition of teaching-by-objectives standards for teacher evaluation. None of the teachers taught to prepare for standardized tests, or valued technical knowledge above narrative, intuitive, experiential warrants for knowledge claims. None had adopted a social-science model of history, although materials for doing so were available in their school systems and professional associations. With two exceptions, their theories of politics and historiography admitted conflict and rejected simplistic consensus. They were not stratifying students for the labor force, nor deliberately reinforcing racial or class inequities. Neither the state nor the business community intruded directly into the treatment or, for the most part, the selection of course topics. From their personal values alone, it would seem that these teachers are not "reproducing" technological culture.

Yet their instructional strategies embody the very values they wish to avoid in teaching-by-objective models. In accomodating to institutional priorities for order and efficiency, the teachers demonstrate the very technocratic values that they do not respect in administrators and on which they place much of the blame for the need for efficiency. By reducing course content to its most manageable and measurable fragments, the teachers are splitting the learning process into means and ends and reinforcing a concern for extrinsic rewards. The strategies of classroom control have their basis in the reward system of the institution (teacher pay and student credentials, as examples) and the power structure of the institution (the hierarchy that makes teachers responsible for control of students). The societal factors shaping quiescence, discretion, and autonomy within the institution are beyond the scope of this discussion, but what the data show is that theories of the social role of schools must be grounded in the processes within schools that disseminate selected societal values to the students.

At the elementary level, it can be argued that external forces have more directly shaped curricula by deskilling teachers through the adoption of "teacher-proof" materials. Packaged materials, produced by commercial publishers, adopted by state and local school systems under the direction of experts such as child psychologists and reading specialists, have the purpose of reducing teacher discretion and variation. The "teacher-proof" materials contain pre-tests, instructional techniques, sets of content reduced to measurable items, and post-tests for mastery. All the teacher need do is to follow the directions; no decisions, background, experience, or personal knowledge is necessary.

Secondary teachers at the observed schools have resisted such prepackaged materials. They see themselves as professionals, and, as such, responsible for course content and evaluation. So far, no outside experts or political pressures have attempted to insulate their students from their discretion through prepackaged materials. Yet these teachers are participating, and many of them willingly, in their own deskilling. Their assessment of their effectiveness or even survival within the institution has led them to split their personal knowledge from their classroom teaching in much the same way as prepackaged materials divorce elementary teachers' ideas from instruction and evaluation. The secondary teachers express disrespect for administrators who see only needs for hall order or completed paperwork. They feel frustration when faculty meetings month after month focus on graduation requirements and credit equivalencies rather than substantive matters like library acquisitions and course content. They resent having to do hall duty during their planning periods, as though "planning lessons" were nothing more than a coffee break. They feel alienated from institutional goals that subordinate teaching and learning to institutional maintenance.

Yet, within their classrooms they reinforce these goals of order with the justification that doing so is the only way they can protect themselves from the institutional pressures. They feel no encouragement to deal with differences in ability, so they structure lessons that obscure these differences. They get no reward for holding discussions, but feel sanctions for not "covering the material," so they minimize discussion in the interest of speeding up the lecture pace. Each one of the simplification strategies for gaining student compliance could be seen as the participation by high school teachers in their own de-skilling. The gaps between what they are doing and what they could be doing are not the perceptions of an outside observer but are the teachers' own views expressed in interviews as they discuss their personal views of what students ought to learn and what the subject is really all about. Their entrapment in the institutional reward structure could be seen as an excuse for lazy teaching, or as the most potent of the school's ways of reproducing technological culture. Even the teachers who least support that culture resort to instructional strategies aimed at the kind of minimal standards and desire for order that they reject at the administrative level. Their personal ideologies have not been enough to counter this deskilling.

Their splitting of their personal knowledge from the institutional in attempts to gain minimal compliance may be seen as a kind of deskilling of students as well. Yet the data also point to the danger of carrying this conclusion too far and deducing social-control effects from social-control processes. In a separate discussion,[19] I have elaborated the forms of student resistance that have only been mentioned here. What is clear is that where knowledge control is used as a form of classroom control, alienation increases for all participants, further reinforcing patterns of control. Resistance to forms of control does not mean that students are escaping the effects of the way information is processed. One real effect of the alienation students feel toward school-supplied information is the opportunity cost of rejecting much course content without having any sense of how to find (or generate or evaluate) credible information on their own. The teachers seem fairly successful in placing a distance between the students' own questions and concerns and the course content. This seems to make the students withdraw into their own personal information (their "real" knowledge) so that it will not become contaminated by school-supplied knowledge.[20]

The supreme example of teachers' promoting the split between personal knowledge (their own as well as the students') and classroom knowledge occurred in a class on Contemporary Social Problems. This popular elective takes a social-psychological approach to the selection and discussion of social issues such as death and dying, theories of personality, the family, and so on. The teacher uses many lists, despite the discussable nature of the topics, so that a topic such as theories of personality, for example, might include a few handouts and lists of Freudian concepts.

During the unit on death and dying, the teacher handed out a lengthy questionnaire on attitudes toward death. Such ostensibly impersonal questions as "when did you first become aware of death?" were followed by more personal inquiries about one's views on life after death, killing for moral reasons, dying for a purpose, and so on. One set of questions asked whether a student had ever considered suicide, and if so by what means, and with what degree of actual success. On the way out of class, I asked if the teacher had designed the questionnaire and whether he had ever had any qualms about asking about suicide in such graphic terms (such as checking off preferences for different methods). He answered that he got the questionnaire "from somewhere." At first he had had second thoughts about the suicide section until he "checked with a psychologist," who told him it is impossible to put ideas of suicide into another person's head and that people come to this act on their own.

Then he said, "Maybe you wondered what I was doing at the door during class. It was about this boy that sits in this seat [he points]. I was checking with the counselor because of his past background." He went on to say that except for this one course the boy was confined to a mental hospital for attempting suicide about three months before. The teacher had "checked with" the school guidance counselor who in turn had "checked with" the boy's psychologist. It was determined that the boy was indeed a high risk for future suicide attempts but that "it was okay for him to sit in on this." The students would exchange questionnaires, which would bear no names, and count the responses checked for each question. That this boy would, if answering honestly, have been the only student to check "attempted suicide, with high probability of success," was less important than his presence for the "covering of the material." (If he had answered untruthfully he could have been subjected to added strain, because many in the class knew of his suicide attempt.) "Learning the content" was not to be confused with relating to it, even at the risk of a boy's life. The discussion placed the topic on the usual casual level: the field trip for the unit was a trip to a funeral home.

In addition to exacerbating the split between personal and institutional knowledge, knowledge control that was not successfully resisted by students had the effect of individualizing classroom interaction. The individualization of rewards and sanctions in schools, in terms of credits and failures earned, is fairly widely understood. What the control strategies in the observed classes accomplished, beyond the power of the credentialing system, was to make resistance more private. As students acquiesced to controlled patterns of classroom interaction (or noninteraction), their resistance to the resulting content became silent and hidden (knowable to the researcher only through interviews). Because there was no discussion or exchanges of papers (except to mark each other's answers on multiple-choice tests), students tended to feel isolated in their alienation from the content. There was no mechanism for collective response. Occasionally they would grumble together about the tests or about the boredom of the transparencies, or protest with a groan the announcement of a difficult-sounding topic (before the teacher backed off from it). But the teachers had successfully prevented the kind of collective resistance that a few of them recalled being challenged by during the anti-war movement. The vulnerabilities within the patterns of control—including widespread student cynicism toward oversimplifications, student rejection of facts that contradicted their own information, and teacher alienation at having to apologize for assignments in order to get students to cooperate—remained too hidden to be seen as emancipatory possibilities. So long as they are hidden from participants, the cycle of alienation and control will presumably persist. So long as they are hidden from researchers, these patterns of control will be seen as the inevitable result of schooling in a capitalist society. As we have seen, however, domination is not mechanistically inevitable, but highly responsive to institutional variability. And with teachers, domination in the classroom may also be interpreted as resistance to their own alienation and lack of control within the larger institution. These many layers of control and resistance must be examined if our theories of cultural reproduction are to be founded in reality, are to help us understand the complex effects of schooling, and are to be instruments of social change.

Notes

1. Dwayne Huebner, "Curriculum as the Accessibility of Knowledge," unpublished paper presented at the Curriculum Theory Study Group (Minneapolis, March, 1970).

2. Linda M. McNeil, "Economic Dimensions of Social Studies Curricula: Curriculum as Institutionalized Knowledge" (Ph.D. diss., University of Wisconsin, Madison, 1977). The research, funded in part by a grant from the Graduate School of the University of Wisconsin, is the subject of "Making Knowledge Inaccessible" (unpublished ms.).

3. Linda M. McNeil, "Negotiating Classroom Knowledge: Beyond Achievement and Socialization," in *Journal of Curriculum Studies* 13, no. 4 (1981): 313–28.

4. The administrative context is the subject of a two-year study funded by the Organizational Processes division of the National Institute of Education and entitled "The Institutional Context Controlling Classroom Knowledge." The principal investigator and author of the research report, *Contradictions of Con-*

trol, is L. McNeil. The grant was administered by the Wisconsin Center for Public Policy, Madison, Wisconsin.

5. For additional insights into students' perceptions of whether teachers take them and their schooling seriously, see *Classroom and Corridors* by Mary H. Metz (Berkeley: University of California Press, 1978).

6. This study of the effects of student employment on high-school students and their schoolwork is entitled "Lowering Expectations: Student Employment and its Impact on Curriculum," funded by the Wisconsin Center for Education Research, University of Wisconsin School of Education; L. McNeil is principal investigator.

7. Karen B. Wiley, *The Status of Pre-College Science, Mathematics and Social Science Education: 1955–1975. Volume 3: Social Science Education* (Boulder, Colorado: Social Science Education Consortium, 1977). Funded by the National Science Foundation.

8. Frances Fitzgerald, *America Revised* (Boston: Atlantic Monthly Press, Little, Brown, 1979) and Jean Anyon, "Ideology and United States History Textbooks," in *Harvard Educational Review* 49, no. 3 (August, 1979): 361–86.

9. See Frances Fitzgerald, "History Textbooks (Parts I–III), *The New Yorker* 26 February 1979; 5 and 12 March 1979).

10. Samuel Bowles and Herbert Gintis, *Schooling in Capitalist America* (New York: Basic Books, 1976.) (See McNeil, "Economic Dimensions of Social Studies Curricula" and "Negotiating Classroom Knowledge," for my assertion that their data do not entirely support their conclusion.)

11. Pierre Bourdieu and Jean-Claude Passeron, *Reproduction in Education, Society, and Culture* (Beverly Hills, California: Sage Publications, 1977). See also P. Bourdieu, "Systems of Education and Systems of Thought," in M. Young, ed. *Knowledge and Control* (London: Macmillan, 1971).

12. See Madeleine MacDonald's discussion of Bourdieu's contribution to the understanding of tacit, dispositional aspects of cultural reproduction in *The Curriculum and Cultural Reproduction* (Milton Keynes: The Open University Press, 1977). 35ff.

13. Conversation with Geoffrey Whitty, Madison, Wisconsin, December, 1979.

14. See McNeil, "Economic Dimensions of Social Studies Curricula," and "Negotiating Classroom Knowledge."

15. See McNeil "Negotiating Classroom Knowledge." Data on the students' perceptions of the trade-offs they make between jobs and school work will appear in McNeil, "Lowering Expectations."

16. McNeil, "Institutional Context."

17. See Linda M. McNeil, "On the Possibility of Teachers as the Source of an Emancipatory Pedagogy," *Curriculum Inquiry* 11, no. 3 (Fall, 1981): 205–10 and Linda M. McNeil, "Response to Henry Giroux's 'Pedagogy, Pessimism, and the Politics of Conformity,' " *Curriculum Inquiry* 11, no. 4 (Winter, 1981): 393–94.

18. See the *Public Issues* pamphlets series written by Donald Oliver and Fred M. Newmann, and published by Xerox.

19. See note 3, above.

20. See Jurgen Habermas, *Legitimation Crisis* (Boston: Beacon Press, 1971) for an analysis of the implications of replacing the moral and ethical language of personal knowledge with technical language in our large institutions. For application of this idea to students' roles as clients, see McNeil, "Making Knowledge Inaccessible," Chapter 7.

CHAPTER 6

Curricular Form and the Logic of Technical Control

MICHAEL W. APPLE

It does not require an exceptional amount of insight to notice the current attempts by the state and industry to bring schools more closely into line with "economic needs." Neither side of the Atlantic has been immune to these pressures. In Britain, The Great Debate and the Green Paper stand as remarkable testaments to the ability of capital in times of economic crisis to marshall its forces. As the Green Paper notes:

> There is a wide gap between the world of education and the world of work. Boys and girls are not sufficiently aware of the importance of industry to our society, and they are not taught much about it.[1]

It goes on, making the criterion of functional efficiency the prime element in educational policy.

> The total resources which will be available for education and the social services in the future will depend largely on the success of the Industrial Strategy. It is vital to Britain's economic recovery and standard of living that the performance of manufacturing industry is improved and that the whole range of Government policies, including education, contribute as much as possible to improving industrial performance and thereby increasing the national wealth.[2]

In the United States, where governmental policies are more highly mediated by a different articulation between the state, the economy, and schools, this kind of pressure exists in powerful ways as well. Often the workings of industry are even more visible. Chairs of Free Enterprise devoted to economic education are springing up at universities throughout the country. Teaching the message of industry has become a real force. Let me give one example, taken from what is known as the

Ryerson Plan, a corporate plan to have teachers spend their summers working mainly with management in industry so that they can teach their students "real knowledge" about corporate needs and benefits.

> The anti-business, anti-free-enterprise bias prevalent in many parts of our American society today is very real and is growing. Unless we quit just talking about it—and do something about it now—it will prosper and thrive in the fertile minds of our youth. It will be nurtured and fed by many teachers who have good intentions but no real knowledge of how a free market operates in a free society.
> American business has a very positive story to tell and one of the most important places to start is with the youth of our country. The last 4,000 years of recorded history proves the interdependence of economic freedom and personal freedoms of all civilizations, countries and societies. We have a perfect example in a present day test tube. Take a look at Great Britain's decline over the last 30 years.
> Our response is simple and effective. Reach the high school teachers of America with the true story of American business and they will carry the message to their students and their fellow teachers. The message, coming directly from the teacher, rather than books, pamphlets or films, will have a far more telling and lasting effect. Convince one teacher of the vital importance of our free enterprise system and you're well on your way to convincing hundreds of students over a period of years. It's the ripple effect that anti-business factions have been capitalizing on for years.[3]

It is an interesting statement to say the least, one that is being echoed throughout advanced corporate economies. While this kind of program seems rather blatant, to say nothing of being historically inaccurate, we should be careful of dismissing this kind of program as overt propaganda that is easily dismissed by teachers. As one teacher said after completing it:

> My experience with the steel industry this summer has given me a positive and practical introduction to the business world that I might never had had, had it not been for the initiative of Ryerson management. Now I can pass a more positive portrayal of the industry on to my students; students who are usually very critical, very distrustful, and basically ignorant of the operation of big industry today.[4]

The Ryerson Plan is, of course, only one of many plans for getting the ideological message across. In fact, though there has been serious resistance to this kind of material by progressive forces in the United States, the movement to "teach for the needs of industry" is growing so rapidly that a clearinghouse, appropriately named The Institute for Constructive

Capitalism, has been established at the University of Texas to make the material more available.[5]

Now I do not want to minimize the importance of such overt attempts at influencing teachers and students. To do so would be the height of folly. By focusing only on these overt attempts at bringing school policy and curriculum into closer correspondence with industrial needs, however, we may neglect what is happening that may be just as powerful at the level of day to day school practice. One could fight the battles against capital's overt encroachments (and perhaps win some of them) and still lose within the school itself. For as I shall argue here, some of the ideological and material influences of our kind of social formation on teachers and students are not most importantly found at the level of these kinds of documents or plans, but at the level of social practice within the routine activities in schools.[6]

In essence, I want to argue that ideologies are not only global sets of interests, things imposed by one group on another. They are embodied by our commonsense meanings and practices.[7] Thus, if you want to understand ideology at work in schools, look as much at the concreta of day to day curricular and pedagogic life as you would at the statements made by spokespersons of the state or industry. In the terminology of Finn, Grant, and Johnson, we need to look not only at ideologies "about" education but ideologies "in" it as well.[8]

I am not implying that the level of practice in schools is fundamentally controlled in some mechanistic way by private enterprise. As an aspect of the state, the school mediates and transforms an array of economic, political, and cultural pressures from competing classes and class segments. Yet we tend to forget that this does not mean that the logics, discourses, or modes of control of capital will not have an increasing effect on everyday life in our educational institutions, especially in times of what has been called "the fiscal crisis of the state."[9] This effect, clearly visible in the United States (though I would hazard a guess it will become more obvious in Europe and Latin America as well), is especially evident in curriculum, especially in some very important aspects of the actual stuff that students and teachers interact with.

In this essay, I shall be particularly interested in curricular *form*, not curricular content. That is, my focus will not be on what is actually taught, but on the manner in which it is organized. As a number of Marxist cultural analysts have argued, the workings of ideology can be seen most impressively at the level of form as well as what the form has in it.[10] As I shall argue here, this is a key to uncovering the role of ideology in education.

In order to gain some understanding of the effects of the ideological and economic pressures being placed upon the school, we need to situate what is occurring within certain long term trends in the capital accumulation process. Recently these trends have intensified, and have had a rather large effect on various areas of social life. Among these trends we can identify certain tendencies such as:

> the concentration and centralization of capitals; the expansion of labour processes that are based on production-line technologies and forms of control; the continuing decline of "heavy industry" and the movement of capital into modern "lighter" forms of production, most notably the production of consumer durables; and major shifts in the composition of labour power—the secular tendency to "de-skilling," the separation of "conception" from "execution" and the creation of new technical and control skills, the shift of labour out of direct production and into circulation and distribution, and the expansion of labour within the state.[11]

As we shall see, the development of new forms of control, the process of deskilling, the separation of conception from execution, are not limited to factories and offices. These tendencies intrude more and more into institutions like the school. In order to unpack this, we shall have to examine the very nature of the logic of corporate deskilling and control.

Deskilling and Reskilling

In corporate production, firms purchase labor power. That is, they buy the capacity one has to do work and, obviously, will often seek to expand the use of that labor to make it more productive. There is an opposite side to this. With the purchase of labor power goes the "right" to stipulate (within certain limits) how it is to be used, without too much interference or participation by workers in the conception and planning of the work.[12] The means of accomplishing this have not stayed the same, of course. Empirically, there has been a changing logic of control that has sought to accomplish these ends.

We can distinguish three kinds of control that can be employed to help extract more work—simple, technical, and bureaucratic. Simple control is exactly that, simply telling someone that you have decided what should go on and they should follow, or else. Technical controls are less obvious. They are controls embedded in the physical structure of the job. A good example is the use of numerical control technology in the machine industry where a worker inserts a card into a machine and it directs the pace and skill level of the operation. The worker is meant to be simply an attendant to the machine itself. Finally, bureaucratic control signifies a social structure where control is less visible because its principles are embodied within the hierarchical social relations of the workplace. Impersonal and bureaucratic rules concerning the direction of one's work, the procedures for evaluating performance, and sanctions and rewards are dictated by officially approved policy.[13] Each of these modes of control has grown in sophistication over the years, though simple control has tended to become less important as the size and complexity of production has increased.

The long period of experimentation by industry on the most successful modes of controlling production led to a number of conclusions. Rather than simple control being used, where control is openly exercised by supervisors or persons in authority (and hence could possibly be subverted by blue- or white-collar workers), power could be made invisible by being incorporated into the very structure of the work itself. This meant the following things. The control must come from what seems to be a legitimate overall structure. It must be concerned with the actual work, not based on features extraneous to it (like favoritism and so on). Perhaps most importantly, the job, the process, and the product should be defined as precisely as possible on the basis of management's, not the workers's, control over the specialized knowledge needed to carry it out.[14] This often entailed the development of technical control.

Technical control and deskilling tend to go hand in hand. Deskilling is part of a long process in which labor is divided and then redivided to increase productivity, to reduce "inefficiency," and to control both the cost and the impact of labor. It usually has involved taking relatively complex jobs, jobs which require no small amount of skill and decision-making, and breaking them down into specified actions with specified results so that less skilled and costly personnel can be used or so that the control of work pace and outcome is enhanced. The assembly line is, of course, one of the archetypical examples of this process. At its beginnings, deskilling tended to involve techniques such as Taylorism and various other time and motion studies. Though these strategies for the division and control of labor were less than totally successful (and in fact often generated a significant amount of resistance and conflict).[15] they did succeed in helping to legitimate a style of control based in large part on deskilling.

One of the more effective strategies has been the incorporation of control into the actual productive process itself. Thus, machinery in factories is now often designed so that the machinist is called upon to do little more than load and unload the machine. In offices, word processing technology is employed to reduce labor costs and deskill women workers. Thus, management attempts to control both the pace of the work and the skills required, to more effectively increase their profit margins or productivity. Once again, as the history of formal and informal labor resistance documents, this kind of strategy—the building of controls into the very warp and woof of the production process—has been contested.[16] However, the growing sophistication by management and state bureaucrats in the use of technical control procedures is apparent.[17]

I have mentioned that deskilling is a complex process as it works its way through a variety of economic and cultural institutions. Yet, when jobs are deskilled, the knowledge that once accompanied them, knowledge that was controlled and used by workers in carrying out their day to day lives on their jobs, goes somewhere. Management attempts (with varying degrees of success) to accumulate and control this assemblage of skills and knowledge. It attempts, in other words, to separate conception from execution. The control of knowledge enables management to plan;[18] the worker should ideally merely carry these plans out to the specifications, and at the pace, set by people away from the actual point of production.

But deskilling is accompanied by what might be called reskilling. New techniques are required to run new machines; new occupations are created as the redivision of labor goes on. Fewer skilled craftspeople are needed and most are replaced by a smaller number of technicians with different skills who oversee the machinery.[19] This process of deskilling and reskilling is usually spread out over the landscape of an economy so that relationships between them are rather difficult to trace out. It is not very usual that you can see it going on at a level of specificity that makes it clear since while one group is being deskilled another group, often separated by time and geography, is being reskilled. One institution in particular, however—the school—provides an exceptional microcosm where these kinds of mechanisms of control can be seen in operation together.

In examining this we should remember that since capitalist production has developed unevenly, the kinds of control being used in social institutions will vary. Some institutions will be more resistant than others to the logic of corporate rationalization. Given the relatively autonomous nature of teaching (one can usually close one's door and not be disturbed) and given the internal history of the kinds of control in the institution (paternalistic styles of administration, in the United States often based on gender relations), the school has been partially resistant to technical and bureaucratic control, at the level of actual practice, until relatively recently. This "relative autonomy" may be breaking down today.[20] For just as the everyday discourse and patterns of interaction in the family and in, say, the media are increasingly being subtly transformed by the logic and contradictions of dominant ideologies,[21] so too is the school a site where these subtle ideological transformations occur. I shall claim that this goes on through a process of technical control. As we shall now see, these logics of control can have a rather profound impact on schools.

Controlling Curricular Form

The encroachment of technical control procedures is exemplified by the exceptionally rapid growth in the use of prepackaged sets of curricular materials. It is nearly impossible now to walk into an American classroom, for instance, without seeing boxes upon boxes of science, social studies, mathematics and reading materials ("systems," as they are sometimes called) lining the shelves and in use.[22] Here, a school system purchases a total set of standardized material usually, one that includes statements of objectives, all of the curricular content and material needed, prespecified teacher actions and appropriate student responses, and diagnostic and achievement tests coordinated with the system. These tests usually reduce the curricular knowledge to "appropriate" behaviors and skills. This emphasis on skills will become rather significant later on.

Let me give an example from one of the better of the widely used curricular systems, one of the numerous sets of materials that are becoming the standard fare in American elementary schools. It is taken from *Module One* of *Science: A Process Approach*. The notion of module is important here. The material is prepackaged in attractively colored cardboard boxes. It is divided into 105 separate modules, each of which contains a set of pregiven concepts that are to be taught. The material specifies all of the goals. It includes everything a teacher "needs" to teach, has the pedagogical steps a teacher must take to reach these goals already built in, and has the evaluation mechanisms built into it as well. But not only does it pre-specify nearly all a teacher should know, say, and do, but it often lays out the appropriate student responses as well. To make this clear, here is one sequence taken from the material which lays out the instructional procedure, student response, and evaluative activity. It concerns colors.

As each child arrives at school, fasten a red, yellow, or blue paper rectangle on the child's shirt or dress . . . Comment on the color of the paper and ask the child to say the name of the color he or she is wearing . . .

Put thirty yellow, red, and blue paper squares in a large bag or small box. Show the children three paper plates: one marked red, one yellow, and one blue. (See *Materials* for suggestions on marking.) These colors should closely match those in the bag. Ask the children to come forward, a few at a time, and let each child take one square from the bag and place it on the plate marked with the matching color. [A picture of this with a child picking out paper from a box and putting it on a plate is inserted here in the material so that no teacher will get the procedure wrong.] As each child takes a colored square, ask him to name the color of that square. If the child hesitates, name it for him.[23]

In the curricular material, everything except the bag or box is included—all the plates and colored paper. (The cost is $14.00 for the plan and the paper).

I noted that not only were the curricular and pedagogical elements prespecified, but all other aspects of teachers' actions were included as well. Thus, in the "Appraisal" of this module, the teacher is asked to:

Ask each of six children to bring a box of crayons and sit together . . . Ask each child to point to his red crayon when you say the word red. Repeat this for all six colors. Ask each child to match one crayon with one article of clothing that someone else is wearing . . . Before each group of children leaves the activity, ask each child individually to name and point to the red, blue, and yellow crayon.[24]

Even with this amount of guidance, it is still "essential" that we know for each child whether he or she has reached the appropriate skill level. Thus, as the final element, the material has competency measures built into it. Here the specification reaches its most exact point, giving the teacher the exact words he or she should use:

Task 1: Show the child a yellow cube and ask, What is the color of this cube?

This is done for each color. Then, after arranging orange, green, and purple cubes in front of a child, the teacher is to go on.

Task 4: Say, Put your finger on the orange cube.

Task 5: Say, Put your finger on the green cube.

Task 6: Say, Put your finger on the purple cube.[25]

I have gone on at length here so that you can get a picture of the extent to which technical control enters into the life of the school. Little in what might be metaphorically called the "production process" is left to chance. In many ways, it can be considered a picture of deskilling. Let us look at this somewhat more closely.

My concern is not the specific curricular or pedagogical content of this kind of material, though an analysis of this certainly would be interesting.[26] Rather, it is the effect of the form itself. What is *this* doing? For notice what has happened here. The goals, the process, the outcome, and the evaluative criteria for assessing them are defined as precisely as possible by people external to the situation. In the competency measure at the end of the module, this extends to the specification of even the exact words the teacher is to say.

Notice as well the process of deskilling at work here. Skills that teachers used to need, that were deemed essential to the craft of working with children—such as curriculum deliberation and planning, and the ability to design teaching and curricular strategies for specific groups and individuals based on an intimate knowledge of them—are no longer as necessary. With the large scale influx of prepackaged material, planning is separated from execution. The planning is done at the level of the production of both the rules for use of the material and the material itself. The execution is carried out by the teacher. In the process, what were previously considered valuable skills slowly atrophy because they are less often required.[27]

But what about the element of reskilling that I mentioned earlier was essential to understand how ideological forms can penetrate to the heart of institutions like the school? Unlike the economy where deskilling and reskilling are not usually found operating at one and the same moment with one and the same poeple, in the school this seems to be exactly the case. As the procedures of technical control enter into the school in the guise of pre-designed curricular/teaching/evaluation "systems", teachers are being deskilled. Yet they are also being reskilled in a way that is quite consequential. We can see signs of this in teacher training institutions, in inservice workshops and courses, in the journals devoted to teachers, in funding and enrollment patterns, and not the least in the actual curricular materials themselves. While the deskilling involves the loss of craft, the atrophy of educational skills, the reskilling involves the substitution of the skills and ideological visions of management. The growth of behavior modification techniques and classroom management strategies and their incorporation within both curricular material and teachers' repertoires signifies these kinds of alterations. That is, as teachers lose control of the curricular and pedagogic skills to large publishing houses, these skills are replaced by techniques for better controlling students.

This has significant consequences for both teachers and students. Since the material is often organized around and employs specified outcomes and procedures and these are built into this kind of material itself (with its many worksheets and tests often), it is "individualized" in many ways.

Students can engage in it themselves with little overt interaction on the part of the teacher or each other as they become more used to the procedures, which are usually highly standardized. The students' progress through the system can be individualized, at least in regard to speed; and this focus on individualizing the speed (usually through worksheets and the like) at which a student proceeds through the system is becoming even more pronounced in newer curricular systems. Since the control is technical—that is, management strategies are incorporated into it as a major aspect of the pedagogical/curricular/evaluative "machinery" itself—the teacher becomes something of manager. This is occurring *at the same time* that the objective conditions of his or her work are becoming increasingly "proletarianized" due to the curricular form's logic of technical control. This is a unique situation and certainly needs further thought. The possible effect of these forms of technical control on the students is just as serious and is something to which I shall return shortly.

Yet there are other important consequences as well as the process of deskilling and reskilling. As the literature on the labor process reminds us, the progressive division and control of labor also has an effect on social relations, on how the people involved interact. The effects were momentous in factories and offices; they will undoubtedly be felt in the school. There too, as in the workplace, the results may sometimes be contradictory.

Let me be more specific here. With the increasing employment of pre-packaged curricular systems as the basic curricular form, virtually no interaction between teachers is required. If nearly everything is rationalized and specified before execution, then contact among teachers about actual curricular matters is minimized.[28]

If such technical control is effective, that is, if teachers actually respond in ways that accept the separation of planning from execution, then one would expect results that go beyond this mere separation. One would expect, at the level of classroom practice, that, because of their increasing isolation, it will be more difficult for teachers to jointly gain informal control over curricular decisions. In essence, if everything is predetermined, there is no longer any pressing need for teacher interaction. Teachers become unattached individuals, divorced from both colleagues and the actual stuff of their work. While this may be an accurate estimation of one of the results of technical control on one level, however, it does not take into account the fact that most systems of control embody contradictions within themselves. For instance, while deskilling, forms of technical control, and the rationalization of work have created isolated individuals in, say, factories, historically they have often generated contradictory pressures as well. The use of technical control has often brought unionization in its wake.[29] Even given the ideology of professionalism (an ideology that might make it difficult for collective struggles to evolve) which tends to dominate certain sectors of the teaching force, other state employees who in the past have thought of themselves as professionals have gained a greater collective sense in response to similar modes of control. Thus, the loss of control and knowledge in one arena may generate countervailing tendencies in another.

We cannot know yet what the results for teachers will be. In industry, it took decades for the full effect of these contradictory tendencies to be felt. The same will no doubt be true in schools.

Accepting Technical Control

So far in this essay, I have looked at teachers as if they were workers. That is, I have argued that the processes that act on blue and white collar workers in the larger social arena will and are entering into the *cultural forms* that are considered legitimate in schools. Yet schools, because of their internal history, are different in some very important ways from factories and offices, and teachers are still very different from other workers in terms of the conditions of their work. Products are not as visible (except much later on in the rough reproduction of a labor force, in the production and reproduction of ideologies, and in the production of the technical and administrative knowledge "required" by an economy)[30] as in offices and factories. Teachers have what Erik Olin Wright has called a "contradictory class location" and hence cannot be expected to react in the same ways as the workers and employees of large corporations.[31] Furthermore, there are children who act back on teachers in ways an automobile on an assembly line or a paper on a desk cannot.[32] Finally, teaching does not take place on a line, but goes on in separate rooms more often than not.

These conditions do not mean that schools are autonomous or immune to the logic of capital. The logic will be mediated (in part because the school is a *state* apparatus); it will enter where it can in partial, distorted, or coded ways. Given the specific differences of schools from other workplaces, a prime moment in its entry can be found less at the level of overt or simple controls or at the level of bureaucratic form,[33] because individual teachers can still be relatively free from those kinds of encroachments. These controls will go on, of course; but they may be less consequential than the encoding of technical control into the very basis of the curricular form itself. The level of curricular, pedagogic, and evaluative practice within the classroom can be controlled by the forms into which culture is commodified in schools. If my arguments are correct, then how are we to understand the acceptance and growth of this process of control?

These forms do not enter schools because of any conspiracy on the part of industrialists to make our educational institutions serve the needs of capital, contrary to what the earlier quotes from the Green Paper and the Ryerson Plan might suggest. They enter in large part because schools are a rather lucrative market. These sets of material are published by firms who aggressively market where there is a need, or where they can create needs. It is simply good business practice in terms of profit margins to market material of this type, especially since the original purchase of the "system" or set of modules means increasing purchases over the years. Let me explain this by comparing it to another arena where similar techniques are employed to increase capital accumulation. Think of shaving. Large razor blade manufacturers sell razors at below cost, or even sometimes give them away as promotional "gimmicks," because they believe that once you buy the razor you will continue to buy their blades and their upgraded version year after year. In the curricular systems we are considering here, the purchase of the modules (though certainly not cheap by any stretch of the imagination) with their sets of standardized disposable material means the same thing. One "needs" to continue to purchase the work and test sheets, the chemicals, the correctly colored and shaped paper, the publishers' replacements of outmoded material and lessons, and so on. Profits are heightened with every replacement that is bought. Since replacement purchases are often bureaucratically centralized, because of budget control, in the office of the administrator, the additional material is usually bought from the producer (often at exorbitant prices) not gotten from one's local store.

Thus, as with other industries, this "good business sense" means that high volume, the standardization of the product and each of its elements, product upgrading, and then the stimulation of replacement purchasing are essential to maintain profits.[34]

Yet aggressive marketing and good business sense only partly explain this growth. In order to fully comprehend the acceptance of the technical control procedures embodied in curricular form, we need to know something of the history of why these kinds of materials evolved in the first place. Let me note these briefly.

The original introduction of prepackaged material in the 1950s and 1960s was stimulated by a specific network of political, cultural, and economic forces in the United States. The views of academics that teachers were unsophisticated in major curriculum areas "necessitated" the creation of what was called teacher-proof material. The cold war climate (created and stimulated by the state in large part) led to a focus on the efficient production of scientists and technicians as well as a relatively stable workforce; thus, the guaranteeing of this production through the school curriculum became of increasing import.[35] The educational apparatus of the state, under the National Defense Education Act, decided to provide the equivalent of cash credits to local school districts for the purchase of new curricula created by the private sector to increase this efficiency. At the same time, the internal dynamics within education played a part since behavioral and learning psychology—on whose principles so much of these systems rely—gained increasing prestige in a field like education where being seen as a science was critically important both for funding and to deflect criticism.[36] In the more recent past, the increasing influence of industrial capital within the executive and legislative branches of government,[37] as well as in the attendant bureaucracy, no doubt is an essential element here since there is recent evidence that the federal government has backed away from the widespread production and distribution of large scale curricula, preferring to stimulate the "private sector" to enter even more deeply into such production.[38]

This gives us a brief sense of the origins of this trend, but why does it continue today? A key perception here is seeing the school as an aspect of the state apparatus. For the state's need for *consent* as well as control means that the forms of control in school will be encoded in particular ways.[39]

The strategic importance of the logic of technical control in schools lies in its ability to integrate into one discourse what are often seen as competing ideological movements, and, hence, to generate consent from each of them. The need for accountability and control by administrative managers, the real needs of teachers for something that is practical to use with their students, the interest of the state in efficient production and cost savings,[40] the concerns of parents for "quality education" that "works" (a concern that will be coded differently by different classes and class segments), industrial capital's own requirements for efficient production and so on, can be joined. Here two important functions of the state can be accomplished. The state can assist in capital accumulation by attempting to provide a more efficient "production process" in schools. At the same time, it can legitimate its own activity by couching its discourse in language that is broad enough to be meaningful to each of what it perceives to be important constituencies, yet specific enough to give some practical answers to those who, like teachers, require them. The fact that the form taken by these curricular systems is tightly controlled and more easily made accountable, that it *is* usually individualized, that it focuses on skills in a time of perceived crisis in the teaching of basic skills, nearly guarantees its acceptability to a wide array of classes and interest groups.

Thus, the logic of control is both mediated and reinforced by the needs of state bureaucrats for accountable and rational procedures and by the specific nexus of forces acting on the state itself. The curriculum form will take on the aspects that best allow it to accomplish both accumulation and legitimation.[41] As Clarke puts it:

> Even where institutions meet a logic required by capital, their form and direction are never the outcome of a simple unidirectional imposition by capital. They involve a complex political work of concession and compromise, if only to secure the legitimacy of the state in popular opinion.[42]

This is exactly what has occurred in the use of this kind of curricular form.

The Possessive Individual

So far I have examined the encroachment into the work of teachers of the technical control systems embodied in curricular form. Teachers, however, are not the only actors in the setting where we find this material. There are the students as well.

A number of writers have noted that each kind of social formation "requires" a particular kind of individual. Williams and others, for instance, have helped us trace the growth of the abstract individual as it developed within the theoretic, cultural, and economic practices of capitalism.[43] These are not simply changes in the definition of the individual, but imply changes in our actual modes of material and cultural producing, reproducing, and consuming. To be an individual in our society signifies a complex interconnection between our day-to-day meanings and practices and an "external" mode of production. While I do not mean to imply a simple base/superstructure model here, it is clear that in some very important ways there is a dialectical relationship between economic and ideological form. As Gramsci and others would put it, ideological hegemony sustains class domination; subjectivities cannot be seen as unrelated to structure. Yet the questions remain: How are they related? Where are the sites where this relationship is worked out? The school provides a critical arena. As Richard Johnson notes, "It is not so much a question that schools . . . *are* ideology, more that they are the sites where ideologies are produced in the form of subjectivities."[44]

But what kind of subjectivity, what kind of ideology, what kind of individual may be produced here? The characteristics embodied in the modes of technical control built into the curricular form itself are ideally suited to reproduce the possessive individual, a vision of self that lies at the ideological heart of corporate economies.

The conception of individualism embedded in the material we have been examining is quite similar to those found in other analyses of aspects of the cultural apparatus in our society. As Will Wright has demonstrated, for example, in his recent investigation of the role of cultural artifacts such as film as carriers and legitimators of ideological changes, important aspects of our cultural apparatus respresent a world in which the society recognizes each member as an individual; but that recognition is dependent almost entirely upon technical skills. At the same time, while heightening the value of technical competence, these films direct the individual to reject the importance of ethical and political values through their form. They portray an individualism, situated in the context of a corporate economy, in which "respect and companionship are to be achieved only by becoming a skilled technician." The individual accepts and does any technical job that is offered and has loyalty to only those with similar technical competence, not primarily "to any competing social and community values."[45]

An examination of these curricular systems illuminates the extent to which this kind of ideological movement is occurring in increasingly dominant curricular forms. Here, the rate at which a student proceeds is individualized; the actual product, however, as well as the process to be accomplished is specified by the material itself.[46] Thus, it is not just the teacher who faces the encroachment of technical control and deskilling. The students' responses are largely prespecified as well. Much of this growing arsenal of material attempts as precisely as possible to specify appropriate student language and action as well, often reducing it to the mastery of sets of competencies or skills. Here Wright seems correct.

The notion of reducing curriculum to a set of skills is not unimportant in this regard since it is part of the larger process by which the logic of capital helps build identities and transforms cultural meanings and practices into commodities.[47] That is, if knowledge in all its aspects (of the logical type of that, how, or to—i.e., information, processes, and dispositions or propensities) is broken down and commodified, like economic capital it can be accumulated. The mark of a good pupil is the possession and accumulation of vast quantities of skills in the service of technical interests. As an ideological mechanism in the maintenance of hegemony this is rather interesting. In the larger society, people consume as isolated individuals. Their worth is determined by the possession of material goods or, as Will Wright noted, of technical skills. The accumulation of such goods or of the "cultural capital" of technical competence—here atomistic bits of knowledge and skills measured on pre-tests and post-tests—is a technical procedure, which requires only the mastery of the prior necessary technical skills and enough time to follow the rules, at one's own pace, to their conclusion. It is the message of the new petty bourgeoisie writ large on the ideological terrain of the school.

In fact, one might hypothesize just this, that this kind of movement speaks to the increasing importance in the cultural apparatus of the ideologies of class segments with contradictory class locations, in particular what I have called the new petty bourgeoisie—those groups who make up middle management and technical occupations.[48] The kind of individualism we are witnessing here is an interesting shift from an ideology of individual autonomy, where a person is his or her own boss and controls his or her destiny, to a careerist individualism. Here the individualism is geared towards achieving organizational mobility and advancement by following technical rules. As Eric Wright puts it, for the new petty bourgeoisie, "individualism is structured around the requirements of bureaucratic advancement."[49] It may also be a coded "reflection" of the increasing proletarianization of white collar work. Individualism formerly signified some degree of real autonomy over how one worked and what one produced, but for a large portion of white-collar employees autonomy since that time has been trivialized.[50] The rate at which one works may be individualized, but the work itself, how it is accomplished, and what the exact specifications of the final product will be, are increasingly being specified.

We are left with many questions. When technical control means that the form that the curriculum takes is highly specified, that it is individualized to such an extent that little interaction is required among the students so that each activity is by necessity viewed as an individual intellectual act of skill; that answers often take the form of simple physical activities; that answers are either correct or incorrect based on the application of technical rules; and this kind of form is what one follows throughout one's elementary school life, what impact does it have on the teachers and students who interact with it at the level of practice each day?

We do have evidence to suggest what procedures of this type do to workers in industry and in offices.

Increasing rationalization and a more sophisticated level of control tends to encourage people to manifest an interesting array of traits: a "rules orientation," where workers are aware of rules and procedures and have the habit of following them; greater dependability, where they perform a job at a relatively consistent level; being reliable and getting the job done even when rules have to be modified a bit to meet changing day-to-day conditions; and, the "internalization of the enterprise's goals and values," where conflict is minimized and slowly but surely, there tends to be a homogenization of interests between management and employees.[51]

Will this happen in schools as well? This clearly points to the significance of engaging in analyses of what actually happens within the black box of the school. Do teachers and students accept this? Will the gradual introduction of the logic of technical control generate resistances, if only on a cultural level? Will class and work cultures contradict, mediate, or even transform the expected outcomes?[52] It is to this that we shall now turn.

Resistances

I have not presented an optimistic appraisal here. As the activities of students are increasingly specified, as the rules, processes, and standard outcomes are integrated through and rationalized by the materials themselves, so too are teachers deskilled, reskilled, and made anonymous. Students work on material whose form both isolates individuals from each other and establishes the conditions of existence for the possessive individual; the form of the material and the embedded nature of the technical control process does nearly the same for the teacher. Surrounded by a specific logic of control, the objective force of the social relations embodied in the form itself tends to be quite powerful.

Yet I am not arguing for a kind of functionalist perspective, where everything is measured by, or is aimed toward, its ability to reproduce an existing static society. The kind of ideological hegemony "caused" by the increasing introduction of technical control is not "naturally" preordained. It is something that is won or lost in particular conflicts and struggles.[53]

On the one hand, teachers will be controlled. As one teacher said about a set of popular material even more integrated and rationalized than the ones I have pointed to here, "Look, I have no choice. I personally don't like this material, but everyone in the district has to use this series. I'll try to do other things as well, but basically our curriculum will be based on this."

On the other hand, resistances will be there. This same teacher who disagreed with the curriculum but used it, also was partially subverting it in interesting ways. It was employed only three days a week instead of the five days that were specified. As the teacher put it, "Listen, if we worked hard we'd finish this stuff in two or three months and besides it's sometimes confusing and boring. So I try to go beyond it as often as possible, *as long as I do not teach what is in the material to be covered by this series next year."* Thus, as we can see from this last part of her comment, internal conditions make such overt resistances more difficult.

Yet these internal conditions need not preclude teachers from also making these commodified cultural forms their own, generating their own creative responses to dominant ideologies, in much the same way as some counter-cultural groups have responded to commodified culture. These groups transformed and reinterpreted the products they bought and used so that they became tools for the creation of alternative pockets of resistance.[54] Students and teachers may also find ways of creatively using these systems in ways undreamed of by state bureaucrats or corporate publishing. (I must admit, however, that my repeated observations in classrooms over the last years make me less than totally optimistic that this will always or even very often be the case.)

Other elements in the environment may provide a site where different meanings and practices can evolve, though, even within the curricular form itself. For we should remember that there may be progressive elements within the *content* of the curriculum that contradict the messages of the form.[55] And it is in the interaction between the content, the form, and the lived culture of the students that subjectivities are formed. No element in this set of relations can be ignored.

This last point about the lived culture of the actors, the students themselves, must be stressed. One would expect resistances by students as well, resistances that will be *specific by race, gender, and class*. My earlier quote from Johnson is correct here. The formation of ideologies— even those of the kind of individual I have examined in this analysis—is not a simple act of imposition. They are produced by concrete actors and embodied in lived experiences that may resist, alter, or mediate these social messages.[56] As Willis demonstrates, for instance, segments of working class youth partially defeat the ideology of individualism. The same may be true for many women and "minority" students. While we can and must focus on these resistances, though, their actual meanings may be unclear. Do they, like those of the lads in Willis's book, also reproduce at an even deeper level ideological meanings and practices that provide quite powerful supports to relations of domination?[57]

Take teachers, for example. While technical controls could possibly lead to unionization, within the school most resistances will be, by necessity, on an individual not a collective level because of the social relations generated by the curricular form itself.[58] The effects, hence, can be rather contradictory.

We must remember as well that, as I mentioned earlier, these more "invisible" modes of control may be accepted if they are perceived as coming from a legitimate overall structure. The fact that curriculum selection committees give teachers a say in the curriculum they will employ means that some of the prior conditions for the consent necessary for this kind of control to be successful have already been established. The choice is made, in part, by the teachers themselves. It is hard to argue in the face of that.

It is easy to forget something else. This is not a good time, ideologically or economically, for teachers who engage in overt resistances. Given a difficult ideological climate and given the employment situation among teachers today—with thousands having either been laid off or living under the threat of it—the loss of control can progress in a relatively unthreatened way. Deskilling and reskilling, progressive anonymization and rationalization, the transformation of educational work, somehow seem less important than such economic concerns as job security, salary, etc., even though they may seem to us clearly to be a part of the same dynamic.

We must recognize, however, that these powerful social messages, while embedded in the actual experiences of teachers and students as they go about their day to day lives in classrooms, *are* highly mediated by other elements. The fact that individual teachers like most other workers may develop patterns of resistance to these patterns of technical control at the informal cultural level alters these messages. The contradictory ideologies of individualism and cooperativeness that are naturally gener- ated out of the crowded conditions of many classrooms (an individual cannot be isolated all the time when there are twenty or thirty other people around with whom one teacher must cope) also provide counter- vailing possibilities. And lastly, just as blue-collar and white-collar work- ers have constantly found ways to retain their humanity and continually struggle to integrate conception and execution in their work (if only to relieve boredom) so too will teachers and students find ways, in the cracks so to speak, to do the same things. The real question is not whether such resistances exist—Aronowitz, myself, and others have claimed at length elsewhere that they are never far from the surface[59]—but whether they are contradictory themselves, whether they lead anywhere beyond the reproduction of the ideological hegemony of the most powerful classes in our society, whether they can be employed for political education and intervention.

Our task is first to find them. We need somehow to give life to the resistances, the struggles. What I have done here is to point to the terrain within the school (the transformation of work, the deskilling and reskill- ing, the technical control, and so on) over which these struggles will be fought. The resistances may be informal, not fully organized or even conscious; yet this does not mean that they will have no impact. For as Gramsci and Johnson remind us, hegemony is always contested.[60] Our own work should help in this contestation.

Notes

An earlier version of this essay appears in *Economic and Industrial Democracy* 2 (August, 1981): 293–319.

1. Quoted in James Donald, "Green Paper: Noise of a Crisis," *Screen Education* 30 (Spring, 1979): 44.

2. Ibid, 36–37.

3. "The Ryerson Plan: A Teacher Work-Learn Program," (Chicago: Joseph T. Ryerson and Son, Inc., no date). I wish to thank Linda McNeil for bringing this material to my attention.

4. Ibid.

5. See, for example, Diane Downing, "Soft Choices: Teaching Materials for Teaching Free Enterprise," (Austin, Texas: University of Texas, Institute for Constructive Capitalism, 1979, mimeo).

6. This is not to deny the importance of analyzing official documents, especially those emanating from the state. James Donald's essay on the Green Paper noted above provides an excellent example of the power of discourse analysis, for example, in unpacking what these documents mean and do.

7. Raymond Williams, *Marxism and Literature* (New York: Oxford University Press, 1977).

8. Dan Finn, Neil Grant, Richard Johnson and the C.C.C.S. Education Group, "Social Democracy, Education and the Crisis," (Birmingham, England: University of Birmingham Centre for Contemporary Cultural Studies, 1978), pp. 3–4.

9. James O'Connor, *The Fiscal Crisis of the State* (New York: St. Martin's Press, 1973).

10. See, for example, Fredric Jameson, *Marxism and Form* (Princeton: Princeton University Press, 1971), Williams, *Marxism and Literature*, and Michael W. Apple, "Ideology and Form in Curriculum Evaluation," in George Willis, ed., *Qualitative Evaluation* (Berkeley: McCutchan Publishing Corp., 1978), pp. 495–521.

11. John Clarke, "Capital and Culture: The Post-War Working Class Revisited," in John Clarke, Chas Critcher and Richard Johnson, eds., *Working Class Culture: Studies in History and Theory* (London: Hutchinson, 1979), p. 239. See also the impressive discussion in Harry Braverman, *Labor and Monopoly Capital* (New York: Monthly Review Press, 1974) and Michael Burawoy, "Toward a Marxist Theory of the Labor Process: Braverman and Beyond," *Politics and Society* 8, no. 3–4 (1979): 1–77.

12. Richard Edwards, *Contested Terrain: The Transformation of the Workplace in the Twentieth Century* (New York: Basic Books, 1979), p. 17.

13. Ibid., pp. 19–21.

14. Ibid., pp. 110.

15. See David Noble, *America By Design: Science, Technology and the Rise of*

Corporate Capitalism (New York: Alfred A. Knopf, 1977) and Michael Burawoy, "Toward a Marxist Theory of the Labor Process."

16. See Michael W. Apple, "The Other Side of the Hidden Curriculum: Correspondence Theories and the Labor Process," *Interchange* 11, No. 3 (1980–81): 5–22, Stanley Aronowitz, "Marx, Braverman and the Logic of Capital," *The Insurgent Sociologist* 8 (Fall, 1978): 126–46, and David Montgomery, *Workers' Control in America* (New York: Cambridge University Press, 1979).

17. Edwards, *Contested Terrain*.

18. I have discussed the school's role in producing this knowledge in Michael W. Apple, "The Production of Knowledge and the Production of Deviance," in Len Barton and Roland Meighan, eds., *Schools, Pupils and Deviance* (Driffield, England: Nafferton Press, 1979), pp. 113–131.

19. See, for example, Jane Barker and Hazel Downing, "Word Processing and the Transformation of Patriarchal Relations," (Birmingham, England: University of Birmingham Centre for Contemporary Cultural Studies, 1979).

20. Roger Dale points this out in "The Politicization of School Deviance," in Barton and Meighan, eds. *Schools, Pupils and Deviance*, pp. 95–112.

21. Todd Gitlin, "Prime Time Ideology: The Hegemonic Process in Television Entertainment," *Social Problems* 26 (February, 1979): 251–266. The work of Philip Wexler on the commodification of intimate social relations is important here. See especially Philip Wexler, *Critical Social Psychology* (Boston: Routledge and Kegan Paul, 1983).

22. This is not only an American phenomenon. The foreign subsidiaries of the companies who produce these materials are translating and marketing their products in the Third World and elsewhere as well. In many ways it is similar to the cultural imperialism of Walt Disney Productions. See, for example, Ariel Dorfman and Armand Mattelart, *How to Read Donald Duck*(New York: International General Editions, 1975).

23. *Science . . . A Process Approach II, Instructional Booklet: Module 1* (Lexington: Ginn and Co., 1974), pp. 3–4.

24. Ibid., p. 7.

25. Ibid.

26. See, for example, my analysis of science curricula in Michael W. Apple, *Ideology and Curriculum* (Boston: Routledge and Kegan Paul, 1979).

27. I do not mean to romanticize the past, however. Many teachers probably simply followed the textbook before. However, the level of specificity and the integration of curricular, pedagogical, and evaluative aspects of classroom life into *one* system is markedly different. The use of the system brings with it much more technical control of every aspect of teaching than previous text-based curricula. Obviously, some teachers will not follow the system's rules. Given the level of integration, though, it will undoubtedly be much more difficult to ignore it since many systems constitute the core or only programs in that curricular area in the entire school or district. Thus, accountability to the next grade level or to administrators makes it harder to ignore. I shall return to this point later on.

28. This may be similar to what happened in the early mills in New England, when standardized production processes drastically reduced the contact among workers. See Edwards, *Contested Terrain* , p. 114.

29. Ibid., p. 181.

30. See Apple, "The Production of Knowledge and the Production of Deviance," Apple, *Ideology and Curriculum*, and Noble, *America By Design*. One

could also claim that schools operate to produce use value not exchange value. Erik Olin Wright, personal communication.

31. Erik Olin Wright, *Class, Crisis and the State* (London: New Left Books, 1978), pp. 31–110.

32. Therefore, any outcomes of schooling must be analyzed as the products of cultural, political, and economic resistances as well as determinations. See Paul Willis, *Learning to Labour* (Westmead, England: Saxon House, 1977) and Michael W. Apple, "Analyzing Determinations: Understanding and Evaluating the Production of Social Outcomes in Schools," *Curriculum Inquiry* 10 (Spring, 1980): 55–76.

33. I do not want to ignore the question of the relationship between capitalism and bureaucracy. Weber and others were not wrong when they noted that there are needs for rationalization specific to bureaucratic forms themselves. However, neither the *way* bureaucracy has grown in corporate economies nor its effects have been neutral. This is treated in considerably more detail in Daniel Clawson, "Class Struggle and the Rise in Bureaucracy," (Ph.D. diss.; State University of New York at Stony Brook, 1978). See also Wright, *Class, Crisis and the State*.

34. Jane Barker and Hazel Downing, "Word Processing," p. 20. See also Noble, *America By Design*, for his account of standardization and its relationship to capital accumulation.

35. Joel Spring, *The Sorting Machine* (New York: David McKay, 1976).

36. Apple, *Ideology and Curriculum*.

37. O'Connor, *The Fiscal Crisis of the State*.

38. Among the reasons for the fact that the state has slowly but surely backed away from such production and distribution is the controversy surrounding "Man: A Course of Study" and, no doubt, the intense lobbying efforts on the part of publishing firms. Corporations will let the government socialize the costs of development, but obviously would prefer to package and distribute the curricula for themselves. See Michael W. Apple, "Politics and National Curriculum Policy," *Curriculum Inquiry* 7, no. 4 (1977): 351–61.

39. Donald, "Green Paper," 44.

40. This is not meant to imply that the state always directly serves the needs of industrial capital. It in fact does have a significant degree of relative autonomy and is the site of class conflict as well. See Donald, "Green Paper" and Wright, *Class, Crisis and the State*.

41. We should remember, however, that accumulation and legitimation may be in conflict with each other at times. See Wright, *Class, Crisis and the State*, for a discussion of these possible contradictions and for an argument about the importance of understanding the way the state and bureaucracies mediate and act back on economic determinations.

42. Clarke, "Capital and Culture," p. 241.

43. Raymond Williams, *The Long Revolution* (London: Chatto and Windus, 1961) and C. B. MacPherson, *The Political Theory of Possessive Individualism* (New York: Oxford University Press, 1962).

44. Richard Johnson, "Three Problematics: Elements of a Theory of Working Class Culture," in Clarke, Critcher, and Johnson, eds., *Working Class Culture*, p. 232.

45. Will Wright, *Sixguns and Society* (Berkeley: University of California Press, 1975), p. 187.

46. Bernstein's work on class and educational codes is interesting here. As he notes, "The pacing of educational knowledge is class based." It is based upon

middle class views of socialization. Basil Bernstein, *Class, Codes and Control, Volume 3* (Boston: Routledge and Kegan Paul, 1977), p. 113.

47. See Stanley Aronowitz, *False Promises* (New York: McGraw-Hill, 1973), p. 95.

48. Wright, *Class, Crisis and the State*, p. 79.

49. Ibid., p. 59.

50. Ibid., p. 81. See also Braverman, *Labor and Monopoly Capital.*

51. Edwards, *Contested Terrain*, pp. 150–51. This does not mean that important resistances and countervailing practices do or will not occur. But they usually occur on the terrain established by capital.

52. I have suggested elsewhere that this will be the case. See Apple, "The Other Side of the Hidden Curriculum" and Apple, "Analyzing Determinations."

53. Richard Johnson, "Histories of Culture/Theories of Ideology: Notes on an Impasse," in Michele Barrett, Philip Corrigan, Annette Kuhn, and Janet Wolff, eds., *Ideology and Cultural Production* (New York: St. Martin's Press, 1979), p. 70.

54. Paul Willis, *Profane Culture* (Boston: Routledge and Kegan Paul, 1978).

55. Geoff Whitty of Kings College, University of London, has been particularly helpful in enabling me to see this point.

56. See Johnson, "Three Problematics."

57. Willis, *Learning to Labour.*

58. Compare here to Edwards, *Contested Terrain*, p. 154.

59. See, for example, Aronowitz, "Marx, Braverman and the Logic of Capital," Apple, "The Other Side of the Hidden Curriculum," and Burawoy, "Toward a Marxist Theory of the Labor Process."

60. Johnson, "Histories of Culture/Theories of Ideology,"

IDEOLOGY AND
LIVED CULTURE

CHAPTER 7

Classroom Management, Student Opposition, and the Labor Process

ROBERT B. EVERHART

The idea of teachers as moderators and mediators of student learning is increasingly manifest. While scarcely discussed a decade ago, the concept of classroom management now appears repeatedly in the literature on teaching and generally refers to the active process by which teachers, through the use of scientific findings on classroom-related patterns and behaviors, can systematically regulate those patterns and behaviors toward intended instructional ends.

Yet there is another side to classroom management, one that focuses not so much on organizationally desirable instructional outcomes as upon the student activities that require teacher management. It is useful to understand the context for student activities, particularly the generation of activities by students as they attempt to establish their role. We can then ask, "What is the nature of the activities being managed, and why do they exist in the form they do?" Such an approach focuses upon the complexity and context of the activities rather than on just their concordance with instructional objectives. It also raises for critical examination the very assumptions that undergird the idea of classroom management and the subsequent application of those assumptions to classroom life.

The approach used in this chapter differs significantly from the recent traditions of classroom management research.[1] One such tradition, almost totally prescriptive, examines the organizing of activities designed to keep students attentive, basically on-task, and invokes a myriad of pedagogical strategies designed to help teachers more effectively control classroom agendas.[2] A second tradition, more deeply steeped in the social science literature, examines classroom management from a systems/ecological perspective. These models, while more sophisticated than those found in the more prescriptive literature, center upon those outcroppings of student behavior, largely structurally determined, which teachers must manage in order to carry out efficient instruction.[3] A third research genre addresses the cultural context of classroom management, and extends the limits of the systems approach in an attempt to understand the manner in which students generate beliefs and behaviors with which teachers must contend.[4]

Yet all three of these traditions seem to pay scant attention to the social-political context of classroom management. My own work, as well as that of Michael Apple, Jean Anyon, and Paul Willis, among others, indicates that the social-political context of the classroom cannot be ignored, and in fact is critically important for understanding classroom life.[5] As Apple notes, "Each aspect of the social process in the state and politics, in cultural life, in our modes of producing, distributing, and consuming serves to affect the relations within and among others."[6] As social relations are affected in schools, students learn, and teach each other, critical aspects of their role in institutional life. For this reason I begin with the assumption that one way in which the technological consciousness of the state is woven into the daily life of schools is through the pragmatics of classroom management. Students, furthermore, as they interpret these pragmatics, both adapt to and contest the management of classrooms and their role within them. It is in this sense that students learn and teach themselves about their role, and it is this line of thinking I wish to extend. Classroom management must be understood not just within the context of the classroom as a social system, but also as an interface between the state educational system and students. Classroom management mediates social life as students attempt to "make" themselves in a world in which political consciousness, class interests, and cultural regularities enter into the calculus of appropriateness and certitude by which students define themselves.

The purpose of this chapter is to examine student opposition to the management of instruction and schooling by focusing upon opposition as a form of learning in itself. By opposition I refer to manifest acts on the part of students that reflect ambivalence or resistance to the imperatives of a managed environment. Teacher-managers view this ambivalence or resistance as a threat to the maintenance of school-determined instructional objectives, and thus as a target for potential "management" strategies.

Student opposition is an important activity because it is part of a lived culture that is created and recreated in their everyday life. It must be seen as part of the students' understanding of their own present and historical role in the school. This understanding will be conditioned (but not necessarily determined) by factors such as class, culture, and gender.

Opposition has attached to it, however, a number of important conditions. First, student opposition will never be completely understood by students and may manifest itself in unpredictable ways. In this sense, while intentionality is assumed, total awareness is not a precondition, since the oppositional behavior may in fact be symbolic. Second, opposition, even if intended as such, might not be disruptive, but instead might blend into the classroom structure. Finally, opposition to the regularities of classroom management procedures must be seen within a cultural context and not just within the environment of the classroom. Culture here refers not to a "thing" out there to which people conform, but rather to an ongoing social process that is formed and reformed by the changing relationship of individuals and groups to basic material forces. The relationship of human groups to the forces of production—the very basis of class—is central to any attempt to understand student opposition as a class phenomenon.

This study is the result of work in four schools over a seven-year period. From 1973 to 1975, I did fieldwork in a public junior high school. In 1979 and 1980 I worked, with an assistant, in three public and private "alternative" schools. The junior high school (which I will call Harold Spencer Junior High) contained about 1,000 students and in it I observed two groups of seventh grade boys (whom I later followed into the eighth grade).[7] The alternative schools (which I will call schools A, B, and C) were much smaller in size.[8] School A, which enrolled students for junior high, had 53 pupils. School B was a public alternative school of 90 students in grades one to eight. I spent most of my time there with the sixth to eighth graders. School C was a private "free" school with an enrollment of about 15 students all, again in grades one to eight. In all the schools except school A, students were predominantly from skilled blue-collar or white-collar families. Students in school A came from families whose parents were in the managerial and professional categories. I include information from all four schools to illustrate how the consequences of opposition were affected by the students' class backgrounds.

I will concentrate on two forms or regularities into which student opposition is channeled. Within the first form, the instructional, there are various classroom strategies that center upon the actions that students are required to do as part of the task structure of the school. Students use these strategies to regulate that structure to their own advantage. The second form focuses not as much upon adaptations to the instructional mode as various forms of escape from it. In this form, "beating the system" means removing oneself from the task structure of the school. In the subsequent section of the chapter, I will address the student world view regarding their participation in such oppositional forms. The last section explores the relationship between student opposition and the labor process.

Classroom Strategies

How do students oppose the management of instruction in the class-room, and thereby attempt to control events? Despite the subservient position of the students, a number of strategies are available. Many of these strategies invoke the same practices, altering them to fit the context.

One strategy was the use of humor to control the direction of instructional activity. Anyone who has spent time with early adolescents knows their pervasive sense of humor. The following dialogue on governmental regulation of laws, from an eighth grade social-studies class at Spencer, illustrates the spontaneous and cumulative effect of humor on the direction of classroom discussion.

The first area to be discussed was traffic law. A girl volunteered. "We were in Montana last summer and my mom was going 100 and there wasn't a cop in sight. We were in Wyoming and the sign said, 'Daytime Speed - Safe Speed.' "

"Oh, wow!" Chris exclaimed, mocking the girl.

"Your mom is a real baddie," chipped in Marty.

"How many think traffic regulations are made by the federal government?" asked Mrs. Paul. A few hands were raised.

"How many think it is controlled by the states?" A few more hands were raised.

"How many think it is shared?"

"Cher?" Chris inquired. "Yes. I watch the Cher Show." Most of the hands went up.

"Okay, let's turn to the laws for crimes," Mrs. Paul said. "Who sets the laws on capital punishment?"

A girl raised her hand. "Some states use electrocutions because they have a lot of electricity." This brought rounds of laughter from the entire class. Chris doubled up; Pete was shaking his head. Mrs. Paul looked back at me and I, like her, was laughing heartily.

"Oh brother," Pete said above the laughter, "I suppose that means that states that raise beans feed them to criminals and then put them in an enclosed room to gas them."

"Then they offer them a cigarette and a match and BOOM," said Chris, filling in.

We might expect that such activities would be most explicit in settings where students had few opportunities to actively participate in instructional decisions. Yet humor was used no less in the alternative schools to direct, redirect, and regulate discussions. At school B, for example, as part of the daily routine the students and instructor gathered at midmorning for 15 to 30 minutes to discuss items from home, community, or the world. While allegedly open, the agenda often was subtly manipulated by the teacher in order to turn the discussion to something of more "educational" benefit. Yet more often than not, students indicated by their actions that they preferred to maintain their own agenda at their own level, as the following discussion illustrates.

David: "Jackson County says that they may have electrical buses to go up and down State Street."

Scott: "Get down!"

Teacher: "What is the advantage of battery buses?"

"Less pollution."

"Cheaper."

John: "Eleven people were killed in concert when 'The Who' were playing, they just got totally wiped out. Wow. Pow."

Teacher: "Why do you think that happened?"

John: "Because 'The Who' is cool."

Scott: "Get down!"

Ruby: "That's what happened with Jimmy Hendrix, he died of an overdose."

Teacher: "Why does that happen?"

Scott: "What about on 'Network.' The Hell's Angels come up and this dude blows him away. Pow! Wow!"

Teacher: "I want to ask Don/Ruby what they would do in something like this."

Don: "I'd camp out five days ahead of time."

Scott: "I'd cruise! Get up on the top seat with a pair of binoculars."

Scott: "Then I'd tell all these dudes to move out of my way."

Teacher: "But Scott, you can't do that, you can't change the situation!"

Humor was used most effectively by the students as a lever to change the direction of agendas. Other strategies of agenda setting involved everything from simple refusal to participate in instructional activities to outright manipulation of agendas. Activities of the first kind often began as individual efforts (such as an "I don't know" response to a teacher's question). Yet quite often such efforts were continued collectively as the student's friends joined in the nonparticipation.

Agenda manipulation, on the other hand, was almost always a collective effort as students attempted to alter the imperatives of instruction. This was accomplished in different ways, again contextually determined. At Spencer, for example, students typically would provide a series of irrelevant answers to questions asked by the teacher. Questions about U.S. history often prompted students to initiate discussions about TV programs, movies, or personal experiences only peripherally related to the subject at hand. Still other delays were created in response to requests by the teacher for a homework or class assignment, using statements to the effect that the material was not available because "I did the wrong assignment" or "I forgot to bring my books." Such efforts, when collectively planned, were effective in delaying previously planned agendas or initiating new ones.

Among the three alternative schools, such agenda changing differed in execution but not in intent. The execution differed because two of the three schools were "open" schools, and so students less often were under the direct control of teachers. In these schools, "contracts" negotiated between students and teacher predominated, where a specific agreement was struck as to the end product of work. The presence of student initiative, in this area, coupled with the difficulty teachers had in keeping informed of exactly what they were doing on any given day (since this depended on the contract) gave the students considerable leeway. Often, for example, they would propose to do less than they knew they could do, realizing (as one student said to me), "the teacher won't find out about it for a few weeks." Once the low output had been agreed upon, the student could spend a considerable amount of time sitting at the tables talking to friends, under the guise of working on a group project or helping a friend with an assignment.

The primary target of agenda-changing strategies in all the schools was the timing and content of class assignments and homework. Whether the focus was the contract at the alternative schools or the length of assignments at Harold Spencer, students continually and collectively made attempts to parley better terms for themselves. The negotiation over an assignment between a group of students and a teacher at school A exemplifies both this process and a frequent outcome.

"When can we turn it in?"

"How about Sunday?"

"All the other teachers say the next day at school is only one day late."

"Why can't we turn it in Sunday when we go for our trip to San Francisco?"

"Yeah, we have to be here anyway at 10 A.M. in order to go to San Francisco."

"What difference does it make if it's only a day late?"

"Yeah, does our grade go down a point for each day it's late?"

Teacher: "Yeah."

"Oh, ok, that's not a bad deal, only one point."

(Teacher, after some thought.) "I'll let you turn it in only if it is witnessed by three adults over twenty-one."

"Ok, ok, Paul and Donna on Sunday A.M."

Teacher: "That's only two."

"My parents!" (Teacher looks questioningly.)

"You said, you said."

Teacher: "Ok, it goes down only one point."

"Far out, that's a good deal."

Another fundamental classroom strategy attempted to create, maintain, or control patterns of communication among peers in settings where communication of this kind typically was considered to be counterproductive to instructional outcomes. At a school like Harold Spencer, where students sat in rows of six or seven, facing the front of the class, such patterns were not always easy to form. Yet it became evident that the students had, in fact, developed several strategies, which worked in various ways. Among girls, note passing was common, particularly where the arrangement of the class led to separation of peers, or where the instructional technology minimized the potential for face-to-face interaction.

A number of methods for passing notes were evident. For example, students often passed notes to the person behind by raising one hand as if to answer a question and, putting the other hand behind the head as if to rest it, dropping the folded note on the desk behind. This would be repeated until the note reached its destination. One might think that such notes would routinely be "intercepted" by unfriendly students, and read or not passed on. This never happened in all the time I was at Spencer. Students passed on the notes, treating them as the private business of the parties involved, thereby showing their respect for the dissemination process. It was as if there was an unspoken law requiring reciprocity—to have the sanctity of one's private communications respected, then one must extend the same courtesy to others.

Control of communication patterns took a somewhat different form in the alternative schools, for here interpersonal communication was such an accepted part of the routine that students could interact almost at will. In these schools, students sat at tables rather than in rows, and teacher-directed instruction was the exception rather than the rule. Hence, many opportunities for student interaction were built into the instructional process, and were therefore not considered by teachers to be deviant.

Yet in these environments too students felt the need to circumvent institutional imperatives and to establish their own communication links. Indeed, when I asked students at school B what they spent most of their time doing at school, the most common response was "socializing." And this socializing continued despite the clear expectation on the part of teachers that there were times and places in which attention to academic issues was required, and that this attention precluded excessive socializing. Students, however, apparently saw things differently as daily they voted with their feet and expressed their opposition to instructional demands.

For example, one of the continuing problems at school B was the tendency for students to temporarily simply absent themselves when they decided they wanted more social interaction than was possible in the classroom. Such absences were selective and contextual, depending upon the situation and the student's knowledge of how to use it. One group of seventh and eighth grade girls often left class for the bathroom for periods of fifteen minutes at a time. When I asked them what led to this routine, one girl said they simply had discovered that it was a good place to talk. Another group of girls routinely slipped out into "the trees," a clump of low bushes alongside the school where they normally smoked cigarettes. A group of boys had a private space in the basement of the school, which they called their "territory" and which permitted them the interaction they desired.

Such means of socializing were possible at school B because of the relatively unstructured nature of the instructional process and the constant movement of students from activity to activity (sometimes in different parts of the school). Students attempted to maintain open communications within that setting by restructuring it to fit their own needs, thereby resisting the institutional imperatives for teacher-directed knowledge.

Beating the System

Students showed opposition to their assigned role in ways other than by manipulating the agenda. In many instances, students engaged in illegal activities that could, if discovered, have serious consequences.

Smoking, for example, which only a minority of students engaged in, was considered by those indulging in it to be important. I have already briefly mentioned smoking in the bushes at school B. At Harold Spencer, smoking regulations were more rigidly enforced, making it more difficult for students to get away to smoke. As a result of the challenge, a well-developed body of knowledge about smoking was readily shared among certain students, thereby optimizing their chances for success.

The most likely spots for smoking at Spencer were the "cans" (bathrooms), and students were well aware of which "can" offered the best opportunities. The best "cans" had cold-air return vents. Smoking near the vents resulted in some smoke being exhausted, leaving less of a telltale cigarette odor. Yet the odor itself did not particularly bother many of the student smokers because the teachers had to catch them cigarette in hand to prove that they were smoking. To minimize the risk of this, when smoking was done collectively (as it normally was between classes and at lunch), a "lookout" was posted at the door. This person's responsibility was to provide a signal (a tap on the wall, a loud cough) when a teacher was seen coming down the hall. But the ideal way to smoke in the "cans" was to use the toilets inside the stalls, a trick that could be used only if one was lucky enough to get out of class and into the "cans" when they weren't crowded. The smokers went into the stall, closed the door, and stood on the seat of the toilet, being careful not to stand so high that they could be seen over the top of the door. Thus, the closed door shielded them completely: if teachers entered to make a spot check on the "cans," they would see no telltale feet in the stalls and make a quick exit while the smoker was, all the while, puffing away. Whenever they did check more carefully, the smoker simply dropped the butt into the toilet and the teacher could not prove a thing.

In schools A and B schedule flexibility and the nonroutine nature of the schedule provided much greater opportunity for students who wished to smoke. Since they did not always have to be in a certain class at a certain time, and were permitted to move in and out of instructional activities, the constraints on smoking were less binding. Yet this did not mean that they did not have to consider carefully how, when, and where to partici-pate. At school B for instance, the "tree" was a good spot until one day a stray spark set some leaves on fire. The smouldering fire alerted a nearby neighbor, who in turn called the school. After this incident, students had to find other locations in which to light up. At school A, forty-five minute lunch breaks when students could leave the school provided ample opportunity to go to the nearby park and smoke a cigarette or a joint. But even here, one person usually served as an informal lookout, for teachers also visited the park at lunch. Frequent long trips to natural areas, and historical spots for educational and recreational purposes also provided considerable opportunity, although on one occasion six students were suspended for three days for smoking on one such trip. One of the six commented, after being informed of the punishment, that "next time, we ought to have someone looking out for the teachers."

"Skipping" was another oppositional strategy engaged in by students, regardless of the structure of the school. For, in all the schools, students were expected to attend some classes or activities arranged for them by the school staff. Absence from all or some of these activities was referred to as "skipping" or "skipping out," of which there were two types—illegal and legal. Students took advantage of whatever situation was presented to them in order to exercise their prerogatives and maximize self-determination.

One form of skipping could be called "illegal skipping,"—absence from the school for illegitimate reasons. Generally, illegal skips involved not showing up for school for a day. Normally students attempted to present some evidence to indicate that the absence was in fact legitimate.

At Harold Spencer, such absences were usually in concert—that is, with other students of the same friendship group. For example, Don and Steve frequently skipped together as did Don and some of his older friends. Usually, this entailed going to the local park (if the weather was good), to one of two local shopping centers, or just hanging around the house if the parents were not home.

Students didn't always skip for the entire day, instead taking off one or more periods. Typically this was more difficult because attendance was taken in each class, and if a student was absent from that class the chances were he or she would be called to the office for an explanation. But there were ways around this. Sometimes, students simply went to the counselor's office instead of to class, told the secretary they were waiting to see the counselor, and then spent the time reading magazines or, better yet, talking to other people who were also waiting to see the counselor. Even if the counselor was unavailable until some later time, students would wait until a particularly "boring" class was over, tell the secretary they needed to return to class, and then obtain an admission pass from the secretary, thereby legitimating the absence.

The "individualized" classes at Spencer were the easiest to skip because there attendance was not taken by checking assigned seats, as there were no assigned seats. Instead, each student had an individualized packet that was kept in a file when not in use. When students entered the class at the beginning of the period, they took the packet from the file, after which the aide simply noted the names of those students whose packets were still in the file, and assumed all others to be present. The students of course, had figured this system out, and one simple way to skip in such classes was to have a friend pull the folder.

Skipping for all or part of the day at school B, where all of the classes were individualized, was much easier. Here, attendance was taken at the beginning of the day, and even then somewhat sporadically. After that, precise knowledge of where a student was to be at any given time was difficult to obtain. Students used this to their best advantage, absenting themselves from classes with little fear of serious repercussion. Strategies ranged from arriving at or departing from a class almost at will, to staying away from school for an entire day. It was not unusual to see students from school B hanging around the bus terminal in town during the day, or riding the mopeds down the street. When these same students returned to school the next day, they often did so with little more than a verbal excuse that they were ill the previous day. No note from home was required (as it always was at Spencer) and the staff appeared unconcerned about following up on student absences unless they became regular.

If there were ways to skip illegally, then there were also ways to skip legally for all or part of the day. By legal skipping, I mean the process by which students took advantage of their status in the school to "get away" from certain academic requirements they might not be able to otherwise avoid. Illegal skipping was engaged in by a minority of students (and a certain type of student) while legal skipping tended to be more widespread and, again, practiced by a certain type of student. The opportunities for this were numerous, as a review of the daily bulletin at Spencer reveals.

> The Thespians will be excused at 10:00 A.M. today to go to a special performance of a play in Port City. Those students who are to be excused are noted on the enclosed list.

> Students listed below shall be excused at 9:30 A.M. to attend a science seminar at the high school. They should be back by 11:30.

> Pep Club members will be excused at 2:00 P.M. today to attend the football game with Edgewood. Students to be excused are the following . . .

> Honor society members please report to the cafeteria at 10:15 tomorrow morning for group pictures.

Of course, such general meetings usually were supplemented by more specific meetings, which involved the participation of the "elite" within the school, most especially athletes and those active in student government.

> Would the following members of the football team please report to the stage this morning at 11:00. These boys missed the last picture session and they cannot be included in the annual unless they have their picture taken at this time.

> There will be a student council meeting this morning at 8:35 in room B–16. Everyone please attend. This is an important meeting.

> There will be a special meeting of the 9th grade room representatives today at 8:35 to discuss plans for the graduation dance. Meet in the library conference room.

Again, greater opportunity for such legal skipping was built into the structures of schools A, B, and C. Yet these opportunities often were in conflict with the necessity to fulfill contracts, to be at specific tasks at specific points in time, or to fulfill the need of teachers for a certain product indicative of their academic achievement. Thus even here students placed considerable emphasis on their ability to control their own time by taking advantage of opportunities to absent themselves from directed activities. At school B, for instance, some students always seemed to "have to" work on a drama presentation that was coming up. Among the upper-grade students, half the class could be absent from "learning block" (the 90-minute period when most of the basic subjects were covered) to practice a play. Other specialized classes in music, drama, the yearbook, and the existence of a school restaurant, all drew students from learning block for periods of time throughout the year.

At school C, legal skipping occurred in other ways as well. Here school structure was of a free school variety wherein students often were the sole determinants of whether or not they would engage in academics on a given day. Students often decided not to participate in anything, to "veg out"—sit, doodle, play. This was considered legal (at least for some unspecified period of time) at school C, and gave students the right to skip assigned learning tasks without fear of serious consequences.

Of course, correlation does not mean causation, and it is reasonable to ask the extent to which student participation in such legal skips was with the deliberate intention of avoiding classes and other required activities. Answers are provided by the students themselves. For example, at Spencer I had occasion to be present at lunch when a group of eighth-grade boys asked Chris, and a friend, why he participated in almost all of the school's drama activities.

"You really like that stuff, don't you?" one boy asked.

"Sure I do, it's great," Chris replied. "Not only is it fun but I get out of lots of classes. I can get out of almost any class I want."

Jack replied, "The only way I can get out of class is to get kicked out; the bastards don't trust me at all."

"Me either," said Marty. "The only thing I can get out for is wrestling."

Chris continued to describe his ability to get out of class.

"I guess the main thing is that it's an honor system kind of thing. If Mrs. Mackle wants me to get out for rehearsals or to get pictures taken or to work on costumes or something, she just writes a note and I take it to the teacher . . . they [the teachers] know that they can trust me, so they're willing to let me out. They know I won't be behind the 'B' building smoking dope."

Don, a student at school B, had a similar perception of the alternative school and the role of trust in attempts to broker opportunities for greater self-determination. In a conversation, he reflected upon his abilities to negotiate preferences, using as leverage his high standardized test scores and the awareness on the part of teachers that he always could do well if he really wanted. This knowledge permitted him to remove himself from many required activities under the implied threat that he would evidence his boredom and thus become a distraction to the rest of the class.

I asked Don how he was able to manipulate the teachers management of the classroom to achieve his own objectives.

> I don't really know—I guess it's because I can do pretty well in school and I know that my tests are pretty high; [the teacher] has even admitted that. So I can do pretty well in school but not have to do a lot of work and I don't think the kids like the fact that I can do what I want to and they can't because they have to work more to do what they do. I can do not much here and still get good grades and everything, and that's why I spend a lot of time kinda walking around and doing what I feel like doing. I can get away with things, and I have power because this school supposedly lets you make your own decisions. They don't like that.

As we can now see clearly, legal skips were in fact intentionally carried out, but mostly by those students who perceived that they had the power to do so. Trusted students were more likely to skip legally than were students whom the teachers did not trust. Chris could get out of many classes when a play or musical production was being scheduled, since he had access to a *carte blanche* pass. Other students used different avenues to legally skip.

Student Perspectives on Opposition

I now wish to discuss how students viewed actions that were resistant of teacher directed classroom routines. First it is important to differentiate those student actions engaged in consciously to express self-determination from those that are conscious but without a clear understanding of motive. Finally, we will examine the presence of the more generalized sense of disaffection that existed without a clear understanding of either its presence of its source.

There is little doubt that most students were aware to some degree of their attempts to alter the direction of classroom instruction. More often than not, the motivation for these actions seemed understood, although it was not always explicit. For instance, Roger, a seventh-grader at Harold Spencer, often played "dumb" in certain classes, especially English class, which he saw as demeaning and unproductive because students were asked to read aloud. Roger simply refused to answer questions posed him by the teacher, and he once told me he felt the class to be a "baby" class because of the reading of poetry. That many students felt that way led to frequent collective withdrawal of participation, as groups of students recognized the power of group action against the demands of a single teacher. Such collective action was most prevalent in classes students did not like—where they felt the instructor to be unfair, or not a good teacher.

In one English class, collective actions were so common that the students seemed to assume that they, rather than the teacher, determined the flow of events during the class. Furthermore, normative forces were such that once a group of students decided to withdraw their participation in the class, they expected other students to do likewise. Students who conformed too much to the demands of the instructors' management strategies were routinely sanctioned by other students, to the extent that even the "pets" eventually cooperated to some degree.

Typical strategies in this class involved forgetting supplies, doing the wrong assignment, leaving papers in the locker, and "ad-libbing" on teacher-directed stories—all activities that maximized the students' control in a class that virtually all of them disliked. John, a student in the class, once told me that the students in another class all "know that the teacher is insecure and if you get him talking about something he likes, he'll keep on talking about it. One day he cracked a joke about streaking and we started talking about it for twenty minutes and missed a quiz and everything."

"It sounds as if you get them off the subject on purpose then," I responded.

"Sure," John replied, "it makes things more interesting and sometimes we even get out of work."

The intentionality of such resistance was more pronounced when students used agenda changes as a way to "get back" at a teacher they didn't like. Students at Spencer particularly disliked the music teacher, so they frequently "forgot" to pass out the music books before class (a task they were supposed to do every day), often pretended to be singing when they really were mouthing the words, and continually confused eighth notes for half notes when asked to beat out the time. Such acts were engaged in collectively by groups of students as a way of revenging themselves on a teacher who, as one student said, "treats us like babies."

Students did not seem to use humor and joke telling with the specific intention of disrupting the flow of classroom procedures, though there is little doubt that they realized that it did, in fact, serve that purpose. Its use was closely connected to student attempts to force teachers off the subject and into areas of greater interest. Constant plays on words, the use of mixed metaphors, and so on, often resulted in quizzes being postponed, assignments being redefined, and changes in the manner in which time was spent in the classroom. While I believe that students realized the humor and joking could often lead to those consequences I have no way of knowing whether they consciously indulged in joking behavior with those ends in mind. I believe that students often participated in or created oppositional forms not so much out of an explicit and outward realization of their oppositional nature as from a generalized recognition of the absence of involvement and control over their labor in the school and the fact that, quite often, "there is nothing to do."

Opposition often signaled, at least in the student's mind, a recognition of their role as members of an organization wherein they had been relegated to positions of low status where, almost invariably, they were the passive recipients of knowledge or activities planned for them by adults. The assumptions of these adults, well-intended though they were, were predicated on the assumption that, while some liberties could be extended (especially in the alternative schools), students still should not be actively involved in understanding their role as consumers and producers of knowledge.

To the extent that opposition was a reaction against passivity, "bugging the teacher" (a strategy nominated by students as one of their most common) then takes on an added dimension, for it consisted of a set of strategies engaged in because students were aware that their place in the school often left them as mere observers. Thus, not only did they bug the teachers because, oftentimes, "they deserve it," but also because, as a number of students emphasized, "there is nothing else to do."

A case in point from Spencer. One teacher, Mr. Richards, was particularly strict and his close supervision of the class made oppositional behavior difficult. Yet such difficulty was overcome by students because they found their own relation to the productive system in the class to be alienating. In a conversation with Dave and Steve, two students in the class, I found that both said that they did things "to piss him off," like smiling when he lectured, deliberately piling up textbooks the wrong way on the counter at the side of the room, and tapping their feet in class. I asked them why they bugged him. The combination in their answer of active response and reactive stand against aimlessness is instructive:

"It's boring all right."

Dave responded, "You just can't get away with doing that much."

Steve provided an illustration. "He'll sit back in the room and fake like he's watching a movie, looking around at the other kids to see what they are doing. Then if you go to sleep he'll find a book or a yardstick and just slam it right, practically right in their face, right on the desk."

"He'll give you detention if you pick your nose. One day I fell asleep in geography."

Steve laughed knowing full well what Dave was talking about, "Everyone falls asleep in social studies. One time I fell asleep holding my book. Pow, right on the floor."

Schools A and B were more philosophically inclined to provide their students with choices and some degree of self-direction, and thus the lines between adult authority and student passivity were not as clear as those at Spencer. Indeed, one rarely heard comments from students about the worthlessness of the school, the unresponsive nature of the teachers that warranted constant "bugging," or their resentment at being in the school in the first place. One would not expect such comments since parents and pupils chose the school on a voluntary basis. Yet opposition was not absent from these schools; its presence was merely masked by different strategies. Students, while they often claimed to be satisfied with their role in the schools, still resisted participation in activities that they did not approve of or understand.

For example at School A (the school with the most comprehensive offerings and facilities) half the members of a science class refused for one entire week to take seriously their involvement in science experiments because the purpose of the experiments was unclear to them and the meaning marginal. An excerpt from my field notes indicates the state of affairs for most of the period:

"Kirk to Star Base, the temperature is dropping, its below 50 degrees C. I can't hold the course much longer."
"Star Base to Kirk. See what you can do, we must have that mission complete."
"Mr. Spock, this is Kirk. Beam me to the engine room, I must check on the temperature of that solution. Its dropping rapidly."
"Scotty, Scotty, do you have a fix on that heat exchange yet? Why is the temperature dropping?"
"I don't know Captain, I guess the solution is changing!"
(All in English Brogue accent)

This despite the fact that the students said they like the instructor and saw him as a person "you can talk to." They did not, however, feel they could talk to him about their dislike of having "science crammed down our throats" because they felt that his mind was already made up; "he says it's good for us because we'll need it in college." Students thus felt justified in opposing their role as receivers of this information because, as one student put it, "if we have to be there, at least we can play 'Star Wars' to make the time go by faster."

This was especially true for those who did not see themselves as "college bound," and who were in the school because of its reputation for permitting independent work on the part of students. Two students in the class, David and Terry, indicated clearly that they did not have aspirations beyond high school, and that all of the talk of needing knowledge for college "cuts no ice with us." This further justified their continual creation of Star Wars-like games, for the future rewards promised for the acquisition of science knowledge were not part of the manual-labor tradition of their family background.

We are beginning to see how, regardless of the amount of flexibility students had in choosing extracurricular activities or times when they would complete some academic tasks, student labor by its nature did not involve them in active decisions about their work or facilitate any consideration of the present or future meaning of that work. Most students were estranged from the labor they performed, and it was, for the most part, simply a process by which their role in the social structure of the school was extended for vague reasons emphasized by parents and teachers. Students felt estranged from much academic work, even in the alternative schools, because it was carried out as part of an undefined relationship wherein students generated a product whose value was defined by others (teachers, acting as agents for parents and society). The level of estrangement is illustrated clearly in the following discussion. Barry, a student at Spencer indicated that he saw time "dragging" in some of his classes. I asked him which classes dragged. He said:

"This one [English]. We sit here and we do the same thing over and over and over and every day it gets boring. We sit there and do assignments three and four times. This class really drags because I know we are going to do the same thing again and again."

"Is that what makes the classes go slow?"

"Yeah, doing the same thing all the time."

This pattern is changed somewhat in the alternative schools, but the change is more one of degree than of kind. Students at school B, for example, told me repeatedly that they attended the school mostly at their parents' request, and partly to learn responsibility (a concept that most did not know the meaning of). Yet in this school students still saw work as "that which teachers tell us to do" and it made little difference that such work could be done in a more flexible time frame. The student was still required to accept the logic of those who created the work, to recognize that it was "useful," and to agree that it should be done for its own sake.

In all four schools most students firmly believed that, when it came to academic knowledge, they were merely passive recipients. Any knowledge in whose creation they played a part came not through the formal dimensions of instruction but through informal peer culture and, at the alternative schools, in the choice classes and in discussions pertaining to interpersonal relations. Their feeling of estrangement from active and conscious knowledge production became manifest, in part, through the presence of oppositional forms and the numerous strategies that were part of them.

To understand what was "learned" as students created this culture, we need to examine the significance of opposition in school in relation to the labor process endemic to capitalist economic systems.

Opposition and the Labor Process

While some oppositional strategies do, in fact, disrupt the instructional routine of the school, such disruption is not the most critical aspect of student opposition, the preponderance of literature on classroom-management techniques notwithstanding. I say this because a focus on disruption leads to an emphasis on the management of disruption—an orientation that takes as given the presence of opposition and does not inquire into its source. Student opposition, however, because it commands such important objective and subjective aspects of the student culture, must be seen as being as "instructive" as the very manifest purposes of school itself. The information just presented demonstrates the pervasiveness of opposition and makes clear the nature of the student culture that creates and interprets it. Students learn something about themselves and their role as a result of these experiences. The fundamental question, however, is what is learned.

In all the schools, student understanding of their relationship to the labor process suggests some answers to that question. Their perception was based on the fact that, regardless of the organizational arrangement of the school, students found themslves separate from the academic work they performed, which constituted their labor in the school. Rarely, if ever, did students discuss their labor as an extension of themselves—that is, as a means that they had formulated and were using toward some self-defined and conscious end. Rather this "work," as they called it, always seemed to be an activity that separated them from the productive process by affirming the right of others to uniformly define and ultimately control the academic labor they performed.

If this analysis is correct, then experiences of students in school are rudimentary forms of what Marx called "alienated labor"—a system wherein workers produce products which they have little control over in exchange for direct remuneration decided by the owner of the product created. They work for wages, selling their labor power to the owner. In so doing, workers surrender their right to the control of their labor and, in turn, come to see that labor as functional not for its own sake (use value) but more for what it buys (exchange value).

Marx's discussion of the relationship between labor and the forces of production is equally applicable to schools, despite the fact that students do not sell their labor power for wages. The product that students "sell" is school-sanctioned knowledge rather than some tangible product. This knowledge is turned into a tangible product or commodity through its translation into grades, points, or evaluations. Since the origin and utility of such commodities makes little sense to most students, and because these commodities are made for someone other than the producer of the knowledge, then students become alienated from that knowledge and the labor it takes to produce it.

This collective estrangement from the basis of labor process means that students can be considered as a subjugated "class." Here I use the term "class" less in an economic sense than as it refers to the relationship of the worker to the productive process. Collectively, students had little control of their situation, even in those schools where adults thought that they were allowing some by letting students choose when they would finish an assignment. Because of this minimal control, and the realization that they were systematically excluded from decisions about their labor and its meaning, students came to understand their role in the school organization in class terms—as a group sharing phenomenological estrangement from labor and collectively acting out this estrangement through oppositional strategies.

Understanding the class basis of alienated labor helps us to better understand the collective nature of opposition. As noted throughout this chapter, most oppositional strategies generated by students were collective, norm-referenced activities engaged in or understood as group activities. Oppositional strategies then, be they as inoffensive as telling jokes in class or as drastic as skipping a class, were all shared activities. By shared I mean that the activity required the participation and understanding of other members of that class, and that the standards regulating the behavior were generally understood. Such standards were demonstrated daily: no student would ever "nark" on a fellow student seen skipping a class, sneaking a smoke, or throwing a book across the room, no matter how much personal animosity might exist between them. The class basis of student experiences, then, grew out of the system of shared meanings derived from those experiences, and out of the oppositional strategies supported by that interpretive world.

Yet the presence of collective opposition does not necessarily indicate a shared consciousness of the purposes of resistance. Opposition often grows out of a muted resistance to forces and situations whose basis is not understood. Quite often, as we have seen, it grows out of boredom and the minimal involvement of students in activities that are meant to consume much of their time. This is especially true at schools like Spencer. Strategies such as the use of humor, joke telling, and changes of agendas are all part of a general unarticulated but still vaguely understood way of filling in the time and gaining some control over its limits.

Boredom serves as the catalyst toward a muted reappropriation of the control of the labor process.

The strategies themselves, while oppositional in structure, may be minimally so in fact, because they may serve not to oppose the basic structure of school life but rather to form a separate reality parallel to formalized school life. In the schools I studied, the collective belief systems about boredom, noninvolvement, and filling in the time did often generate adaptive strategies that led to a reassertion of student control and that helped make time go faster. The basic class position of students in the school, however—that is, their position as a group characteristically separated from control over the labor process—continued and in many ways was reaffirmed by the very oppositional strategies themselves.

It may seem ironic that student oppositional strategies, while of different dimensions, were as common in the alternative schools as at Spencer, despite the intentions of the staff to create conditions where learning was more an agreed-upon process. This becomes more understandable when we realize that the practice in these schools was to limit student choices primarily to the selection of "choice" classes and to negotiating the specific terms of contracts, while the overall authority for establishing the parameters of knowledge still rested with the teachers. In most cases, students perceived this knowledge as handed down rather than socially developed by the students in concert with the teachers. Thus, despite being on a first-name basis with students, teachers still made them do "work," "work" here referring to the students' perception of their minimal control over their academic labor. Teachers, because of their persistent tendency to consider core academic knowledge as "basic" and universal information, rather than as material whose origin and boundaries were socially determined, assumed that a basic un-reflexive system of knowledge production in this core, or academic, material was permissible because "choice" classes (particularly at school B and C) were also available.

Students, however, through their opposition to the general content of school, reinforced the belief that the "benefits" of alternative schools were not sufficient to compensate for what they still perceived to be a subservient role. The freedom that existed as a context within which to do work (freedom meaning flexibility of time to complete tasks) often created frustration and anxiety as students had little foundation which they could use to understand what was to be done and why. At schools B and C in particular, many of the older students reacted to their freedom by faulting the school for "not teaching us much" and thereby not preparing them well for surviving in the real world. The following statement by Don from school B illustrates this rather common point of view.

But one thing about this place is they don't teach you much here. You know you have those choice classes but they don't teach you anything like that. It's really kind of tough like if you're going on to junior high school. I don't really feel like I know very much. I think they ought to teach more here you know like hard language stuff and mathematics and dictionary work and things like that.

This statement illustrates that when students do not share in the creation of the conditions of labor to an extent that they either share control over that labor or understand and accept its purpose, then the creation of "freedom" is really the creation of the illusion of freedom. Such an illusion turns back to support the conditions of opposition because students are vaguely aware of their continued lack of control over their labor. Oppositional behavior resists attempts to "manage" student labor. But such behavior may, on the other hand, also serve to further incorporate the student into the productive process being resisted. This is why opposition must be seen as containing internal contradictions.

The Contradictions of Opposition

The contradictions existing in oppositional behavior are especially clear when we examine the consequence of such actions. Most important as a consequence is what students learn through their oppositional behavior.

Peter Woods and others have pointed out that it is important to recognize the ability of students to make adaptations to a culture as they come to experience it. Accordingly, students do not uniformly accept their condition and role, but modify that role so that they can live in but not be totally of the formal organization of the school. However, we also need to recognize that, as well as this process of adapting to a culture "out there," students also are creating and making their own culture. They are, in fact, living out a culture where they "learn" the cultural roles and form the world views which they themselves have been instrumental in creating. In resisting certain imperatives of schooling, they are learning not only how to survive in situations where labor is extracted from them, but also are forming belief systems about institutions, organizations, and the place of human actors within them.

The learning that takes place through opposition to classroom management parallels the making of class relations in the workplace.[9] Indeed, what students liked most about school related to their interaction together or to the situations they could choose (for example, the "choice" classes at the alternative schools). What they found almost uniformly unacceptable was "work" where they had minimal control over their labor, and most oppositional strategies were formed around these activities. These strategies consisted of forming a separate cultural form—a separate reality—in order to re-appropriate control over labor. In so doing, students created, lived out, and reinforced the very forces of production that damns people in the workforce in most capitalist (and indeed even in nominally socialist) societies.

Yet, as in the workplace, we need be aware of the differential effects on learning created by opposition to productive forces. In the case of student opposition, I am speaking specifically of the manner in which oppositional behavior grows from and re-enters the student's cultural-historical context. For example, I observed many instances where students from more affluent backgrounds were able to compensate for the manner in which the productive forces of the school removed them from control over their labor. This occurred, for example, through involvement in certain voluntary organizations (YMCA, sports clubs, creative arts organizations), participation with families in educative activities, and a general familiarity with high-status knowledge, gained by continual contact with it at home and elsewhere. Many of these compensatory activities emphasized knowledge and skills that paralleled the high-status knowledge emphasized by the school, and thereby provided an opportunity for the student to conclude that the knowledge resisted at school (as well as the control they lacked over the labor process) could be gained elsewhere.

Students from predominantly laboring families usually did not have such resources available to them. The activities in which they engaged outside of school (dirt biking, "cruising," working on motorcycles) were of a type that could not be considered conducive to the acquisition of high-status knowledge. For these students then, resistance to classroom activities may have had more serious consequences, for in resisting that knowledge (or the framework in which it existed) they were resisting the very epistemology on which "success" in life was based.

The contradictions of student opposition are evidenced in other ways as well. Students, as Paul Willis has pointed out, can and do "penetrate" the fundamental dimensions of the labor process in such a way that they begin to conceptualize their own place in the material world that they are in the process of entering and making. Perhaps such insight was evident in the comments by Don, who recognized the false promise of free choice in school B.

As students learn to make oppositional action conscious and to concretize its origins and consequences, it can come to serve as a vehicle for future education as well as a catalyst for political action. Teachers can help students in this process by a critical understanding of their own "management strategies" and by viewing uncritical acceptance of these strategies as the continuation of a system of production whose basis is the extraction of "value" from student labor. Classroom management then, rather than continuing to be a tool of the modern state for the regulation of its young, can become the vehicle around which both students and teachers strive for awareness of their place in the production of knowledge and in systems of social relations.[10]

Notes

1. A recent overview is provided in Daniel Duke, ed., *Classroom Management: The Seventy-Eighth Yearbook of the National Society for the Study of Education* (Chicago: University of Chicago Press, 1979).

2. A complete inventory of these hortatory sources would consume pages. Representative of this type of discussion are Katherine C. LaMancusa, *We Do Not Throw Rocks at the Teacher* (Scranton: Intex, 1966); William E. Amos and Reginald Oren, *Managing Student Behavior* (St. Louis: Warren Green, 1967); Harvey F. Clarizio, *Toward Positive Classroom Discipline* (New York: John Wiley, 1971).

3. For appropriate illustrations, see Walter Doyle, "Making Managerial Decisions in Classroms," in Daniel Duke, ed., *Classroom Management: The Seventy-Eighth Yearbook of the National Society for the Study of Education* (Chicago: University of Chicago Press, 1979), pp. 42–75; Jacob Kounin, *Discipline and Group Management in the Classroom* (New York: Holt, Rinehart and Winston, 1970); Stephen Bossert, *Tasks and Social Relationships in the Classroom* (Cambridge: Cambridge University Press, 1979).

4. See, for example, Philip Cusick, *Inside High School* (New York: Holt, Rinehart and Winston, 1973); Peter Woods, *The Divided School* (London: Routledge and Kegan Paul, 1979).

5. Michael Apple, *Ideology and Curriculum* (Boston and London: Routledge and Kegan Paul, 1979); Jean Anyon, "Social Class and School Knowledge," *Curriculum Inquiry* 11, no. 1 (1981): 3–42; Paul Willis, *Learning to Labor* (Teakfield: Saxon House, 1977).

6. Michael Apple, "Reproduction, Contestation, and Curriculum: An Essay in Self-Criticism," *Interchange* 12, no. 2/3 (1981): 27.

7. For more detail on student life at Harold Spencer see Robert B. Everhart, *Reading, Writing, and Resistance: Adolescence and the Labor Process in a Junior High School* (Boston and London: Routledge and Kegan Paul, in press).

8. An examination of programs characterized by student "choice" and their relation to adolescent cultures is described in my unpublished monograph, *Adolescence, Ideology, and Symbolic Community: A Study of Alternative Schooling*.

9. See, for example, Michael Burawoy, *Manufacturing Consent: Changes in*

the Labor Process Under Monopoly Capitalism (Chicago: University of Chicago Press, 1979); Richard Edwards, *Contested Terrain* (New York: Basic Books, 1979); Richard M. Pfeffer, *Working for Capitalism* (New York: Columbia University Press, 1979).

10. For an illustration of this process in action, see Ira Shor, *Critical Teaching and Everyday Life*(Boston: South End Press, 1980).

CHAPTER 8

School Structure
and Teachers' Work

ANDREW GITLIN

Current theorists point out the powerful influence society has in shaping schools as agents of cultural and economic reproduction.[1] Although helpful, this perspective appears rather deterministic because the schools are not shown to contain any contradictory or oppositional trends. Instead schools are often portrayed as "puppets" carrying out capitalist needs to perfection. One explanation for this simplistic perspective is that the internal everyday practice of the schools is not analyzed. By excluding such an analysis it is possible that these theorists are ignoring not only how schools act in reproductive ways but also the contradictory trends that exist in the schools.

To challenge the deterministic nature of the relationship between school and society, recent analyses have focused on the internal workings of the schools. Some of these studies have looked at what knowledge gets into schools,[2] how knowledge in the schools is used,[3] what values and meanings "get in,"[4] and how informal groups may, in their rejection of the school, actually help reproduce their class position.[5] What is common to all these analyses is that they have pointed out the complexity of the relationship between school and society.

To continue the tradition of analyzing the internal workings of the schools, and their effect on societal relations, this study will focus specifically on the relationship between school structure and teachers' work. To understand the establishment of particular school structures and their impact on teachers within a societal context, work structures and their impact on workers outside the educational context will be used as a comparative framework. Three major points will be argued. First, changes in the work structure of teachers have affected them in similar ways to structural changes influencing workers outside the educational arena. This indicates that constraints on teachers are not unique to their profession, but rather derive from the priorities and values guiding labor reforms as a whole in this country. Second, teachers do not passively accept these changes and their response to these structural changes is an important factor influencing what happens in schools. Third, the result of such changes is to limit the transformative potential of teachers and encourage them to act in ways which contribute to the reproduction of dominant societal relations. This analysis will begin by investigating the reforms affecting work outside the educational arena.

Reforms Outside the Educational Arena

The question of control was central to the changes in work structures outside the educational arena. In the early phase of the Industrial Revolution, management attempted to exercise control by using foremen or middle management to supervise workers and to make sure they were doing the "proper" job. There were several problems with this arrangement. First, the allegiance of foremen was often split between management and the workers, and second, foremen often used their positions to gain favors from workers. It was also difficult to know exactly what a worker should be doing at a specific time. Consequently, the use of foremen for supervision was not by itself very effective in increasing production.

Thus, it was not long before a new approach was tried. This approach, made popular by Frederick Winslow Taylor, was called scientific management. Scientific management not only standardized procedures, supposedly to increase production, but also allowed middle management or supervisors to know exactly what a worker should be doing at a specific time and what the next step should be.

In addition to innovative managerial systems, technological developments such as the assembly line also affected the labor process. A worker performing a particular task within this type of work structure had the speed of his or her work determined by the speed of the machine. With the development of advanced technologies and completely automated systems, the worker was removed from any direct connection with the product and instead became a watcher. "Patrolling becomes the main human contribution (with highly developed automated plants). The 'operator' if he is still there, becomes a sort of watchman, a monitor, a helper. We might think of him as a liaison man between machines and operating management."[6]

The introduction of these types of managerial systems and accompanying technological developments affected workers in significant ways. One effect was that control became embedded in the technical aspects of the plant (technical control) rather than being completely in the hands of individual managers.[7]

Having control embedded in the technology of the workplace makes it difficult for workers to negotiate with foremen about the pace of work or to intentionally try to slow it down. Advanced automation plants, by "disconnecting" workers from the direct production process, make it even more difficult for workers to affect production at all.

In addition, technological and managerial changes limited workers primarily to the role of executing an operation while management became responsible for its conceptualization. This condition became apparent under Taylor-like management systems. Although workers always retained a certain understanding of the conceptualization of the work process, the emphasis on executing an operation made it difficult for them to react to and overcome the constant difficulties that grew out of variations in tools, materials, and work procedures. Consequently, by being primarily involved with executing an operation, workers became more dependent on management to conceptualize the work processes that would make them employable. "This process (separation of execution and conception), it is evident, separates skills and knowledge even in their narrower relationship. When it is completed, the worker is no longer a craftsman in any sense, but is an animated tool of the management."[8]

The type of skills a worker needed to do his or her job effectively were also influenced by labor reforms. If the technology and managerial systems limited a worker primarily to executing an operation, as was true in assembly lines, the worker tended to be deskilled. This deskilling process allowed management to replace high-skilled labor with cheap, low-skilled labor. Conversely, other advanced technologies required that workers develop new skills. For example, those workers who patrolled the automated plants needed new types of skills to understand if the system was working. The acquisition of these new skills necessitated a reskilling process.[9] Therefore, with the changes in the labor process workers used a different set of skills than was common in craft or cottage industries.

A final way that labor reforms seem to have affected workers involves their relationships. Worker relationships are at best partially dependent on the organization of the plant. If workers are allocated in serial fashion, instead of having a group of workers converge on the same material, it is likely that their relations will be atomized. Thus, where workers "work in series, each separately adding some modification or part, [and] where in addition serial production is spread out over vast physical expanses, the isolation of workers can be extreme. In a mile-long steel mill, workers in one department have no contact with those in other departments."[10]

Other causes of atomization include noise, speed of operation, and the attention demanded of the operator. Not only do high levels of noise make communication difficult, but high-speed operations that require close attention to the work process leave little time for workers to interact. Since the assembly line has the above characteristics, it seems fair to conclude that this particular reform contributed to an atomization of workers.

Other labor reforms, however, seemed to reverse this trend. For in highly automated plants workers were no longer "tied" to their machine. "In the first place, automation reversed the trend towards an ever-increasing division of labor. The worker was no longer confined to one highly specialized and trivial task, and he was no longer tied to the rhythm of the machine; instead he was now responsible for the overall operation of a complex unit of production."[11]

Thus it appears that although the first advances in technology created situations where workers found it difficult to interact, later technologies somewhat reversed this trend by "freeing" the worker from direct operation with the machine, thereby providing a potential for worker interactions. Investigation into how workers relate will provide insights into how (or if) workers compete for rewards and status, and whether they focus on constraints as a group or as individuals.

It is important to point out that workers did not passively accept the changes in their working conditions. The increased pace of work, isolation, separation of the worker from the finished product, and loss of autonomy for many workers encouraged them to find ways to resist. These resistances took a variety of forms, ranging from simply making "homers"[12] to purposely sabotaging a part of the production line, thus causing the whole operation to shut down temporarily. Burawoy argues that the implementation of management systems such as scientific management caused such strong worker resistance that profits and productivity actually decreased when the system was introduced.[13] This suggests that attention to worker resistance should be an important part of any attempt to understand what occurs at the "point of production."

With this perspective in mind, we can ask, how have reforms involving the school structure affected teachers? Data from a study I conducted on an Individually Guided Education (IGE) school (which will be referred to as Meadow School) will form the basis of my attempt to answer this question.

Methodology

To analyze the relationship between teachers' work and school structure, I chose an ethnographic approach. My primary sources of data came from observations, taped interviews, school documents and local newspapers. Specifically, two teams of five teachers were observed for approximately thirty-five days each. In addition, fifteen interviews, lasting between thirty minutes and an hour were conducted. The interviews tried to probe the relationship between the school structure and teachers' work.

To keep in touch with wider school issues, I obtained specific directives affecting the teams observed, and as many school documents as possible. These included minutes of team meetings and IIC (Instructional Improvement Committee) meetings, school events, memos to the team, evaluation of teachers, and so forth. Finally, because the observations took place during one year only, data about the school's history that might help explain observed behaviors were collected. These data were collected primarily from interviews with parents and senior members of the staff, as well as from an extensive review of a local newspaper.

Care was taken in choosing a representative school structure for study. The IGE structure seemed representative of many recent attempts at school reform for several reasons. First, the curriculum form used—a set of predetermined, sequentially laid out objectives—has become associated with the individualized movement. Not only do many schools try to individualize at least some of their programs, but almost all the major publishers have some individualized materials that use this form.[14] Secondly, the staff structure used in IGE schools consists of teachers grouped into teams, each with a team leader. Although many schools use teaming in a variety of ways, the organization of teachers into groups with a team leader has become increasingly popular in the last decade. Finally, the physical layout of an IGE school incorporates an open-plan design that eliminates many of the walls in the school building. Following the example of British primary schools, many schools in the United States have done away with egg-crate architecture and "opened up" their buildings. Although not all IGE schools are similar, these basic features seem to indicate that the school structure is representative of the conditions many teachers work in today.

Meadow School is located fifteen miles away from a medium sized Midwestern city. The surrounding community is suburban and middle class. Community expansion has resulted in increased enrollment for Meadow School, which currently has about 650 students in grades K to 6. Instead of formal grades, students move through units, each of which corresponds to approximately two grades. For example, unit five has students whose age corresponds to those in the traditional fifth and sixth grades. Each unit is made up of between three and five teachers (not including resource help or student teachers) and approximately 120 students. Teachers in the unit work together to coordinate activities and to plan. One of the teachers in the team is designated as a team leader.

The staff is for the most part very hard-working. It is not unusual for a teacher to arrive at 7:30 A.M. and leave after 4:30. All teachers instruct from 8:30 to 3:30, with a half an hour lunch break and either one or two "free" periods where students go to special classes, such as art, gym, music, and so on.

The physical structure of the school is open. The Instructional Media Center (IMC) is in the middle of the building and the unit areas around the periphery. There are few interior walls, and from the IMC one can see all the activity going on in the unit areas.

The school has modern, high quality facilities. The floors are carpeted, walls brightly colored; there are new desks; the IMC has an excellent supply of books, and audiovisual equipment and curricular and office supplies are plentiful.

The curriculum used at Meadow School, in almost all areas, allows for an individualized rate of learning by using a curricular form with predetermined, sequentially laid out objectives and pre- and post-tests. For example, in math a student starting at the beginning of the year takes a pre-test for the first predetermined objective of the course. If the student passes this test, a second one, relating to the second predetermined objective, is given. If he or she fails this pre-test, the student works through activities suggested by a booklet, after which he or she takes a post-test. Upon passing the post-test the student proceeds to the next pre-test, where the process starts all over. The math, science, language arts, and social-studies programs at Meadow School all use this curricular form. Although such areas as art and gym do not, as yet, the principal has stated that he hopes they will do so in the future.

The Effect of Reforms

Control

Reviewing data collected on teachers' work at Meadow School, I did not find one example of an administrator or even a team leader telling a staff member that something *had* to be done. Although it is possible that these sorts of interactions could have gone unnoticed, data suggest that direct control played a minor role in influencing teachers' work. Instead, it was observed that the curricular form was one of the prime factors in influencing teacher behavior. This curricular form controlled teachers by limiting their flexibility in determining what to teach. In describing it, a teacher of unit 5 said:

> It's definable in that it has the objectives there for the content of what you are teaching; from that point of view you would have little flexibility in your goals of teaching.

These sentiments were reiterated by another teacher:

> Occasionally you're looking at the end of the book at what the unit is going to be. These are the goals that you have to obtain, that the children are going to be tested on. That may affect your teaching in some way, in that you may bypass other learning experiences simply to obtain the goal. These goals are going home to parents. It's a terrible thing to do, but parents like to see 90s and 100s rather than 60s on skills.

It should be noted that having control embedded in the curricular form is different from separating those who conceptualize from those who execute. For if teachers were controlled simply by the separation of conception and execution, then in situations where teachers both conceptualized and executed the curriculum there should be an absence or decline in control. The social-studies curriculum used at Meadow School provides an example of how teachers can be controlled even when conceptualization and execution are united.

The social-studies program had a curricular form that broke down learning into a set of predetermined objectives. For example, one objective stated: "The student will discover that the period of Industrialization was a time of rapid and great change in the production of goods." After passing the post-test for that objective the student would go on to the next predetermined objective. These objectives, as opposed to those in the math course, were conceptualized not by "experts" but by the teachers themselves. This curricular form, however, even given the unity of conceptualization and execution, puts limits on teachers's work for several reasons.

One reason is that the objectives and suggested activities were predetermined and interwoven in sequential order. This meant that changing an objective or developing new activities required a significant amount of extra effort. Given the intensity and pace of work at Meadow School, it is not surprising that many teachers relied on and used the objectives and activities embedded in the curricular form. Furthermore, any change in an objective or activity affected not only a single class of students but the entire team. This created the need to standardize these activities and objectives among teachers working with a particular skill so that all the students within a team could work through the same material and have an equal chance on the post-test. Therefore, even if teachers were willing to put in the extra effort to change an objective, this change would have to be discussed and approved by other teachers.

The curricular form also constrained teachers because, in many cases, the objective being taught had been developed by another teacher. Teachers who had not contributed objectives or tried to relate them to practice at the time of the development of the curriculum were responsible nevertheless for executing these objectives so that as many students as possible would obtain mastery. Since they had no input into the process of curriculum development, such teachers did not always agree with the objectives or the associated practice. An example may clarify this point. One of the topics developed by teachers for the social-studies program concerned the Industrial Age. The particular objective of the lesson I observed was: "The student will discover that the period of Industrialization was a time of rapid and great change in the production of goods." The activity that was used in class to meet this objective was a fun-filled, practical event in which the teacher, with the students' help, demonstrated how, if the class broke down all the functions necessary to make a peanut butter and chocolate on graham cracker dessert, the dessert would be made more efficiently than if each person made a complete dessert and everyone would eat sooner. This seemed to meet the stated objective, in that the assembly-line approach provided an example of how the Industrial Revolution changed the nature of the production of goods. In an interview I had with this teacher after class she seemed satisfied with the lesson. She thought the students understood that the assembly line could increase production and that it was a prominent feature of the production process during the Industrial Revolution. Although the teacher could feel satisfied that her practice met the stated objective of the lesson, some of the implications of the lesson were not illuminated by the teacher's practice. The assembly line does more than simply increase the quantity of goods. It also affects workers' autonomy and craftmanship, as well as enabling industrialists to make larger profits from the deskilled repetitious work done by those on the assembly line. Why were these theoretical implications not realized in the teacher's practice?

One possible explanation is that the teacher was unaware of these implications or did not want to include them. This teacher was aware of these implications, however, but she suggested that her primary job in teaching social studies was to give students the information they would need to do well on the post-test.

This example suggests that even though teachers conceptualized and executed the program, their work was limited primarily to execution, because of the influence of the post-test, the difficulty in changing objectives, and the separation of those who conceptualized the objective from those who taught it.

In trying to understand the constraints imposed by the curricular form in relation to constraints affecting other workers, Edwards's notion of technical control is useful. Edwards argues that, with the technology developed during the Industrial Revolution, work was primarily controlled by the physical structure of the labor process. Although curricular form is not physical in the way that a machine is, both teachers and other workers seem to be constrained more by the characteristics of what they use to do their work—whether this is a machine or a curricular organization—than by the "direct" influence of management. For this reason, the category of technical control accurately describes the constraints imposed on teachers by their use of a particular curricular form and suggests that teachers are affected in similar ways to other workers employed in structures influenced by advanced technologies. Yet, as was true of other workers, teachers did not always passively accept these limitations on their work.

One specific response of teachers to the limitations embedded in the curricular form used at Meadow School was to rework programs. An example of this occurred in the science program. Teachers were dissatisfied with this program because they felt that some of the objectives were inappropriate and that the materials to be used with the program were ineffective. Consequently, teachers developed new objectives, as well as suggesting and designing new materials to be used with the program.

Teachers also responded to constraints in the curricular form by cancelling a subject area for a period of time. Specifically, teachers using the Science Research Association (SRA) reading kit and the individualized spelling program deviated from this program at least once a week. For instance, teachers might have SRA reading or individualized spelling for two days, and then take a day off. These "gaps" also occurred in math. Occasionally a team would decide to abandon the entire math program for a time and allow teachers to work with their homeroom students in an area of the teacher's choice. In one case when the math program was halted, a teacher who had an interest in birds did a fascinating unit on bird recognition, migration patterns, and the general characteristics of local species.

These examples suggest that although teachers did not respond to constraints in powerful or blatant ways, they could actively confront curriculum constraints by reworking or cancelling for a time the use of the individualized curricular form.

Relations With Students

In addition to providing new modes for control, the curricular form used at Meadow School made it likely that teachers would spend a large part of their time trying to contend with the ever-increasing line of students waiting to see if they had mastered a particular objective, could take a post-test, or had correctly solved the problems in the workbook. What effect did this "technical" priority have on teacher/student relations?

The emphasis on the "technical" aspects of work limited a teacher's ability to use his or her personal knowledge to influence a student's learning direction. Often, when a student came up to the teacher, the objective to be covered, the problems to be solved, and the post-test to be taken had been predetermined. The priorities and guidelines predetermined by the curricular form were the central mechanism for teacher/student relations, making it difficult, in many cases, for a teacher to appropriately interact with a student.

Another consequence of the "technical" nature of work is that the influence teachers could have on less motivated students was limited because it was difficult to keep a close watch on students working independently while trying to cope with those waiting in line to have their work or tests checked and recorded. These limitations "disconnected" the personal impact of a teacher on what a student learned. Although this "disconnection" is clearly less extreme than that experienced by, for example, assembly line workers from their product, there does seem to be a similarity in the *type* of impact between product and producer.

As was true of others affected by labor reforms, teachers did not simply accept this "disconnecting" limitation. One example of resistance was observed during a spelling period where a teacher was so busy trying to keep up with the never-ending line of students waiting to have work marked or evaluated that she was clearly frustrated. When the frustration reached a certain level, the teacher simply stood up and told the students to put their work away and gather as a group. When they had done so, she asked, "What would you like to know about me?" By changing the curricular direction in this way, the teacher minimized the effect of curricular form on her relations with students, and emphasized the personal relations between them.

Teachers also responded to the "disconnection" of their influence on students by limiting the amount of time for teaching a certain subject. Specifically, almost all the teachers on one team openly expressed a dislike for the language arts program, which used predetermined objectives with pre- and post-tests. Their dislike stemmed from the routine nature of the program and their perception of the inappropriateness of some of the objectives. Yet they could not abandon this program, because it was used throughout the school. Furthermore, because the program used computer-managed instruction, teachers were under pressure to meet *all* the predetermined objectives. Despite these limitations teachers minimized the impact of the curricular form by using the program for the least amount of time that still allowed them to get through a majority of the objectives.

Although these resistances do not have the same effect as workers shutting down the assembly line, they do show that teachers do not simply accept changes in their roles with students, and that they can influence to a degree the effect of these changes. These actions also suggest that responses to constraints are not necessarily progressive and can act in contradictory ways. For example, it is possible that by limiting the amount of time for the language arts program, the teachers would come to accept it, and any constraints embedded within it. In this way, their response may actually perpetuate the constraints found in the curriculum.

Skills

The school structure at Meadow School also affected teachers' skills, in that areas of expertise were either encouraged or discouraged by the school structure. For example, if the use of teams makes it difficult for a teacher to use a particular expertise, this process may be considered to be deskilling. Conversely, if the team structure encourages or obliges a teacher to use particular expertise, this may be considered as reskilling. Therefore, the use or disuse of expertise in practice is a key to analyzing changes in teachers' skills.

One skill that teachers at Meadow School rarely had a chance to use was in the conceptualization of a curricular activity. This constraint was directly related to the curricular form that prescribed the objectives that teachers were to follow, leaving teachers primarily with the role of executing objectives conceptualized by others.

Although teachers did respond to their relative inability to use conceptualization skills, there is evidence to suggest that this did not significantly increase the use of this skill. One indication of this was that the minutes of team meetings were dominated by execution and scheduling questions, while conceptual issues were rarely raised. For example, teachers often discussed the amount of time a particular math objective would take up, but never in any of the minutes of team meetings analyzed did they address the problem of what objectives they should be teaching or the implication of the objectives currently used. This suggests that the conceptualization of curricular activities was either not thought to be important enough to discuss at team meetings, or was not a major part of the work required of the team of teachers.

A further source of evidence that teachers rarely had the opportunity to conceptualize comes from a close investigation of the work schedule of one of the observed teams. The teaching day for all teams at Meadow School officially started at 8:30 A.M. and ended at 2:50 P.M. For the team observed, approximately an hour and three quarters of that time was "noncontact." This was the time that students were at special classes, at lunch, or at recess. This left approximately four and a half hours of teacher instruction. In the areas of language arts, science, spelling, and math there was almost no opportunity for teachers to conceptualize, because those programs had predetermined objectives (or content, in the case of spelling). Although in other subject areas, such as social studies and reading, teachers had more opportunities to conceptualize learning activities, as was mentioned previously the pace of work limited the time teachers had to conceptualize activities, and the use of post-tests encouraged teachers to concentrate on getting students to master an objective rather than think about what the objective should be. In practice, then, teachers taught in ways based on their own conceptualization for less than an hour and three-quarters (the time allotted for social studies and reading) out of the four and a half hours of instruction time per day.

The lack of opportunity teachers had to work on their own conceptualizations, along with the indication that conceptual questions did not appear in the minutes of team meetings, is strong evidence that teachers rarely used this skill. This deskilling process affected what happened at Meadow School by allowing, for the most part, persons not in direct contact with a specific group of students to make curricular decisions for that group.

Teachers were also limited in their ability to use creative skills by the school structure, which encouraged teachers' work to become predominantly routine and specified, or noncreative. This was so because the challenge of the workday (or week) was to get through the required number of objectives. In the words of one teacher, describing an objective she was working on: "I just want to get his done. I don't have time to be creative or imaginative."

Furthermore, since the demands of the curricular form increased the amount of time teachers spent recording, checking, and organizing students' work, teachers had fewer opportunities to work with the curriculum in other ways. For example, during math a teacher typically spent half the period correcting and recording students' work. If teachers were relieved from some of these requirements, they would have more time to construct math games for less motivated students, develop new approaches to master a math concept, develop integrated math activities, and either explore new objectives or refine some of the present objectives. Although these activities might not fit every possible definition of creativity, there is little doubt that they require more creative energy than do the "technical" responsibilities imposed on teachers by the curricular form. It must be stressed that the limitations on the use of creative activities do not imply that teachers lacked creative talent, but rather that to be "effective" in the school, other abilities generally not considered creative were given priority.

As well as creating this deskilling process the work structure also had the effect of creating situations where teachers were obliged to use certain abilities quite often and, therefore, reskilled teachers. One such skill was in bureaucratic tasks, such as checking post-tests, recording scores, and regrouping students.

The need to develop bureaucratic skills occurred because each teacher was involved with 130 students who were constantly being grouped and regrouped because of the individualized nature of the curriculum. The importance of bureaucratic skills was indicated by the number of agenda items at team meetings that asked questions such as, "How can we regroup students after a mastery test?" "How can we organize our reading program so students can go to swimming lessons?" "What will the 'late recess' do to our math program?" "How can we organize our afternoons to integrate the use of student 'helpers?' " Although not every teacher displayed the same expertise, these examples suggest that the priorities of the school structure necessitated the use of these bureaucratic skills. Consequently, teachers would probably use them more often at Meadow School than at a school that assigned 30 students to a teacher and did not use a curriculum that required the grouping and regrouping of students.

Teachers at Meadow School also needed to get a specific number of objectives covered in a specified time. This need to be "focused" resulted from the coordination required by the team, which made it necessary for all teachers to change classes at specified times. If a class ran late, other groups of students would be either held up or they would come rushing into the class still in session. The importance of being "focused" became quite evident for teachers just coming into the school. "The hardest thing for me to get used to from having all the time to myself (as in the self-contained classroom) to teaming was thinking small enough so that you could teach and zero in on the class and get it done in a period of time."

In one case, an intern who was considered outstanding by the team was criticized for either finishing the lessons too soon or running over the allotted time. In trying to cope with this criticism the intern struggled to complete a lesson in the required time. The rewards were obvious from her evaluations:

> Excellent time—half an hour was perfect for this lesson.

> Timing—very good.

These comments suggest that the priorities of the work structure were communicated to the intern, and her attention and practices became concentrated on this aspect of teaching. The need of teachers to concentrate on accomplishing a number of objectives in a specified time indicates that they were reskilled in this area.

As in any classroom, teachers at Meadow School spent a great deal of time on classroom control. The need to work on developing control of the class was especially important in Meadow School because of the open-area design, which allowed noise from one learning area to spread to the surrounding classes. A lesson taught by a new intern provides an example.

It became obvious that the noise from the intern's room was creating difficulties for the neighboring teacher. Not only were the students distracted by this noise, but it was difficult to hear the teacher's instructions or the students' answers. This made the discussion move at a painfully slow rate, annoying the teacher. Later, the teacher—in the nicest way possible—approached the intern about the implications of the noise in her class. The teacher's arguments about the need for quiet classes were not based on personal preference or on how much control she thought a teacher should have; rather she used the argument that a degree of quiet is *needed* in the open-area design if each class is to be able to function effectively. The teacher's argument obliged the intern to move toward asserting greater control over her students. Thus, in this case, the need to develop skills in classroom control depended, at least in part, on the physical structure of the school.

In analyzing the effect of the school structure on teachers' skills, the arguments put forth by Aronowitz, Edwards, and Benson seem helpful.[15] They claim that with industrialization and subsequent labor reforms, workers were not simply deskilled, as was argued by Braverman, but were actually both deskilled and reskilled.[16] This process accurately describes the effect of school structure on teachers, suggesting a similarity between workers outside the field of education and teachers.

Relations With Other Teachers

Meadow School's work structure also influenced relations among teachers. The use of teams influenced teachers' relations by making them more likely to view themselves as a group. It became clear after several months of observation that while some teams did not communicate well, most teams took on a singular identity. The development of this group identity was reflected in some of the minutes from team meetings:[17]

> *We* are in charge of November birthday party, be thinking of good ideas for food and activities.

> *We will* be listeners for morning poems sharing time.

> *We'll do* our "sharing skit" the afternoon of in-service. (Emphasis mine)

Teachers showed their awareness of certain group identities by referring to the "discipline" team, the "science" oriented team, or the "open" team. These identities came about not only because the team structure encouraged the standardization of rules, and consensus decision-making, but also because the team structure made it likely that teachers on a team would plan together and eat together.

While the team structure promoted collective relations among teachers at the team level, other aspects of the school structure, including the curriculum, encouraged competition and noninteraction between groups.

One reason for this was that the work structure made it likely that teachers would have to compete over issues of educational autonomy. A common issue involved a team's ability to determine the scope of objectives to be taught during the year. Conflicts occurred because if one team did not cover the predetermined number of objectives for the year, or covered too many objectives, this affected the team that would teach the students the following year. Although all the teams were in this predicament, it was not uncommon for one team to view problems in this area as resulting from the position of another team.

> We're so happy Unit II has agreed not to watch "2¢ worth" or "wordshop." We'll offer options to the kids who have already seen it.

> Is Unit II still using the skillroom from 9:40 to 10:15? We sure could use it!

> Unit III was unable to come to a compromise in meeting with Unit II regarding recess time change, so Unit III will have to go with early recess and early P.E. classes cutting into reading. Hopefully, we'll be able to plan with related arts so we don't have the problem again. We did check plan books and we have had to send kids to 8:20 P.E. since 1974 except for the year at the church. We must come up with something better for the kids.

We feel that Unit II should not do D level but instead plug in comprehension, study skills, to enrich, work on punctuality, sentence structure and paragraph writing.

These examples show that the school structure can create situations which encourage teams to compete in trying to retain their autonomy over scheduling.

Another reason for the noninteraction between teams was that the work structure limited communication. Specifically, the design of the building meant that teams were dispersed, and even when they could get together during lunch, the existence of two separate lunch areas and varying lunch schedules made interteam communication and interaction difficult.

The nature of the relations between groups had a significant influence on how teachers responded to constraints. The noninteractive nature of teams diverted attention from the fact that all teachers were affected by the limits imposed on their work by the school structure (such as the need for precise scheduling, coordination of the scope of curriculum, or use of space), minimized their likely response to structural constraints, and, therefore, strengthened the effect of the school structure on their work. On the other hand, the collective consciousness of teachers within teams *helped* teachers be aware of and act on some constraints, as exemplified by one team's response to a consultant who was selling computer-managed instruction. The team rejected the consultant's pressure to teach certain study skills, arguing that they would be difficult to teach and unnecessary. By responding as a team they not only created a strong response, but avoided having individual teachers pointed out as the reason why the skills were not taught. The team structure, in other words, gave teachers a greater potential ability to minimize the constraints imposed by the overall school structure.

This pattern of collective interaction at the team level and competitive noninteraction between groups strongly supports Gallie's contention that with advanced rationalized work structures the potential for worker collectivity occurs alongside the separation of groups of workers at the same level. What both this case study and Gallie's descriptive study of an automated oil refinery found was that although workers had opportunities to interact socially and work together at the team level, there was little interaction at the plant level (that is, between teams) because teams were in competition for various "rewards." In the case of teachers, the "rewards" dealt with their ability to control the scope of the curriculum and the scheduling of the day, while workers in Gallie's study competed for higher status and jobs with greater salary. This suggests that teachers, as was true of many other workers, may be given an opportunity to act as a group on the team level, but are discouraged from relating collectively at the "plant level."

The Influence of School Structure on Teachers' Roles

Teachers can influence the values, attitudes, and perspectives of students. This influence can be in any direction from helping students function in society as it presently exists (reproductive influence) to helping them to question and transform societal relations (transformative influence).[19] In analyzing the roles teachers play, this discussion will not deal with the question of motivation, focusing instead on the feasibility of teachers acting in particular ways, regardless of what their motivation might be.

Teachers can view their roles in at least two significantly different ways. One way is concerned with questions of efficiency and implementation. The other is to look critically at the curriculum form and content, thereby questioning what is and making judgments about what should be. Those who view their role primarily in terms of efficiency and implementation will act to facilitate the values and attitudes embodied in the curriculum form and content, because they do not consider confronting values to be part of their job. Those who investigate the curriculum in terms of what is and what should be have the potential to question and present alternatives to curriculum values and attitudes because this *is* part of their job. Since the questioning of curricular values and the determination of alternatives are prerequisites for one who wants to act in transformative ways, they must be included in the work of teachers for them to have a transformative influence. Given that teachers' beliefs can fall anywhere between these two foci, what influence, if any, has the school structure at Meadow School had on them?

One factor militating against teachers critically analyzing the curriculum and providing alternative conceptions is that what they teach is predetermined by the curricular form used at the school. Their main function is to facilitate the curriculum, not question what is or what should be. The social-studies lesson mentioned previously that dealt with the topic of the assembly line is a case in point. The values, attitudes, and knowledge presented were greatly influenced by the predetermined post-test. The teacher's job was to facilitate good scores on the post-test, not to question the values, attitudes, and knowledge embedded in the lesson. Although teachers did respond to the constraints put on their ability to conceptualize, and certainly were not eliminated from the conceptualization process, the curricular form used at the school made it difficult for them to significantly influence thinking about what is to be taught.

Therefore, the use of a curricular form with predetermined, sequentially ordered objectives made it likely that teachers would act to facilitate the perspectives found in the curriculum instead of providing alternatives. There were few curricular areas where teachers *could* act in transformative ways.

Teachers at Meadow School were somewhat "disconnected" from the students because of their involvement with bureaucratic tasks such as checking and recording post-tests. This made it difficult for them to use their personal knowledge to relate to students, leaving them less opportunity to confront the priorities and values that filtered through the curriculum. This could only minimize their ability to act in a transformative way.

The fact that some skills were encouraged and others discouraged also had an effect on the way teachers influenced students. Dewey argues that action that occurs without reflection is guided by an "external attention."[20] This "external attention" is more likely to accommodate reality than try to transform it because there is no reflective growth or understanding of what makes reality the way it is. Without considering how or why reality is formed, one is unlikely to change it. Teachers at Meadow School were deskilled in the area of conceptualization, and thus discouraged from reflecting on their practice. On the other hand, they were reskilled in areas such as focused teaching, organization, and classroom management, all of which help further an objective or curricular idea. The priorities given to the development of particular skills at Meadow School suggest that teachers were encouraged to act without reflection.

The perspective encouraged by the work structure narrowed teachers' role so that it was difficult for them to ask questions about how reality is or should be constructed. This narrow focus made it more likely that they would accomodate school reality as opposed to trying to transform it.

The way that relations between teachers was structured also influenced the role of teachers in the school. One factor influencing what teachers do in the classroom is the power they have to act in ways that might be considered unacceptable by others (the administration, for example). The school structure at Meadow School encouraged collective relations at the team level, which increased the teachers' ability to gain autonomy over what is taught. The school structure, however, also encouraged a competitive noninteraction between teams. These divisions at the staff level made it difficult for teachers to see the commonality of their positions and instead made it likely that they would compete over issues of teacher autonomy, minimizing the power they could have by acting collectively at the staff level.

How do these influences affect teachers' ability to act in reproductive or transformative ways? If teachers have little or no power or autonomy, the attitudes, values and perspectives currently held in curriculum programs are likely to have a dominant influence on students. Although this powerlessness may not be reproductive, it does diminish the teachers' opportunities to provide alternative perspectives: if they had a significant amount of power and autonomy, they would have a greater opportunity to present alternative attitudes and perspectives. Reviewing all the data about Meadow School, it seems clear that this type of school structure encouraged teachers to act in ways more likely to help reproduce dominant societal relations than to transform them. There are contradictory influences, however. The collective relations encouraged on the team level along with the indication that teachers did not passively accept limitations imposed by the school structure suggests that school structure cannot totally determine the role teachers will play in influencing society. Teachers always retain *some* autonomy. The future role of teachers in helping to reproduce or transform societal relations will depend both on the school structures we build and teachers' responses to those structures.

Notes

1. See Samuel Bowles and Herbert Gintis, *Schooling in Capitalist America* (New York: Basic Books, 1976).

2. Raymond Williams, *Marxism and Literature* (Oxford: Oxford University Press, 1977).

3. Jean Anyon, "Social Class and School Knowledge," *Curriculum Inquiry* 11 (January, 1981):3–42.

4. Michael Apple, *Ideology and Curriculum* (London: Routledge and Kegan Paul, 1979).

5. Paul Willis, *Learning to Labour* (Westmead: Saxon House, 1977).

6. James R. Bright, *Automation and Management* (Boston: Pergamon, 1958), p. 188.

7. Richard Edwards, *Contested Terrain* (New York: Basic Books, 1979), p. 117.

8. Robert Hoxie, *Scientific Management and Labor* (New York: Kelley, 1918), p. 131–32.

9. Edwards, *Contested Terrain*, p. 109.

10. James Ehrenreich and Barbara Ehrenreich, "Work and Consciousness," *Monthly Review* 28 (1976): 13.

11. David Gallie, *In Search of the New Working Class* (London: Cambridge University Press, 1978), p. 7.

12. See Michael Burawoy, "The Politics of Production and the Production of Politics," *Political Power and Social Theory* (forthcoming).

13. See Michael Burawoy, "Towards a Marxist Theory of the Labour Process," *Politics and Society* 8 (1979): 1–77, about the effects of workers' resistance on factories using scientific management.

14. Examples of programs using a curriculum with predetermined objectives are Individual Guided Education (IGE) schools (about 3,500 schools nation-

wide), Individually Prescribed Instruction (IPI) and Goal Based Educational Management Systems (GEMS). Furthermore, teaching has been explicitly stated to be a central component of the Middle School.

15. For a discussion of the impact of work structures on the deskilling, reskilling process see Stanley Aronowitz, *False Promises* (New York: McGraw-Hill, 1973).

16. Harry Braverman, *Labor and Monopoly Capital* (New York: Monthly Review Press, 1974).

17. It is important to point out that although the team structure promoted a group consciousness, this did not eliminate the competitive nature of teachers within a team. Competitive or individualistic consciousness coexisted with the group identity.

18. Gallie, *In Search of the New Working Class*, p. 7.

19. In claiming that teachers affect the way students are socialized, I am not implying that they are the only or determining factors. Teachers influence students along with family, peer groups, media, and so on.

20. For a discussion of an "external attention" see Archambault, *On Dewey in Education* (Chicago: University of Chicago Press, 1964), p. 319.

CHAPTER 9

Becoming Clerical Workers:
Business Education and
the Culture of Femininity

LINDA VALLI

The purpose of this chapter is to map out the relation between the ideological messages of a high-school office education program regarding appropriate sex roles and gendered subjectivity, and the cultural orientations of a group of primarily working-class girls.[1] The chapter delineates the ways in which the young women acquire a basically feminine work identity, the role of the school program in strengthening that identity, and the manner in which educational practices can reinforce or contribute to the reproduction of a sexually divided labor force, in which men and women not only fill different occupations, but have different relations to wage and domestic labor as well.[2]

Since boys generally select themselves out of vocational preparation for office work before their high-school years, I was not able to study the gender-based occupational selection process.[3] I focus exclusively on the production and reproduction of gender-related meanings, behaviors, and orientations that make up the world of the office worker.

Although this chapter falls into the broad category of the study of socialization processes, I attempt to avoid a basic flaw of that approach. I do not presume that the messages that are taught or transmitted to students are the ones that are received or accepted. This assumption creates a model of the world that is far more static than reality, and produces agents who are passive recipients of their own "internalized structures." Following the models of Willis and McRobbie, I reject this concept of socialization, replacing it with a notion of cultural orientations that implies involvement by individuals and groups in the ongoing creation of their own identities, in a way that is neither mechanistic nor wholly voluntaristic, but is rooted in their social and economic pasts and in their perceived futures.[4]

Three general relations to cultural reproduction processes seem possible: acceptance, negotiation, and resistance.[5] Although it is difficult to predict which relationships will be chosen, certain factors appear to structure the choices. Acceptance of specific aspects of culture (in this situation, gender-related work aspects) tends to occur when these messages are congruent with the past and the perceived future, and when no alternatives are perceived. Negotiation and resistance, both of which imply rejection of the cultural messages and practices, occur when there is an element of incongruity, when the culture is experienced as imposed, when it does not fit with a sense of self. Negotiation will be the chosen course of action when the individual or group perceives some element of control or power over the situation, and when the struggle seems worth the effort. Resistance is chosen when, from the participants' point of view, there is no room to negotiate. In this particular context, overt resistance can take such varied forms as saying no to a directive given by a boss or teacher, entering into argumentation, or quitting a job. Covert or hidden resistance is the chosen course of action when the person or group involved is unwilling to bear the consequences of overt resistance, consequences such as being fired. Hidden resistance looks like passive acceptance only to the outsider.

As the details of this ethnographic study suggest, the ideological messages the students received were fairly congruent with the gender-specific patterns and relations they had become accustomed to both in their homes and at school. Their primary mode of behavior, therefore, was to accept, almost to fall naturally and spontaneously into, a sexual division of labor and the subordinate roles for women it implies. In the process of elaborating their lives at work, the students utilized a fairly conventional culture of femininity that identified them not as raw labor power, but as sex objects, on the one hand, and as office wives and mothers, on the other. In so doing, they partially realized (in the dual sense of created and were aware of) their double subordination, in domestic labor and in wage labor. But because this awareness was only partial, and because they saw no alternative, they tended to fantasize an ideal future in which they worked part time and stayed home part time, regardless of the fact that this solution would only strengthen their subordination, keeping them dependent on a male provider and condemning them to low-level positions in the job market.[6]

This chapter develops by giving a brief account of the methodology employed in the study, and descriptions of the cooperative office education program, the teacher, and the students upon which it is based. The main part of the chapter is devoted to an account of those parts of the program that emphasized a work identity that was gender specific, the ways in which the students dealt with those messages, and the implications of those practices.

Methodology

The analysis presented here is based on an ethnographic study of a cooperative office education program, a vocational program in which senior high students go to school part time and work part time in an office. This methodology was selected because I was interested in analyzing the processes of cultural transmission. I focused on a group of senior high-school students who were being prepared for office work because I was primarily concerned with women's acquisition of a work identity. Since office occupations employ the largest single group of the female labor force, and since many of the areas are currently expanding, office education was the compelling choice for this study.

The data were collected during the 1980–81 school year. The site was a comprehensive, urban high school, which I will call Woodrow High, in a Midwestern city. I was present at Woodrow from September through June on approximately half the school days, scattered throughout the year. Three related techniques were used to collect the data: participant observation in the school and at work (fourteen sites in all); formal and informal interviewing, throughout the year, of significant subjects (for example, teachers, students, supervisors, alumnae and coworkers); and analysis of curricular materials and other related documents. These techniques allowed me to study the transmission of ideological messages and to understand why students accepted, negotiated, or resisted attempts to socialize them in certain ways.

In addition to sixteen students, I interviewed seventeen alumnae: ten from the previous graduating class and seven from the years 1972 to 1979. My goal was threefold: to obtain more information on family backgrounds and influences, since I had no direct contact with parents; to collect reflective accounts of their decision to take, and their experiences within, cooperative office education; and to obtain information on work life and perspectives after high school. I anticipated that these accounts would both confirm and elaborate upon the information I was gathering from my work within the school, and this expectation was realized.

The Program

Cooperative education is a specific form of vocational education, that, unlike most educational programs, which take place primarily within school buildings, alternates work experience with school experience. Students receive help in finding career-related jobs and are to receive on-the-job, as well as classroom, training. The implicit rationale of the program is that the work site is a valuable source of learning and should

be utilized as an educational tool. The stated expectation is that cooperative education will help students identify their career objectives, that this
identification will lead to appropriate training in attitudes, skills, and
knowledge, and that the training will lead to careers. These careers are
then supposed to create a better community, a community that will
"experience a productive growth of its citizens, schools and businesses."

The cooperative office education program at Woodrow High was organized in a fairly typical manner. During their senior year, students who
selected the program attended classes in the morning and worked for
three to four and a half hours in the afternoon. They received both one
school credit and pay for their work. Both students and teacher believed
that at least two credits should be given for work. In their behavior and in
their conversations with me, work was a far more salient aspect of the
cooperative experience than what went on in the classroom.

Students were supposed to carry three morning classes in addition to
the "related" office education class, which was specifically designed to
relate to their afternoon work experience. This class was scheduled to
meet five times a week for forty minutes each day. Students would often
miss class, excused or not, but would report for work that afternoon.
Four times a year, the teacher (referred to here as Mrs. Shapiro) met with
each supervisor for a student evaluation session. Within a day or two,
Mrs. Shapiro would then meet with each student in her private office to
discuss the evaluation.

While a full analysis of cultural reproduction mechanisms would have
to take all aspects of the curriculum into consideration, it should be
apparent from the above description that in this particular context too
much attention to the formal corpus of knowledge would distort rather
than illuminate the ideological messages actually conveyed and received.
The fact is that although most of the formal syllabus was organized
around the teaching of particular skills (for example, how to reconcile a
checkbook, how to fill out tax forms, how to type using a dictaphone, how
to proofread), in actual practice little class time was devoted to concentrated work in these areas, and the development of these skills was not
the primary concern of either the teacher or the students. During interviews with the teacher, the students, and the graduates, the same refrain
was consistently repeated.

> I don't attempt to teach much in the class because, unlike the other city
> high schools, we have a junior prerequisite. I'm also less demanding in
> this class than in my others because the students and I spend a long time
> together. I'm more relaxed in here because I want to build up personal
> relationships. I see myself as more in a counselor's role.
>
> —Mrs. Shapiro

The hour in school seemed wasted. We didn't discuss problems at work and what we were doing. That's what I thought it would be like—saying what problems we had at work and discussing what we could do about them.

—Kathryn '80

I don't think I'd want the class part again. I don't think it taught that much. I don't think there needs to be a class part. It doesn't help that much in the jobs most of us are in. I don't see the point of having it.

—Dorothy '81

My parents thought I was skipping when I got home early. They didn't believe she was letting us out, or that there was nothing to do.

—Jane '80

My contention is that the absence of a rigid syllabus created a gap, a space that was filled with incidental teaching and learning. The absence of an overt curriculum created a situation in which the messages students received from casual comments, relationships, school and work structures and practices were stronger than they would otherwise have been.

The Teacher

Mrs. Shapiro had been directing the program at Woodrow High for twelve years. She perceived herself and introduced herself as a feminist, as a person who believed in and worked toward women's equality with men, particularly in the business world. Having had parents who encouraged her to succeed just as much as they encouraged her brothers, Mrs. Shapiro belonged to numerous professional and women's organizations, and had a life history that was very much career oriented. She was married, the mother of two, and, at the time of the study, a recent grandmother.

Mrs. Shapiro was quite verbal about her feminism. On the bulletin board in her office was the saying "All discrimination against all women must be removed" and Erica Jong's poem "Woman Enough." When the principal distributed the faculty roster, she confronted him over the asterisks placed after the names of married women. A new roster was distributed the next day with the asterisks removed. During class time, she told the students she considered the term "Gentlemen" to be an inappropriate salutation since the unknown addressees could be women and, during a filing unit, she told the class that the formulation "Mrs. John Smith" was incorrect, that a woman always kept her own first name.

Because of Mrs. Shapiro's feminist orientation, this case study should be one of the strongest in testing the school's role in the reproduction of a culture of femininity in the labor force and the reinforcement of traditional, sex-typed work orientations. Since gender-related occupational training definitely and explicitly occurred in this situation, I infer that it also occurs in a large percentage of other office education programs in secondary schools across the country.

The Students

Although an elite subdivision is within its catchment area and it draws its students from a wide range of social class backgrounds, Woodrow High is located in the industrial part of town and is basically considered a working-class high school. The seniors who elected cooperative office education did not seem any different from their female counterparts who did not. A few were unusually wealthy; a few were unusually bright. One of the graduates I interviewed was the valedictorian of her class. She went on to take the two-year Executive Secretary course at the community college. Some of the students went on to four-year universities, but the vast majority stayed in office work, occasionally supplementing their preparation with community college or on-the-job training.

Many of the students had mothers, and sometimes older sisters, who had worked in offices. This work was often done on a part-time basis, or had been returned to once families had been raised. Mothers who did not work in offices tended to be employed as sales clerks or cafeteria workers. The fathers of the students, on the other hand, generally had histories of full-time manual labor or civil-service work; most of them were loading-dock workers, mechanics, truck drivers, factory workers, or building custodians. A few students had fathers who were mail carriers or police officers; one father was a high-school teacher, and one was listed as an industrial engineer although he had never been to college.

The division of labor in the home as well as at the workplace basically followed the traditional sexual pattern. Although, for example, three students mentioned fathers who cooked for the family, in no instance did the activity flow out of a basic role identity. In one case, the mother had suffered a mental breakdown and had been institutionalized. The father, thereafter, assumed the role of housekeeper. In another instance, the father started sharing the responsibility for cooking with his high-school daughters after his wife had died. In the third instance, the father had been retired for some time because of disability. Gourmet cooking had become a hobby for him.

The usual pattern, however, was the mother-as-homemaker. Not even a working mother and retired father guaranteed that the father would partake in routine housekeeping chores. In these cases, the running of the vacuum cleaner once a week seemed to vindicate the father, in his own eyes at least.

But the fact that students came from homes with a traditional division of labor did not necessarily mean that these practices were automatically internalized. Some of the students had older sisters whose marriages did not follow the traditional pattern of their parents, others took child-development or other classes in school that raised the possibility of other marital patterns. One student, for instance, who tenaciously clung to a strict sexual division of wage labor ideology, arguing that "men are stronger than women and that's just the way it should be," simultaneously argued that men should help with everything in the house, although her own father did not, because that was the way her mother said it should be and that was what her brother-in-law did.

The reverse situation also obtained: some students envisioned a world in which women had better jobs than men without it being harmful to business or to personal relationships, and yet believed in the dominance of the man in the home. As one graduate put it,

> I like men paying for my food and opening doors for me. All this stuff about keeping your own name and being equal to your husband, I don't go for.
> —Jane '80

To a few of the students, there seemed to be a fairly clear distinction between gender relations in wage labor and those in personal relations and domestic labor; they saw no need for congruence between the two.

Such were the sex-role orientations with which the students began the cooperative office education program. Because of these orientations, the students were predisposed to accept a work world that men and women related to in naturally different manners. Their job training and work experiences reaffirmed this basic sexual division of labor ideology.

The Office Worker as Sex Object

Messages about sexual appearance and sexual behavior were integral elements of the students' office education training both at school and in the workplace. On the level of appearance and self-presentation, the young women were encouraged to emphasize and use their gender identities. But on the level of practice, when it came to actual behavior, they were warned to control their sexuality. The subtle message was that they would be blamed if sexual improprieties occurred at work.

In terms of their mode of self-presentation, students were informed in numerous ways of how important it was to cultivate a feminine, even provocative, appearance if they were serious about getting a job and being promoted once they had a job. Early in the school year, for instance, a woman from a job placement center spoke to the students about interviewing, stressing the importance of their appearance:

> Look professional. Your best source for that is *Glamour* magazine. It regularly runs sections for the professional woman: her image, what to wear, how to get a job. Dress like you already have the job, like you would to find a boyfriend. That's a good parallel. You have to attract someone.

Later that week, Mrs. Shapiro re-emphasized how important it was for the students to sell themselves at an interview. In encouraging them to listen calmly and collect their thoughts before they answered a question in order to organize their ideas and speak intelligently she used the phrase, "just like the finalists in the Miss America contest."

This association of job with sexual attraction was graphically depicted throughout the year by an advertisement on a classroom bulletin board. Although the overt purpose of the bulletin board display was to show examples of new office machines and technology, in so doing, it also presented a certain image of women office workers. The most striking example was the advertisement for Dictaphone's Dual Display Word Processor. In an attempt to encourage readers (presumably male managers) to purchase Dictaphone's new equipment, the creator of this advertisement cleverly equated obsolete office equipment with the Stone Age and used a photograph of a young, attractive woman clad only in a leopard skin to demonstrate the point. Because this picture was displayed without comment in a business classroom of a public school, it seems that an unspoken approval or legitimation of the image was necessarily conveyed.

The issue of appearance was also regularly discussed during Mrs. Shapiro's evaluation sessions with supervisors. Appearance was, in fact, one of the criteria on the formal student-trainee evaluation report, which included such items as quality and quantity of work, attitude, attendance, reliability. On the evaluation sheet, appearance was defined in a sex-neutral way as "neatness and personal care, appropriateness to the job." But in conversation Mrs. Shapiro often added a gender-specific element;

> You might do her a favor. She's a pretty girl. She could do a lot with herself and I don't think she's doing it. A lot of women in businesses are making appearance an important part of their day. She could capitalize on that.

She puts herself together very nicely. She was wearing some very sexy shoes the other day.

While not forbidden, clogs and slacks, particularly those cut like men's, which were the fashion at the time, were frowned upon. One supervisor talked about how her student-trainee had a figure for skirts, not slacks, how slacks put twenty pounds on her, and how you could see the look of disgust on the older men's faces when young women came to work dressed casually. Appearance, she said, was a definite factor in promotability, even for a woman who was extremely capable.

The accuracy of this perception was born out in the students' experiences with job placement. One student's difficulties in finding a job best highlight the employment obstacles some women are faced with. By the end of their first two weeks in the cooperative program all the students in the class had found jobs, except one. This student, Dorothy, stood out from the rest of the class in that she was overweight and, while always neat, dressed in old, inexpensive jeans, blouses, and shoes. Not until the end of the second month of school did Dorothy find a job. Unlike the other students, who all found afternoon jobs, Dorothy was hired for an evening shift in an assembly-line type department of a large insurance company with no public contact.

Mrs. Shapiro explained to me during those initial weeks that she was not able to place Dorothy very fast because her business background was slim and her appearance poor. In fact, however, Dorothy had more business background than many of the students in the class, had the third highest senior class rank among the cooperative office education students, and had taken a more rigorous academic program than the two students who were ranked ahead of her. In an eleventh grade standardized test, Dorothy had placed in the 99th percentile for math computation and in the 90th for math concepts. She was one of the fastest, most accurate typists in the class, and was the only student who took classroom work home to finish. The other students were apparently quick to perceive her capabilities, for they often went to her for help on their own work. It became clear that her mode of self-presentation was the only reason she was experiencing difficulty in finding a job.

One of the places to which Dorothy applied was a small bookstore, where she was turned down in favor of Cynthia, a tall, slender model-type. I was told later in the year by a graduate (a nice-looking, but plain, honor roll student who had also been rejected for the job in favor of a more attractive but less capable students) that the man in charge of hiring at the bookstore had a "penchant" for a certain type of female employee—blond and well built. Nor did this appear to be an isolated example. Mrs. Shapiro told the class that a bank employer called one day a few years back to complain that she was not sending him very pretty girls.

These examples indicate that there is not only a dual labor market, in which men and women fill different occupational categories, but that there is also a dual market within women's work. Apparently, not only are women primarily relegated to lower-level jobs, but certain types of women are excluded from the best of even these jobs.

Cultivation of a feminine appearance is only one aspect of the situation that women must deal with, for they must learn not only how to cultivate their femininity, but how to control it as well. Sheila Rowbotham makes this point in *Woman's Consciousness, Man's World*, when she says that a certain "contained sexuality" is required as part of the office worker's job.[7] Both Mrs. Shapiro and the students seemed to understand this requirement.

During a classroom discussion of a magazine article on the topic of sexual harassment this issue of "contained sexuality" arose. Mrs. Shapiro stressed the importance of an appropriate degree and type of sexual conduct on the job. While on the other occasions she had been subtly encouraging the students to present themselves with a certain amount of "sexiness," on this particular day she highlighted the importance of knowing what the limits should be if they wanted to avoid detrimental consequences. She told them they would be asking for abuse if they were too timid to control the situation or if they wore attire that was too skimpy, giving signals that they wanted to be noticed. She cautioned them to be aware of what they were communicating through their dress and bodies, indicating an awareness that their sexuality was not only something they could use to gain job benefits but was also something that could be used against them.

In order to make the most of opportunities on the job, then, young workers apparently have to be skilled not only in running typewriters and photocopiers, but in monitoring their sexuality and sexual lives as well. But in case workers do not internalize the "proper" sexual code, companies often have either formal or informal policies about social and sexual relations.

One personnel department, for example, discouraged employees from dating each other. If two employees married, one had to quit the job; that was official company policy. (The one who quit was generally the woman, of course, since she typically had the lower-paying job.)

Eleanor, a 1980 graduate, told the story of a bachelorette party for female employees held at a local bar. As part of the entertainment, a young male employee clad in bikini underwear and bow leapt out of a gift box during the course of the evening. He ended up quitting his job shortly thereafter because of the treatment he was receiving from his supervisor because of the incident, treatment that included a demotion.

Needless to say, students and employees did not always appreciate or accept attempts to control their sexual identities and practices. One student, for instance, explicitly rejected the "image of the secretary" that was conveyed to her. As she put it,

> Mrs. Shapiro had this obsession with secretaries looking gorgeous. Getting up at 5:00 in the morning to do their hair and nails. She taught us a lot about appearances, eye contact, interviews, dressing up. I thought that was good, but you don't have to put on all that make-up. Cleanliness is the important thing.
>
> —Jane '80

Most students, however, did not verbalize any opposition to suggestions that were made about their appearance. But in their nonverbal behavior, in the manner in which they actually dressed for work, there were indications that they, like many office workers, were not passively accepting imposed standards, but were negotiating and creating their own style. This style combined the popular men's cut slacks with open toed, spiked, "sexy" shoes. It was a definite blend of a unisex work look with a feminine social look, and appeared to be an attempt to control the issue of appearance while still emphasizing sexuality.

Resistance to company definition and control of their identities as women workers was also exemplified in a widely distributed cartoon graphic. The graphic simply added two words and a visual to the universal phone memo that is the staple of the secretary's office life. The originally staid and official memo thus read, "While you were out fucking off . . . " and displayed a naked boss "making it" with an extremely buxom nude woman. The term "fucking off" here obviously connotes both sexual intercourse and screwing around, having fun, wasting time, using company time for personal pleasure. It thus attacks both the sexual and the work identity of the boss, projecting onto him the demeaning identity women office workers feel is at times attributed to them.

But all in all, most of the students seemed to internalize definitions of themselves as women workers that took into account traditional notions of feminine appearance. Many of the reasons they could or could not imagine themselves doing certain jobs hinged on physical criteria.

> I would never be a mechanic. You get messy. I really like to fly and travel and I like to meet new people, but you have to have a lot of qualifications to be a stewardess. You have to be tall and skinny. They want you to be really perfect.
>
> —Kris '81

I'm not into all that liberated stuff. I still want to be pampered. I don't want muscles or to get dirty.

—Debbie '80

I thought of being an airline stewardess, but I weighed too much. You have to only weigh 120 or something.

—Jennifer '80

I can't imagine myself getting my hands all gooey, being sweaty and dirty all the time.

—Tanya '80

I wouldn't want to work in a garage—to be a mechanic. I wouldn't want to come home greasy.

—Priscilla '79

So, although there was some disagreement, resistance, and negotiation about the exact amount and type of "femininity" women office workers should cultivate and display, there was basic agreement on a more fundamental level. In general, a gender-specific, feminine appearance that could be contrasted to a masculine appearance was accepted and adopted.

This internalization of a gender-specific identity, an identity defined in many ways in relation to men, was strikingly evident in graffiti written on a sign posted on one of the company's bulletin boards. The sign announced "Fun and Games" at a Women's Christmas Party. The graffiti responded, "How can we have fun without men?" and "Who are we going to play games with?" While obviously acting to reject what they perceived to be the company's attempt to control their social and sexual lives, the women, at one and the same time, affirmed and reinforced their dependence on men. They could not visualize an identity, or even an activity, for themselves apart from a relation to men. What they appear to object to is not their subordination to men, but to interference from the company in the way they acted out that identity.

The Office Worker as Wife and Mother

A second way in which office work roles were linked to the students' gender identity was through an association of office work with domestic labor, either through the equation of the work with women's work in the home or through the subordination of their role in the office to their role in the home.

The observation has often been made that the role of women in the office parallels their role in the home: picking up after men; doing the daily, repetitive, tedious housekeeping tasks; and keeping men's lives organized and undisturbed, so they can concentrate on their important work. Quoting a 1935 *Fortune* magazine article, Margery Davies claims that male bosses preferred women over "pushy young men" as office workers because, as *Fortune* stated, women "are capable of making the offices a more pleasant, peaceful, and homelike place."[8] Taking on this kind of work, which has changed little in half a century, deepens women's wage labor identity as secondary and peripheral, for it patterns a gendered subjectivity already deeply etched into their day-to-day existence.

The objective structuring of these assymetrical roles, of male leading roles and female serving roles, was already so much taken for granted in the students' lives that they were unable to even perceive it. One young graduate told me that during high school "everyone wants to be a cheerleader." She naturally presumed that in this context I would know "everyone" meant "every girl," so that she did not have to make it explicit. In much the same way, the students took the sexual division of labor they found in their offices for granted. During an interview of a graduate who had worked in the same department of the same large corporation for almost two years, I asked her to mention the types of jobs that were filled by men, by women, or by both men and women. After reflecting for a few moments, she said,

> All of the big bosses are men. I've never noticed that before, but that's the way it is. And all the secretaries are females . . . and all the key punch operators are ladies. I've never thought of that before.
>
> —Eleanor '80

At another workplace, a student made daily mail runs, picking up and delivering mail to every office in the building. On the desk of each employee was a name plate. The typical nameplate for a female employee read, "Beth," "Jo," "Susie," or "Pat." The typical male employee's nameplate was "Mr. Mott," "Mr. Gleeson," or "Mr. J. L. Stone." When I brought the distinction to the student's attention it was again apparent it was something she had never really noticed; she said almost in passing,

> I don't think there is anything behind the difference. I think it's just a matter of preference.
>
> —Donna '81

The relation of the woman office worker's status to that of the male worker was objectified in the structure of the workplaces as well as in how the workers were addressed. Men often had offices that were private or closed off, in contrast to the public work areas of the women.[9] Even if women had their own desks, they were generally grouped together in a large, open space. About eight or nine of the places at which students worked were fairly large bureaucracies housed on more than one building level. Inevitably, when this was the case, status differentials were structured into the floor on which one's office was located. So, when referring to bosses, workers would naturally employ expressions like,

> I don't know if there are any ladies up there—up at the very top.
> —Dorothy '81

> One of the big bosses who sits upstairs is over him.
> —Eleanor '80

These linguistic expressions reinforce notions of superiority and inferiority that are so naturally linked with the English concepts of up/down, high/low, over/under, and top/bottom.

While the students often watched upper-level, male employees taking work home, having their work lives spill over into their home lives, so to speak, they usually saw the converse in the lives of the women with whom they worked. These women often worked only part-time so that they could see their children off to school in the mornings and be home before the school day ended. They often brought in candy or cookies to sell for their children's scout troop or hung home-made skeletons they had constructed in their role as den mother. Sometimes they had to take a temporary maternity leave or had to quit work altogether because they were no longer able to juggle working and child care, even though the family needed the money. One of the students vividly recalled how her mother was fired from her clerical job years before because she and her siblings kept walking over to her office (located just blocks from their home) to visit, ask questions, or get permissions.

In many ways, then, the identity of women office workers seems to be closely linked with their identity and work in the home. This was underscored for the students at the Appreciation Banquet given by the class in honor of their supervisors. The two main speeches were given by the teacher and by a retiring supervisor, Mrs. Carter, who was held in high esteem by coworkers, the teacher, and the numerous students whom she had supervised over the years. In both speeches, reference was made to the woman worker as mother. Mrs. Carter told the group:

> My first family was all raised and scattered around the country. I thought my parenting days were over. Then, six years ago, I began a second family. And in six years I've had forty-two offspring.

Mrs. Shapiro's speech was filled primarily with appreciative remarks to those at the banquet who had contributed to the success of the program. A special note of thanks was addressed to Mrs. Carter.

> They gained so much from being in your office. You became the mother at work that I was in school.

It is difficult to imagine male supervisors or teachers so naturally using paternal imagery in speaking about their work relationship to male apprentices.

Mrs. Shapiro also underscored her own identity as mother by knitting baby clothes during class time and used traditional notions about sex-appropriate behavior by advising the students not to express "emotionalism" if they wanted to rise up the corporate ladder, and not to shout, since "it's not ladylike." One of their texts warned them not to "chit-chat" during the workday, since it wasted their employer's dollars.

Another teaching aid, a filmstrip, similarly reinforced traditional notions of the sexual division of labor. Titled "Telephone Impressions," the filmstrip was geared to teaching students good phone techniques: courtesy, clear speaking, and promptness. Mrs. Shapiro made a point of telling the class that although the filmstrip was excellent at demonstrating good phone usage, the school system could not purchase it, because it was sexist. All the examples of the wrong way to answer the phone, she elaborated, were delivered by a male voice; all the correct examples were delivered by a female voice. Therefore, the filmstrip had an antimale bias. It should have portrayed mistakes being made equally by the man and the woman.

It appeared to me, however, that there was a deeper, more subtle sexism at work in the filmstrip. The incorrect phone manner was not just a male voice, it was an authoritative, busy, important-sounding male voice, one that was irritated that it had to be bothered by answering the phone. The female voice, on the other hand, sounded trained for the job: that was her proper work and the task for which she was perfectly suited. Far from being antimale, the filmstrip reinforced the age-old notion that men have more important things to do than answer the phone. Since women are not doing anything of value, they are the ones who should be constantly interrupted to screen and direct messages.

At some of the workplaces women workers were beginning to resist this traditional telephone role, requesting the installation of a decentralized phone system where each person would have to take his or her own messages. Mrs. Carter was one supervisor who was adamant about this. Shortly after she was hired as an executive secretary, she told her boss to take the phones away or she would leave the job. She resented the burden of answering her boss's phone, claiming that if women were relieved of that kind of task they would be freer to do "the administrative work that men won't let women do." Office workers were also starting to resist the secretary's traditional task of serving coffee. Maureen, for example, was startled when a boss asked if she had offered coffee to the men who had arrived for a business meeting. She responded in surprise, "No, was I supposed to?" Her boss replied, "You bet you are, and do it with a smile, too." Maureen characterized this attitude as chauvinistic, but when she checked with other office workers and was told it was appropriate for her to be asked to do that task, she was reluctant to say anything because she feared it would turn people against her, and affect the way she felt about working there. So, even though she thought she would "raise a ruckus" if she were an older worker, employed full time, and if the practice were habitual, because of her structural relationship to the job she ended up complying with the directive.

But, all in all, just as the students partially accept sexuality as a criterion of themselves as office workers, so do they tend to accept being defined as man's helper, as his office wife. Some students saw this as a natural division of labor, some as a social division, and some seemed unable to distinguish between the two.

> Office work is mostly for women because it's typing and a lot of guys don't like to type. Filing and receptionist, that's more for girls too, because that's secretary work and girls are secretaries, you know.
>
> —Kris '81

> I guess there aren't any boys in the class because the role of secretary has almost always been all women. Probably because it's traditional for the man to be the boss.
>
> —Katrina '81

> Women shouldn't do construction work. Men are stronger and that's just the way it should be. Secretary jobs are probably for women mostly. That's just the way things are.
>
> —Terri '81

> Boys don't take the class because boys aren't secretaries. They're more into manual labor. That's just today's society. Men don't sit and push pencils. Being a secretary is a girl's job.
>
> —Marion '80

> A guy should be the boss. I can't see a lady telling a guy what to do. He'd probably be bigger than her. . . . I'm not used to a lady boss. I mean, you

don't see it on television. There a man is always the boss. And that's just the way I think it should be. Sure, there could be a lady doing Robert's job, but that wouldn't be right.

—Cynthia '81

What "is" often became equated with what "should be" and, surprisingly enough, as late as 1981 many of these eighteen- to twenty-year-olds had not seriously considered alternatives. In fact, the ideology of the sexual division of labor remained so strong that many of the students continued to advance arguments that their everyday experiences clearly contradicted (for example, seeing men who pushed pencils, having women as bosses).

When students elaborated on the reasons why men did not or should not do women's work and why women did not or should not do men's work, a striking contrast could be heard. Generally using euphemistic language, they explained that men who ventured into what was traditionally regarded as women's work would be considered homosexual.

I guess there weren't any boys in the class because they have the idea that it's for secretaries and they think boys aren't secretaries. I guess they think a lot of people might get the wrong idea.

—Jessica '80

I really can't picture a man doing a woman's job. My uncle is a nurse, but he's like this [she made a limp-wristed gesture]. That's why it would be hard for guys to have a woman's job. Because it's considered delicate and people might think they're gay.

—Debbie '80

Guys aren't cheerleaders because they think it's too faggy.

—Kathryn '80

I guess guys don't take something like the cooperative office class because they don't think it's right for them. They think they'd be laughed at—wow, what a weirdo!

—Cynthia '81

It's only in big cities that guys are secretaries; because they're able to get lost or hide more there.

—Doris '81

Doris went on to confirm my interpretation of her statement: if men did office work it meant they were gay; and if they were gay they would naturally want to hide their identity.

On the other hand, the young women who thought that the sexual division of labor should be maintained explained that women who were after men's jobs were trying to be like men or trying to prove their (mistaken) equality.

> I don't think ladies should be police or firemen either. They're just trying to show the guys they can do it and have the ability.
>
> —Priscilla '79

> On "Real People" they showed two women who were working on the docks doing loading. I'm sure they needed the job, but I think they were also proving a point.
>
> —Debbie '80

> I think jobs like construction and firefighters should go to men. Some women are trying to prove they're as equal as men, but the jobs should go to the guy.
>
> —Cynthia '81

According to these students, then, when men do women's work, they are denying or rejecting their masculinity, their natural claim to superiority. They are becoming effeminate. When women try to do men's work, they are not accepting their natural limitations and subordination, but are trying to be as good as men, when in fact they are not.

Just as most of these students had a hard time imagining men and women doing the same wage labor jobs, so too did they find it hard to imagine men and women filling the same domestic labor roles. For them, the notion of women's work automatically meant the primary role in domestic labor. In one way or another, they made it clear that men were the primary breadwinners and they, the women, the primary homemakers and childcarers.

> If I were to marrry, I would still want to work part time. Otherwise I'd get bored. But I wouldn't want to work full time if my husband were bringing in a good income. There's a lot to do already with housekeeping and kids.
>
> —Jane '80

> I can't imagine not working unless I had kids. Then I might stay home until they were in school. But then I'd be bored. The perfect situation would be to work half time.
>
> —Charlotte '77

> If I had kids I would sit around the house with them. I wouldn't work. You can tell kids who have been raised by a baby sitter. I don't know if I would let John stay home with them or not. It's not what guys are supposed to do.
>
> —Anne '80

I don't know many guys who would stay home with the kids. It's always been that it's the woman that stays home—because they're the gentle sex. Or that's what I've been told. It's just always been that way.

—Katrina '81

I would like not to be working sometimes. It's hard to come home every evening and just start to do what every housewife has to do. And I'm the one who always has to get the baby off to the sitter.

—Connie '77

I do resent having to have worked all these years, full time, while my kids were little. But there's no way I could have afforded not to. If I were able to find a part time job now, though, I would take it. In fact, I'm looking.

—Mary '72

While they might have been able to imagine themselves having full-time, interesting, or important careers when they were younger or if they were to stay single, the central force directing the students' and graduates' sense of a work identity was the expectation of eventual marriage and family. Interview material from two of the young women illustrates this underlying dynamic.

Kathryn, a 1980 graduate and an accounting student at a major university, was the most career-minded of the students I interviewed. In discussing her future she said,

I want to be independent for my own satisfaction, so I can prove to myself that I can do it, so no one has to take care of me.

She went on, however, to explain that only if she remained single would she ever attempt to be a CPA, an auditor, or the president of a credit union. That type of work, she said, was too stressful to allow other responsibilities as well. Since she definitely wanted a family, she would probably never hold those jobs, but said she would instead look for an accountant's job at a small business or credit union, which would be a good job and offer a good salary "for a woman."

Mary Jo, one of the high-school students, told much the same story from a different perspective. Reflecting on her youthful fantasies rather than her projected future, she explained how she had wanted to be an archeologist when she was in the eighth grade, how she loved to watch accounts of "digs" in various parts of the world. But even at fourteen years of age, she knew that was not practical. She knew that she had to get on with her life: to settle down, get a job, prepare for marriage and a family. So she planned to go to the community college after high school for a degree as an accountant clerk. When I asked why she had decided on a two-year rather than a four-year degree, she responded,

> Why should I waste my time in school? I'd rather get going right away and get it over with.

Mary Jo said she had the old-fashioned ambition of raising a couple of children and working part time.

Conclusion

Experiencing office work as either secondary to or synonymous with a sexual/home/family identity further marginalized these students' work identities. The culture of femininity associated with office work made it easier for them to be less attached to their work and their workplace than men, who stay in paid employment because they must live up to a masculine ideology of male-as-provider. Women's identities tend to be much less intrinsically linked to wage labor than are men's.

The beliefs the young women had about themselves being inferior workers were, thus, reinforced by the ideological messages in the classroom and at the work site, and by their structured experiences as office workers and became even more taken for granted as part of their everyday existence. While in some minimal ways the women may have rejected the ideology of male supremacy, at a more fundamental and persistent level, they affirmed it. They conceded legitimacy to the dominance of men in a way that appeared spontaneous and natural. By denying wage labor primacy over domestic labor, they inadvertently consented to and confirmed their own subordination, preparing themselves "for both unskilled, low-paid work and unpaid domestic service."[10]

The women used a culture of femininity to resist the impositions of wage labor, not just because work was boring and tedious—as it often is, too, for working-class men—but because it created a double work load. So they refused identities as full-time and serious workers; they resisted being subsumed into, and consumed by, capital. But this resistance did not change their primary relationships. Ultimately, the women prepared themselves to become part-time producers and part-time consumers, remaining subordinate to men in the workplace and dependent on them in the home. In this way, office women recreate their own subordinate culture, a culture they have learned to use and benefit from, since they see no way to change the material conditions from which it arises.

Notes

1. I would like to thank Michael Olneck, Michael Apple, and Vandra Masemann for their comments on the draft of this article.

2. An underlying assumption of this article is that while an advanced capitalist economy does not need a sexual division of labor in any absolute sense, a reserve labor force is used to control workers and keep wages down, and is drawn upon in times of economic expansion. In a society where patriarchal practices and ideologies prevail, where it is seen as natural and right that men are the primary breadwinners and women the child-raisers and husband-supporters, the logical group to be that reserve wage labor is women. They can move in and out of the wage labor force with the least disturbance and least strain to the economy because they can be absorbed into the family where, for working class mothers at least, domestic labor is generally a full time job anyway. For detailed discussions see Annette Kuhn and AnnMarie Wolpe, eds., *Feminism and Materialism: Women and Modes of Production* (London: Routledge and Kegan Paul, 1978); and Michelle Barrett, *Women's Oppression Today: Problems in Marxist Feminist Analysis* (London: Verso Editions, 1980).

3. "Selected themselves" is the correct formulation here, since Title IX guidelines explicitly forbid sex-segregated programs in public schools and since there was some evidence of affirmative action attempts to recruit males to the cooperative office education program, at the success rate of two boys in thirteen years. Unfortunately, the term conveys an individual-voluntaristic connotation I do not wish to imply. The weight of cultural pressures on adolescents to choose traditional sex-typed classes is formidable. Generally, they do not even need the type of discouragement reported to have occurred at Woodrow High School in the form of a male counselor asking a hockey player, "What the hell do you want to take a second year of typing for?" For other accounts of the ways in which schools help orient girls and boys to occupations on the basis of gender, see Judith Stacey, Susan Bereaud, and Joan Daniels, eds., *And Jill Came Tumbling After: Sexism in American Education* (New York: Dell, 1974); Rosemary Deem, ed., *Schooling for Women's Work* (London: Routledge and Kegan Paul, 1980); and Nancy Frazier and Myra Sadker, *Sexism in School and Society* (New York: Harper & Row, 1973).

4. See Paul E. Willis, *Learning to Labour: How Working Class Kids Get Working Class Jobs* (Farnborough: Saxon House, 1977), and Angela McRobbie, "Working Class Girls and the Culture of Femininity," in *Women Take Issue: Aspects of Women's Subordination*, ed. Women's Studies Group, Centre for Contemporary Cultural Studies (London: Hutchinson, 1978), pp. 96–108.

5. Similar formulations can be found in Stuart Hall and Tony Jefferson, eds., *Resistance through Rituals: Youth Subcultures in Post-War Britain* (London: Hutchinson & Co., 1975) and by Jean Anyon, "Accommodation and Resistance in Gender and Gender Development," a paper presented at the Ontario Institute for Studies in Education Conference on the *Political Economy of Gender* (Toronto, Ontario, October 30, 1981) and to be published in *Gender, Class and Education*, Len Barton, ed. (Sussex: Falmer Press, 1982).

6. This conclusion is also drawn by Madeleine MacDonald in "Cultural Reproduction: The Pedagogy of Sexuality," *Screen Education*, no. 32/33 (Autumn/Winter 1979/80): 141–53.

7. Sheila Rowbotham, *Woman's Consciousness, Man's World* (Middlesex: Penguin Books, 1973), p. 89.

8. Margery Davies, "Woman's Place is at the Typewriter: The Feminization of the Clerical Labor Force," in *Capitalist Patriarchy and the Case for Socialist Feminism*, ed. Zillah R. Eisenstein (New York: Monthly Review Press, 1979), p. 257.

9. Although this is a basic authority relation that would probably exist irrespective of gender, because gender and authority are strongly correlated in offices, hierarchical authority structures necessarily structure gender relations.

10. MacDonald, "Cultural Reproduction," p. 152.

CHAPTER 10

Schooling and Cultural Production: A Comparison of Black and White Lived Culture

LOIS WEIS

The concept of "lived culture" has assumed increasing importance within recent years. As we move away in studies of education from a base/superstructure model where an economic base explains nearly every aspect of cultural life, the actual practices of teachers and students in schools become more important.[1] These practices, related to an economic base as they are, are nevertheless only partially determined by this base and exhibit a degree of autonomy. Willis's recent study of working class boys in England, for example, suggests that inequalities, and the ideologies that support them, are reproduced only through struggle and contestation.[2] In studies such as these, the school is seen as the arena where tensions and contradictions are worked through, rather than as a place that produces individuals who fit neatly within an unequal social structure. The lived culture of individuals in schools provides a key to our understanding of how reproduction occurs.

This chapter explores the "lived culture" of black students in a community college (which I call Urban College) located in a large Northeastern city in the United States. My purpose is twofold: to articulate elements of student culture at an institution that serves primarily the black urban underclass in a city that is presently experiencing severe underemployment and unemployment, and to compare and contrast black lived cultural forms with those noted in previous investigations of the white working class. The relationship between culture and the economy, and the implications of lived cultural forms for the recreation of dominant ideologies, will also be discussed.

The Urban College Study

The qualitative methods and participant-observation techniques employed here were dictated by my interest in the interplay between culture and economics. As Willis notes, "these techniques are suited to record this level and have a sensitivity to meanings and values as well as the ability to represent and interpret symbolic articulations, practices and forms of cultural production."[3] This is important in that culture is best understood as a set of lived meanings and practices, as the product of collective human praxis rather than the passive result of dominant ideology.[4]

During the academic year 1979–80 I attended classes, conducted in-depth interviews with both faculty and students, and in general immersed myself in the institution. A record was kept of the day-to-day experiences and comments of teachers and students in classrooms, corridors, stairwells, offices, cafeteria, and the local coffee shop and bar. This allowed me to explore the ways in which the direct experiences of education were worked over and through the praxis of cultural discourse.[5]

The college itself is located on the edge of the urban ghetto. Over 70 percent of the students are black and the vast majority reside in surrounding neighborhoods.[6] Approximately 15 percent of the students at Urban College are 19 or younger, and 42 percent are over 25. Although these are not, by and large, students who come to college directly from high school, over 90 percent are attending college on a full-time basis.[7] Since the college is a Full Opportunity Program, all applicants who have high-school or general equivalency diplomas are admitted. More than 90 percent of the students receive some form of financial aid including Tuition Assistance Program (TAP) benefits, Basic Educational Opportunity Grant (BEOG), and Equal Opportunity Program (EOP) benefits.[8]

Urban College does not draw primarily from the black middle class. Fathers of students, if employed, are concentrated disproportionately in the production and service sectors—well over 75 percent are rooted in these sectors and only 7 percent have professional or managerial status.[9] Twelve percent of students report that their father is not in the labor force. Data on mother's occupation largely parallel these findings.[10]

The high percentage of students who did not respond to the question or who indicated that they "don't know" their father's occupation is noteworthy. A full 15 percent of black students said that they did not know what their father did for a living, and over 17 percent did not respond to the question. While it is possible that students genuinely lack such information, it is also possible that a number of fathers are engaged in quasilegal activities that would not be revealed on a questionnaire. In point of fact, the interplay between the "legitimate" and what has been called the "irregular economy" exerts a powerful influence on the day to day lives of ghetto residents. As ethnographers remind us, even those who hold legitimate jobs often participate in the irregular sector.[11]

The parents of Urban College students are, for the most part, rooted in what Edwards and others call the secondary labor market. Jobs in this sector are marked by the casual nature of the employment and the fact that work almost never requires previous training or education beyond basic literacy. In contrast to those in the primary market they provide virtually no job security and movement in and out of such jobs is common. Typically they are dead-end jobs, with few prospects of advancement and little reward for seniority in the form of higher pay or a better job. Most important is the fact that such work is not regular, and intermittent unemployment among individuals in the secondary market is widespread.[12]

Urban College students generally exhibit the same economic marginality as their parents. While most have families of their own, they have not had, nor do they have, steady employment. Those who work tend to have part-time employment in either service or production, engaging in casual hourly wage labor that offers neither security nor benefits.[13] In point of fact, such employment is increasingly difficult to obtain in the city in which Urban College is located. Like their parents then, Urban College students exhibit characteristics that destine them to become part of a permanently trapped population of poor people—the industrial underclass.[14]

Students are aware of this, and they actively perceive Urban College as a mediator between two worlds—the "streets" and the cultural mainstream. Attendance at Urban College must be understood at least in part as a rejection of street life and an attempt to embrace what students see as "legitimate" society.[15] As one student states, the streets mean "heroin, cocaine, marijuana, armed robbery, petty theft, and direct rip-offs—con games." They also mean "pimps, prostitutes, and numbers dealers." "Going legit" (entering the cultural mainstream) means a "good" job, a "three-piece suit and lunch on ———Avenue." One former student describes the role of Urban College as follows:

> [Ghetto kids] are always looking out of a window; looking for money and power and not really knowing where to get it. . . . At a very young age these kids are faced with a choice; they can go the easy way as a pimp, numbers dealer, prostitute, or they can try to make it another way—through the schools. [Urban College] represents a way back for those who took the left fork first and became disillusioned.

The following transcriptions clarify this point. Although the subject was never broached directly, time and time again students indicate that they view the community college as a way off the streets—as a way of dissociating themselves from certain aspects of their community.

James, for example, was born and raised in Columbus, Ohio, and is enrolled in the paralegal curriculum. A black male, aged about forty-five, he is back in school because his mother, dead twenty years, wanted him to be a lawyer, doctor or teacher. For him,

> Everything moves in its own time and I ran the streets enough. Ripping and running back and forth across the country and now it's time for me to take myself back to school and try to fulfill a promise that I made to her.

> . . . I am going back to school to get enough expertise relative to handling oneself, to raise one's employability level, because you can. Because you are not going to get a job legally expediting skills that you have learned streetside way, and this is what I and a number of others [here] were about—street players . . . standing on the corner matching wits with the authorities, that sort of stuff. And you simply don't find jobs doing that, so you got to go back to school—either technical school or you got to be involved in academia in order to raise your employability level.

For James, Urban College is a way of entering a new world—a way of gaining skills, thereby changing his own culture so that he will fit into another sector of society. In order to gain new skills that will enable participation in the "legitimate" economy, the individual must cut himself or herself off totally from former contacts:

> When one *opts* [my emphasis] to change one's lifestyle, he lets go of the streets. I do not go to ——— and ——— anymore although I haven't cancelled out on my friendships, such as they are, in any way over there, but I simply feel that I don't have anything in common with the fellas involved in those crap games in those buildings out there. I don't have anything in common with those fellas who want to hang around the pool hall shooting pool for money all day long. I don't do that anymore. I can always find something that I have to do relative to furthering my education.

This feeling is further illustrated by Anthony, a black male of about twenty-seven, who is working on an associate degree in Business Administration. His was a conscious decision to dissociate himself from street life for fear of its consequences:

> Anthony: I did well living on the streets. I made more money living on the streets than after I went back to school, got me a job and was living the way I guess society expects me to live.

LW: Why did you decide to go back to school?

Anthony: I chose school and society over Attica, because the things I was doing on the streets, they eventually would bring you to Attica, Elmira, or any correctional institution you care to name. I said I better get myself out of this and go straight.

LW: Could you elaborate on that?

Anthony: Nothing I did was legal when I was on the streets. . . . Eventually there was gonna come a time when I was going to have my first bust, my second bust, and I was gonna maybe suspend a sentence, maybe probation, but eventually it was gonna lead to incarceration somewhere. So rather than seeing myself being put into a cage, I started weighing the benefits. I said I don't think it should be that hard for me to go back to school. I was no dummy in the streets, why should I think I'm going to be a dummy in school?

. . . In the black community it [attending Urban College] is an attempt to identify with another group of people and still do what we call 'hang'— you know, 'be in.' [The community] puts a lot of pressure on you. By going back to school, believe me, I have lost friends in the community.

It is apparent that blacks at Urban College view the institution as a way of escaping aspects of their immediate environment. The college becomes the vehicle through which students perceive that they can enter the cultural mainstream and at the same time "hang"—that is, "be in." This is important, and attendance at the school should not be interpreted as a wholesale denial or rejection of the black cultural experience. These students are very much part of the black community and this is a determining factor in the production of located cultural form.

In the remainder of this chapter I will articulate elements of black student culture and compare them briefly with those noted among the white working class. The comparison rests on Willis's data on working-class boys in an English secondary school and London's data on white working-class students in a community college in the United States.[16] Unlike the students in Urban College, those in London's study, have fathers who are members primarily of what Edwards calls the traditional proletariat.[17] These jobs are located within the subordinate primary market; they are better paying than secondary market jobs and involve long-term stable work with prospects for advancement. In the United States, they are distinguished from secondary jobs most fundamentally by the presence of unions.

Willis's "lads" are also of the white manual-labor working class. While the fathers of the students are engaged in generalized rather than in skilled labor, pervasive wagelessness is not a persistent feature of the class landscape. The English equivalent of the wagelessness and economic marginality noted for Urban College students lies with immigrant groups, particularly West Indians. The lads' economic position is therefore closer to that of London's students than that of Urban College students. I will compare the three groups of students along the cultural dimensions attitude toward authority and attendance at class.[18]

Attitudes Toward Authority

Both Willis and London note a distinctly negative attitude toward authority and school knowledge, manifested in incivility toward faculty. While in neither case is this an across-the-board response to teachers, it is sufficiently well developed to be considered an element of each culture.

The most obvious dimension of the lads' culture is "entrenched general and personalized opposition to authority." The lads engage in behavior designed to show resentment while stopping just short of outright confrontation. They scrape chairs, balk at the simplest requirement, and fidget continually. There is, notes Willis, "an aimless air of insubordination ready with spurious justification and impossible to nail down. If someone is sitting on the radiator, it is because his trousers are wet from the rain, if someone is drifting across the classroom he is going to get some paper for written work, or if someone is leaving class, he is going to empty the rubbish 'like he usually does.' . . . A continuous hum of talk flows around injunctions not to, like the inevitable tide over barely dried sand and everywhere there are rolled-back eyeballs and exaggerated mouthings of conspiratorial secrets."[19]

While it is tempting to relate these behaviors to adolescence rather than social class per se, it is important to note that adult white working-class males in the community college exhibit similar attitudes toward authority and engage in comparable behavior.[20] About a month after school opened, students in London's study began injecting *sotto-voce* taunts into class lectures and discussions. This opposition took a distinctly class form in that, for the most part, it was done by students in manual training programs and aimed at liberal-arts teachers or vocational training teachers who were considered too abstract. Law enforcement students did not harass teachers who were ex-detectives for example, but they did harass the lawyer who taught legal aspects of police work. Students reacted negatively only in those classes that were "too intellectual," that is, too centered on mental rather than manual labor.[21]

London's study suggests that working-class whites in the United States demonstrated incivility to the *idea* of teachers if teachers were too abstract or theoretical—toward those who stressed ideas rather than application. While Willis provides no indication that the lads employed this dichotomy with respect to knowledge itself, the lads did emphasize the mental/manual dichotomy in their relations with teachers and conforming students (called "ear 'oles" by the lads because they simply sit and listen). School became identified with mental labor at the same time that manual labor was defined as superior by virtue of its masculinity. Oppositional cultural forms among working-class white males embody an overtly negative attitude toward authority and mental labor in general.

The case of Urban College students is substantially different. Opposition did not take the form described above. Rather than rejecting the idea of teachers or the content of school knowledge as do working-class white males, Urban College students criticized their teachers only insofar as they did not encourage what the students considered a fair transaction. In return for respect or obedience on the part of students, faculty were expected to share their knowledge. As the following transcriptions suggest, negativity was expressed in terms of faculty not caring enough, or not working hard enough, to ensure that students learn. Unlike Willis's or London's students, Urban College students approved of what the faculty had to offer; they simply wanted them to offer it, and they held teachers responsible for student failure.

> Anthony: See, what it is, is that, for one thing, the instructor—he doesn't present the class to make anyone feel comfortable. He could be a much more influential force in the class if he would emphasize certain things and de-emphasize things that he emphasizes right now. As far as participation, don't be so sarcastic because people that are hesitant to get up in class right now are afraid more so of him than they are of the class. . . .
>
> . . . They are afraid of his critical judgement on them as a human being and an individual and a student, instead of him using his influence to make these people feel comfortable.

> LW: Could you elaborate?

> Anthony: He would, I imagine, have a much better class, a greater attendance record, and fewer drop out if he would put himself in the position to realize that the students don't have confidence within themselves yet, and a little more personal understanding. . . . It's a monotone, monotonous type of class, no fluent conversation, no fluent interrelationship between the instructor and the student. (a Business Administration student)

> •

> James: I would like to see more dedication on the part of the faculty.

LW: In what sense?

James: There is a vast difference between a pro and a novice in anything. If you are a professional, you take pride in whatever your speciality is; you take pride in doing a good job. The old fashioned shoe cobbler, he took immense pride in turning out, or trying to turn out, the perfect pair of shoes. I feel a professional person can look at the situation no different. That you must take pride in whatever you are doing and try to do the best possible job. I feel that any teacher over there should be concerned about his students more than the others, and enough to look down the line and pick the paper a student has achieved and he can see his handiwork in the achievement of the individual students.

When I went to school . . . the teacher held the same place of honor and respect that the black preacher did who came to the house on Sunday to eat up all the chicken. Well, a teacher held the same esteem that he did. In my household I *had to study and I had to learn, but in exchange for this my teachers were dedicated.* [My emphasis]

LW: When you say that teachers here are not dedicated, what do you mean?

James: . . . There may be some who don't have what I consider a dedication, they are just there to get the money. They are not unlike the students themselves [referring to the commonly held notion that many students attend school simply to obtain grant money]. They are there to get paid and they are going to do as less they can. . . This works to the detriment of the student because what it does, it lower standards and makes the person think that they are getting an education when they are not. Then they leave this facility and go some place else, they get a job, go to another school, then they cannot pass the entrance test, or they get in class, then they can't maintain because the proper groundwork hasn't been laid over there. . . . I feel that the ones [teachers] who are not dedicated should be held to performance within the scope of their employment. If they cannot perform, then it's about standing aside and allowing someone to assume the position who can. . . . I want my teachers to be dedicated in teaching me, not just there to get the dollar.

(a Paralegal student)

•

Johnnie: As far as the professors, I'd attempt to keep their attendance in line . . . because the professors at Urban College tends to just take for granted the students in this school. . . .

. . . They take the attitude that the student at this school doesn't really want to learn. He's here for some reason or another other than to learn. 'So I'm going to miss this day and I'm going to miss that day.'

Claude: It's bias.

Johnnie: . . . This is my first semester. I started off with five classes and now I'm presently at four. Out of four classes I have two good instructors that are there when they are supposed to be, and the way they go about instructing is compatible, you know, you can really get into it. But I have two other instructors that are hardly ever there; what they teach they don't test on, and they use attendance as their chain on you or something. He says if you don't attend, you don't get a good grade, but if you attend and he's not there, your motivation about getting to this class tends to drop somewhat. You go to class, you break your neck to get there at 9:00 (A.M.) and you go to class and the instructor's not there and he told you you were going to have a test and you studied all nite—stuff like that.

. . . If they [the faculty] couldn't handle the job in the beginning they shouldn't have took the job. 'Cuz you can't go out here and get a job in industry and then expect somebody else to do your job, 'cuz that's too much for you. You shouldn't be there in the beginning . . . . You see, a lot of these professors use teaching as a second job or even a third job. There's a lot of good instructors there, but they don't apply themselves. I know the students don't either and that has the instructor's motivation drop somewhat. . . . I can understand that, but *that is their job.* [emphasis mine] And as far as the students are concerned, they are paying to go to school and if they show up or not, that's their fault.

•

Jerome: At Urban College the instructors tend to make that assumption that everybody is on the same footing when they're not. Certain people can't even understand whiteys, so there's a communications breakdown. Then you have a personality clash between some teachers and students. . . . You know, I take the attitude, you're white, you don't care, you get paid anyway, I know you don't care if I learn. That don't caring attitude—it's transmitted over a period of time. . . . Students are off into that, so there's no communication between students and teachers.

LW: . . . Could you be a bit more specific?

Jerome: In a sense, like, you have various wealth of people, most of them are people you can categorize as being unemployed, underemployed, social-service recipients, you know, uh, poorly educated in the sense that the reading level and the math skills are below par of most high-school kids now. So you know that with that knowledge that most instructors up there have, they are still around there with that Harvard school attitude and that's not Harvard. So to me that's cold and impersonal. 'I'm going to do my job and fail three quarters of them and the two/three good ones can just slip through,' you know.

(a Fashion Merchandising student)

The above discussions suggest that Urban College students do not reject the idea of teachers, nor do they question the legitimacy of their knowledge. Within the context of Willis's teaching paradigm (which is only partly related to a class paradigm), students resent the lack of what they consider a fair exchange.[22] Some students, like Jerome, actively attribute the lack of a fair exchange to racism. As he states, "You know, I take the attitude, you're white, you don't care, you get paid anyway. I know you don't care if I learn."[23] Even those who are most critical, however, adhere strongly to the notion that the content of knowledge is legitimate. Not only do they see knowledge as legitimate, but they also envision it as power. College knowledge has an immediacy and potency that is readily verbalized; it is not an abstract set of codes or principles but rather leads to personal enhancement and collective improvement directly.

> Anthony: (on a Salesmanship class)
> [I've learned] how to make a presentation. It made me aware of public speaking. . . . It made me aware of "know yourself before you try to sell anyone else."
>
> . . . There is a few people in this particular class that are still a little withdrawn. I guess you know from being in the class, a few of them are still sort of hesitant. But now that I know the importance of myself being confident, and confidence to the particular person that I am trying to sell something to, I have no qualms about speaking right out now, because I know not only is it going to benefit me, but if there is anyone who I might be working for in this particular field it is gonna benefit them all, and by benefiting them I know it is gonna benefit me.
>
> LW: So that all these sales presentations that people are making in class are useful?
>
> Anthony: . . . Public speaking is. *I knew it had a definite importance or it wouldn't be offered on a college level*, [my emphasis], but now I have become aware of what it can offer if you are gonna be in this particular field or any field.
> (a Business Administration student)

•

> Jerome: (on Salesmanship)
> No matter what attitude the instructor has, he is presenting some valid material. You can't fight it, nowhere round the world. In the sense that he

is giving it out wrong, that might be another thing, but the material *is* valid. There is a reason behind it; you have to be very naive not to see it.

(a Fashion Merchandising student)

•

James: One of my primary objectives is to write. A man like Mr. ———, the English composition teacher, has helped me immensely in this regard. . . . Now I want to become a writer because I believe I have something to say and heretofore I have done the same thing that a writer would have to have, giving people advice, counseling them, that sort of thing. But today I would like to put it down on paper so that those that come after me will at least have certain guidelines whereas they can get around the pitfalls that I have had experience with. And I have had experience with some pitfalls. You can't be out there [the streets] for twenty years without running into these pitfalls and witnessing the effect of these pitfalls.

LW: So you feel that there are specific skills, like writing, that a school like this can give you. Are there other things besides writing?

James: Sure, the law. The law encompasses it all, that people, random people, ordinary people, to and fro, up and down the street, they run afoul of the law because they have had no experience with the law. They haven't been taught or they haven't been trained in the legal aspects of living. I feel that if people did have a basic working knowledge of the law and how the law works, you would automatically have less crime because they would have learned to appreciate the law.

LW: You are saying something very interesting. You said that people don't know the law on the streets and you also said that if they did know the law there would be less crime. Why is that?

James: This is going to lower crime because if a person understands the legal machinery they can protect themselves better, but the law has heretofore been used to victimize certain people who don't know the law. But this other guy knows and you don't know, like you have a . . . relationship with the preponderance of the dominance resting with the people who have knowledge of the law and he can work the relationship the way he chooses. So you end up being used in your ignorance of the law, and I have seen this happen countless times. It hasn't happened to me, but I have seen it happen to others.

LW: So you want knowledge to be more evenly distributed?

James: I want it to be universal, because you see, law, contemporary law, manmade law is with us from the cradle to the grave, and it is incredulous to me that the system would deny basic legal education to its citizens if you are talking about making better citizens. You have crime because citizens, to a degree, do not want to obey the laws. Now spiraling crime keeps pace with inflation, and, just as inflation can go into a depression, spiraling crime can go into outright anarchy. All because they do not know; all because way down the line you had the tendency to cancel out respect for the law by keeping the knowledge away from ordinary people.

The point here is that black students affirm rather than contradict legitimated knowledge. This goes beyond merely viewing knowledge as legitimate; students see an immediacy and potency to knowledge and some, like James, argue that it will be shared. He wants to write "so that those that come after me will at least have certain guidelines."

James does not argue that the law is unfair or that it works (or has worked) primarily against the poor. Rather, he suggests that knowledge about the law will "automatically" lower crime; it is the fact that knowledge about the law is withheld that is unfair, not the law itself. There is no indication in James's discussion that the law has been overtly discriminatory in many instances and that it was changed only through collective struggle.[24] This suggests a deep faith in knowledge, and a sense that knowledge in its present form can be shared and used for collective action. This is in sharp contrast to the position of working-class whites, where oppositional cultural forms embody a rejection of the idea of teachers and mental labor. As I will argue later, both responses are factors in the reproduction of economic inequalities and the ideologies that support these inequalities.

Chronic Absence

A second cultural element is related to class attendance. For the lads, absenteeism signals their generally oppositional stance; their "struggle to win symbolic and physical space from the institution and its rules and to defeat its main perceived purpose: to make you 'work'."[25] Students are adept at managing the formal system and winning space for themselves. The core skill here is being able to get out of any given class, thus preserving personal mobility within the school. These actions do not contradict their perceptions of schooling and school authority as outlined earlier.

The same point may be made with respect to working-class white students in the community college. In London's study, during the first three weeks of school, attendance averaged from 850 to 950 (out of 1,103) and for the remainder of the year the average head count was 525. London suggests that absence from class is a "means of dissociating [oneself] from slavish adherence to official expectations."[26] As such, it was defined positively.

Absenteeism among white working-class males in the community college, as among Willis's lads, follows more or less logically from perceptions of the institution and its authority. The school "stands for" mental labor, and the implied superiority of such labor is opposed and resented. Student lived cultural form can be understood as simultaneously a rejection of mental labor and a celebration of what they subjectively define as their *own* culture.

An additional point needs to be made here; London does not indicate any formal penalty for missing class. In most colleges, unlike secondary schools, negative sanctions cannot be brought to bear upon offenders. While attendance may affect grades indirectly, it does not, in itself, determine academic outcomes.

This is not true, however, of Urban College. One of the things that the institution attempts to extract from students is regular attendance and a sense of responsibility for such attendance.[27] If students do not take this responsibility, the institution steps in and takes it for them. There is a well articulated attendance policy, which is announced at the beginning of each semester in every class. Students are allowed a predetermined number of cuts in any given class before their names are struck from the class rolls. Attendance *does* count, and student names are removed from class lists if the maximum number of cuts is exceeded within the first three weeks of school.[28] Students are given "W" or occasionally "F" grades if they exceed the maximum number of cuts during the remainder of the semester. If a student's name is dropped from class lists during the first three weeks, he or she is not eligible for grant money. Grant checks amount to approximately $500.00 per semester (tuition is also paid) and are distributed about two-thirds of the way through each term. It is possible for a student to receive all "W" grades and still maintain grant elegibility.

As I argued earlier, Urban College students are the only group under consideration that actively affirm school knowledge and do not reject the idea of teachers. Criticism of the faculty centers around beliefs that they are not trying hard enough, are not meeting their contractual obligations (showing up to class), or are too impersonal. Unlike working-class whites, students do not overtly reject the nature of the knowledge embedded within the institution. At the same time, the absentee rate at Urban College is even higher than that noted for other groups. Students consistently register for classes, obtain grant money, are given "W" or "F" grades for excessive cuts, and register for these same courses next semester when the pattern is likely to repeat itself.[29] Data presented below for courses offered in the 1979 fall semester provide some indication of the extent of absenteeism and associated dropout rates.

Table 1. Fail and Withdraw in College Credit and Remedial Classes, Fall 1979*

	Fail		Withdraw	
Courses	%	No.	%	No.
College Credit				
Mathematics[†]	14.5	12	36.1	30
Science[‡]	8.4	34	26.8	109
English	13.0	65	27.3	150
Social Science	8.5	56	25.5	168
Health and Physical Science	3.1	4	30.5	39
Secretarial Science	25.8	86	27.3	91
Business Administration	4.7	32	33.5	227
Paralegal Assistant	7.5	14	21.3	40
Fashion Buying and Merchandising	—	—	28.4	25
General Studies	—	—	28.5	59
Criminal Justice	—	—	44.1	30
Child Care	6.6	11	22.9	38
Radiologic Technology[§]	4.2	1	4.2	1
Remedial[‖]				
Mathematics	15.9	34	31.3	67
Business administration	6.4	3	29.8	14
English[#]	16.0	66	31.2	129

*Figures were calculated on the basis of grade sheets turned in by instructors at the end of the term. All day classes are included in the tabulations. Data are presented for the combined male and female population. An analysis by gender revealed only slight differences. Figures refer to percent of total enrolled in all courses in each curriculum.

[†]Calculated by curriculum.

[‡]Chemistry, Physics, Biology.

[§]This program has very few black students because of stringent entrance requirements.

[‖]Students are placed in these courses on the basis of test scores on an examination in English and Mathematics. Many of these classes are graded on a satisfactory (S)/Unsatisfactory (U) basis. The "F" and "U" grades are consolidated here.

[#]Over 21 percent of all students enrolled in Remedial English classes received "incomplete."

While these data do not measure absence from class per se, the "W" grade, in particular, provides an indication of such absence. If, as mentioned earlier, a student's name is not struck from the class roster during the first three weeks of the semester, the student is eligible for grant money, and his or her name appears on the final class list. Faculty generally give "W" grades to students who stop attending class, although some faculty fail these students. Since "F" and "U" grades are also given to students who attend class regularly but do not complete the course successfully, they must be interpreted with caution.

The high percentage of withdrawals is noteworthy. An average of 30 percent of males and females end up with "W" grades in college courses. The failure rate is also high, and it is only a slight overstatement to argue that close to half the students do not successfully complete any given course (not including those who drop out in the first three weeks). It is only in the radiologic technology program, which is the only selective program on campus and is reputed to be 99 percent white, that this pattern does not occur. Here the failure and withdrawal rates are each less than 5 percent. This is in sharp contrast with mathematics, where 36 percent of the students receive "W" grades in college credit courses and 15 percent fail them. The data are similarly striking for remedial mathematics courses: 31 percent of students receive "W" grades and 15 percent fail.

Absenteeism is further clarified in Table 2. Faculty were asked to note the number of students attending their classes "regularly" on 14 January and 1 April 1980. Since the semester does not end officially until the middle of May, the data understate actual attrition per semester.

Data again suggest widespread absenteeism. In remedial courses, teachers estimate that 50 percent of students attend regularly by 1 April,

Table 2. Class Attendance as Reported by Faculty, Spring 1980

Courses	14 January	1 April	% Retained
College Credit			
English	386	230	59.6
Mathematics	109	74	67.8
Business Administration	532	324	60.9
Science	426	297	69.7
Social Science	275	204	74.2
Secretarial Science	115	82	71.3
Fashion Buying and Merchandising	64	41	64.1
Child Care	69	64	92.7
Radiologic Technology	24	21	87.5
Criminal Justice	78	67	85.9
Total	2,078	1,404	67.6
Remedial			
English	315	144	45.7
Mathematics	227	125	55.0
Business Administration	72	40	55.6
Total	614	309	50.3
Total College Credit and Remedial	2,692	1,713	63.6

Note: Faculty were asked to note the number of students who attend "regularly" in each class they teach. Data are presented by curriculum.

and the situation is only slightly better in college credit classes: 68 percent attend regularly by the same date.[30]

Chronic absence and stopping in and out are distinct elements of lived cultural form among students at Urban College. As the discussions below indicate, students comment negatively on this practice and are quick, like the faculty and administration, to label it a "problem." At the same time, these students are part of the culture and engage in the very practices they criticize. Among the students interviewed below, only one (Diane) attends class regularly.[31] James was not allowed to register for courses the following semester because of the number of "W's" on his record. Jerome only occasionally attends class and has been enrolled in degree programs at Urban College and other local institutions on and off over ten years.[32] Belinda has been at Urban College for over four years and has still not accumulated enough credits to graduate. The widespread nature of this practice contributes to an exceedingly low graduation rate per entering class. It has been estimated that of the 827 students admitted into degree programs in the fall of 1977, only 93, or 11 percent, graduated in May 1979. The figure is only slightly better for the following year: of 527 students admitted in fall 1978, it has been estimated that 131, or 25 percent, graduated in May 1980. Even assuming a three-year cycle, only 131 of the 827 (16 percent) admitted in the fall of 1977 graduated three years later.[33]

Jerome: The retention rate of the students is awful now, you know. Were you around in September? The campus was full, you know, you couldn't move around. Now it is like an isolated jungle.

LW: I've noticed that . . . Why do people drop out?

Jerome: They lose interest in it. They lose interest in the school. Like what I am saying is, when you sit down and really weigh the advantage, you say now here I am, I got two kids, I know I need a job bad but I don't have the skills to get this job. Now school can provide me with some of the skills that I need to obtain a job that will take me up off subsistence, but I don't have time to go to school. My time now has become so valuable that I have to use it wisely to more or less like make sure that everything stay correct at home. So you cannot study with all them problems on your head, you know, knowing where your rent gonna come from, your next food of mouth, not so much your mouth, it's the kids' mouth, making sure they stay warm and healthy, you know. This is the problem.

So, a lot of blacks are eliminated through a whole lot of social mis-errors, not only blacks I would imagine all people—white too . . . but it is more pronounced, you can see it better in the black community than you can see

[it] in the white, where the average age of the teenage girl at 13, you know, five out of six, you know, got a baby already.

(a Fashion Merchandising student)

•

Belinda: Before I came here I drove a cab. There were pimps waitin' on these girls [at Urban College]. I had one guy, I drove him around for a whole year; four times a year when the BEOG checks came out. He registered, came to a couple of classes now and then, checks came out and he withdrew.

(a Business Administration student)

•

LW: Do you get the impression that most of the students here are pretty serious about their work?

Diane: Well, I find that it splits. I find that some are very serious and others, they could care less . . .

LW: Why do you think they're here if they're not serious?

Diane: Well I don't know. It's hard for me to understand. Like when grant checks come out, classes all of a sudden get very small, and they also get smaller when the work gets difficult and they can't do it, so they drop.

(a Secretarial Science student)

•

James: I feel that the attendance policy, as it is structured, it is unfair. But at the same time I feel that there are some people who go to the school who should be penalized because they are undertaking fraud, because when you register you sign a contract in order to get the BEOG grant, in that you will attend school, etc., etc. Now if you go for a week or two and you don't go back anymore till they hand out the BEOG checks and you go pick up the check and you initiated this knowingly and intentionally, it's fraud and they should be dealt with accordingly.

Now the attendance policy, I think, has a tendency to penalize students who really want to come to class but due to their lifestyle or their problems, or the neighborhood where they live, or problems with children in the household that they sometimes are missed, and I believe a system could be worked out whereas all of these factors can be taken into consideration, whereas these outright wrongdoers can be penalized.

. . . I am almost out of Public Speaking . . . I don't have children, I don't have a wife to go home to, but there are people over there who do and it works to an extreme detriment and it has a tendency to demoralize them and it will drive them off campus. I feel that they should adjust the

attendance policy. There are classes that started out with 35–40 people
and now they have got about 9 or 12 people. And that shouldn't be.

While students are critical of this practice, they engage in the very
behavior they criticize. James admits that he "is almost out of public
speaking," and Jerome rarely attends class, even when he is on campus.
Students are far more critical when, as James puts it, "you go pick up the
check and you initiated this knowingly and intentionally, it's fraud
and . . . should be dealt with accordingly." If it is not intentionally
fraudulent, students label absenteeism a "problem" but are less harsh in
their judgment, locating the source of this problem in the home. Both
James and Jerome clearly articulate this. Unlike that of working-class
whites, the behavior here is not overtly oppositional and is not linked
primarily to the institution. Students instead locate the source of this
behavior in themselves. This is important, and, as I will argue later, must
be linked to the history of black resistance in the United States.

Attendance is low at Urban College and is perceived as such by all
members of the College community. Unlike the low attendance that
characterizes Willis's and London's students, however, the behavior
among Urban College students directly contradicts their attitude toward
knowledge and schooling. While working-class white students actively
oppose institutional authority and all that it has come to symbolize for
them, Urban College students express no equivalent hostility. In these
two lived cultural elements then—attitudes toward authority and
absenteeism—the permutations for working-class whites and urban
blacks are different. In the case of urban blacks we have an example of a
"lived contradiction"; students behave in direct opposition to their collective attitude.

Economic and Cultural Forms

While it is not my purpose here to attempt a thorough explanation of
the production of lived cultural form, I will speculate about the rise of
different cultures and ideologies and the way in which institutions like
schools provide an important site for culture creation. While the school
must be seen as more than a mere reflection of an economic base (even if
we assume contradictions within the base itself), lived cultural forms arise
in part from that base and may act in contradictory ways to sustain it. The
relations between culture (both lived and commodified) and the economy
are exceedingly complex and no simple base/superstructure model will
serve to illuminate them. While the cultural level may be semi-
autonomous, it can bind people to an unequal social structure in more

profound ways than it could if culture and ideology were simply imposed.[34]

The two major categories of Willis's analysis of the lived culture of students—"penetration" and "limitation"—are useful for our understanding of white working class cultural forms and illuminate those of the black underclass as well.[35] "Penetration" is used to describe those instances where students have developed responses to schools and work that show an awareness of the unequal reality they face. The lads' rejection of so much of the form and content of schooling, for example, stems from an unconscious realization that while working class youth can succeed as individuals, schooling will not work for the working class as a whole. Penetration thus designates "impulses within a cultural form towards the penetration of the conditions of existence of its members and their position within the social whole but in a way that is not centered, essentialist, or individualist."[36] "Limitation" refers to "those blocks, diversions and ideological effects which confuse and impede the full development and expression of these impulses."[37] Cultural penetrations are prevented from going farther by contradictions within lived cultural forms themselves.

The distinctions made and acted upon by working class white males in their own lived culture provide an important element in the recreation of the ideological hegemony of the dominant classes. Braverman and others have argued at length that one of the principles guiding the articulation of capitalist social relations is the progressive divorce of mental from physical labor. Planning is separated from execution at every point in production, so that each process is standardized and controlled.[38] When working-class students reject schooling and affirm application and manual labor in the way that they do, they embrace a distinction that lies at the very heart of the economy. Most importantly, they are experiencing it as a kind of cultural autonomy and freedom; they are living it as if they create it. "The rather clumsy but strictly accurate term 'partial penetration' designates the interaction of these two terms [penetration and limitation] in a concrete culture." As Willis notes, penetrations are "bound back finally into the structure they are uncovering in complex ways by internal and external limitations. There is ultimately a guilty and unrecognized—precisely a 'partial'—relationship of these penetrations to that which they seem to be independent from and see into."[39]

It is noteworthy in the context of working-class cultural forms in a changing economy that London's students embrace the very distinctions the lads do—they reject mental labor and resent those who work "too hard" or are "too studious." As Karabel and others have argued, the community college in the United States, "generally viewed as the leading edge of an open and egalitarian system of higher education, is in reality a prime contemporary expression of the dual historical patterns of class-based tracking and educational inflation."[40] While community colleges offer the potential for mobility for the individual, they *cannot* benefit the working class in general. Although London's students have penetrated close to the core of this reality, like Willis's lads, their own culture embodies contradictions that ultimately act back on them and ensure the ideological hegemony of the dominant classes. Since, as Braverman and others have argued, white collar work is becoming increasingly proletarianized, working-class community college students, in rejecting the intellectual and the abstract, embrace the very distinction between planning and execution that lies at the root of modern capitalism. The community college in the United States plays a key role here in that it provides an arena whereby working-class white males, through their own lived culture, produce necessary division in an increasingly proletarianized white collar world.[41]

Although the same basic process is at work in Urban College, the shape and form of student lived culture are different. The black struggle in the United States has, by necessity, taken a less overtly antagonistic form than the struggle for a better life among working class whites in England or the United States. Since times of slavery, overt resistance to the regime has had poor prospects for success and required people of extraordinary daring.[42] It was not until the 1950s and especially the 1960s that overt challenges to the regime emerged in a sustained form.[43]

This is to suggest not that resistance to conditions under slavery or thereafter was absent, but that such resistance was not, for the most part, obvious and direct.[44] White working-class opposition often constituted a direct challenge to management (although not necessarily to capitalism); black opposition was, out of necessity, considerably more subtle.[45]

It is important to point out that day-to-day resistance has its roots in slavery and persists today. While such resistance does not constitute a frontal challenge to an existing order, it can set limits to that order and allow people to live with a minimum of decency. Day-to-day resistance, because it is by its very nature collective, can also impart a sense of community strength and teach the rudiments of organization. At the same time it can imply accommodation to a regime, in contrast to insurrection. Resistance and accommodation thus developed a single pattern in the black community and is reflected at the cultural level in language, notions of time, and work rhythms.[46]

The attitude of Urban College students toward knowledge must be situated within this context. An affirmation of learning has since slavery constituted a form of resistance to dominant ideology and posed a threat to the hegemony of the dominant classes(although not without its contradictory effects).[47] While the nature of the struggle for schooling has changed from one simply of access to one of access and quality, the struggle itself continues. Just as the white working-class affirmation of manual labor is partially determined by the broader white working-class culture, black student affirmation of schooling is partially determined by impulses within broader black cultural form. Among black students, as among the white working-class, these impulses are bound back, finally, in complex ways into the larger social structure. In the case of blacks, these very oppositional tendencies act to limit cultural penetrations regarding the value of education.

Recent research demonstrates that black rates of return to schooling are not the same as those of whites.[48] Numerous studies indicate that "the cost of being black" in the United States is that whites get greater rewards from a given amount of schooling than nonwhites. This is particularly the case for the elementary and secondary level; it is only upon completion of the BA that the expected status advantage is larger for nonwhites than whites. This does not mean that nonwhite BAs work in higher status occupations than white BAs; it simply means that nonwhites with four year college degrees are relatively less disadvantaged in terms of the job market than nonwhites who do not possess such degrees.[49] Completion of the BA is therefore critical in terms of black social mobility.

This is an important finding in light of student lived cultural form at Urban College. While working class white students overtly reject much of the form and content of schooling, black student opposition will be coded differently given different historic struggles. Like working-class whites however, blacks at Urban College have penetrated the unequal reality they face. While they do not overtly reject the form and content of schooling (in part because of oppositional tendencies within the broader black culture), their own lived culture reveals these impulses; they unconsciously and correctly realize that schooling at this level will not work for them as a class. As with working-class whites, this constitutes a realistic assessment of what a community college will do for them.

The pattern of dropping in and out must be seen as an impulse within the culture toward the penetration of the conditions of existence of its members and their position within the social whole. The college cannot work for blacks as a group; the pattern of dropping in and out represents a penetration of this unequal reality. It must be clear, however, that this is not a conscious response nor does it lie in any individual act. Its logic lies only at the group level; the behavior represents a creative response to a set of lived conditions both in and outside the institution. It arises out of definite circumstances in a specific historical relation. While not predetermined and certainly not conscious, it is also not accidental.[50]

As in the case of working-class whites however, these penetrations are prevented from going further by contradictions within lived cultural forms themselves. While student lived culture makes certain penetrations of the conditions of existence of its members, these cultural penetrations and associated practices are only partial and fall short of transformative political activity. In the case of Urban College students this incompleteness is linked to the collective faith in education itself. Despite a cultural form that suggests deep skepticism about what the community college will do for them as a group, Urban College students retain a profound faith in schooling and in the power and immediacy of knowledge. As I argued earlier, this very faith must be seen as an oppositional tendency in the broader community.

The interaction of these elements in a concrete culture has contradictory effects. When students drop in and out of school, thereby reinforcing the collectivity, oppositional tendencies within the broader black culture (which themselves reinforce the collectivity) leave students no one to blame for this practice but themselves. As a result students hold their neighborhood, lifestyle, and problems with children responsible for what is, in fact, structurally induced. Thus the collective aspects of resistance in student lived cultural form are broken down into their component parts by virtue of oppositional tendencies in the larger immediate culture. Like the synthesis that is Black Christianity, lived cultural form in Urban College reinforces that tendency toward atomization at the same time that it reinforces and strengthens the collectivity.[51] It is, then, inherently contradictory. The process of atomization serves to limit cultural penetration and prevents the development of a collective consciousness geared toward transformative political activity.[52]

There is, notes Willis, "precisely a partial relationship of these penetrations to that which they seem to be independent from and see into." When black students take up creative positions within the institution, they ultimately ensure their *own* future as part of the urban underclass, which is precisely what they are attempting to escape. This is not to say that individuals do not make it through the institution and even obtain the BA; the logic examined here is a *group* logic and must be seen in a specific historical relation. Yet this cultural form is not the result of simple outside determination. The institution does not simply "act down" upon students to swell the ranks of an urban underclass. In part the underclass is reproduced at this level—in spite of student desires—because the group logic (which must be seen in relation to broader class and race logics) operates as it does. Impulses within student lived cultural form both reinforce the collective and simultaneously break it into its component parts, thus dissolving its potential for serious political action. Not only is the underclass reproduced, but the potential for transformative political activity is minimized.

In a theoretical sense, this is exceptionally important. Like Willis' and London's students, Urban College students are a product of their own culture. Analyses of the production of culture must proceed carefully, however. It cannot be seen either as being passed down from one generation to the next, as in culture of poverty theories, or as being the passive result of dominant ideology working downwards, as in some base/superstructure models. Schools are best seen as sites where cultures and ideologies are produced and dominant ideologies may ultimately be maintained. This logic operates differently by race, class, and gender in different types of institutions, times, and national contexts. Future work must examine these issues more closely. The role of schools as sites for the creation of ideological hegemony in a nonmechanistic fashion warrants further investigation.

Notes

1. The approaches taken by Bowles and Gintis and Althusser exemplify a base/superstructure model in studies of education. See Samuel Bowles and Herbert Gintis, *Schooling in Capitalist America* (New York: Basic Books, 1976); Louis Althusser, "Ideology and Ideological State Apparatuses," in *Lenin and Philosophy, and Other Essays* (London: New Left Books, 1971). For a recent discussion of this perspective see Henry A. Giroux, "Hegemony, Resistance, and the Paradox of Educational Reform," *Interchange* 12, no. 2–3 (1981): 3–26.

2. Paul Willis, *Learning to Labour: How Working Class Kids Get Working Class Jobs* (Westmead, England: Saxon House, 1977). See also Michael Apple, "What Correspondence Theories of the Hidden Curriculum Miss: An Essay Review of Paul Willis, *Learning to Labour: How Working Class Kids Get Working Class Jobs, The Review of Education* 5, no. 2 (1979): 101–12; Michael Apple, "Reproduction, Contestation, and Curriculum: An Essay in Self-Criticism," *Interchange* 12, no. 2–3 (1981): 27–47; Paul Willis, "Cultural Production is Different from Cultural Reproduction is Different from Social Reproduction is Different from Reproduction," *Interchange* 12, no. 2–3 (1981): 48–67; Michael Apple, "Analyzing Determinations: Understanding and Evaluating the Production of Social Outcomes in Schools," *Curriculum Inquiry* 10, no. 1 (1980): 55–76.

3. Willis, *Learning to Labour*, p. 3.

4. For further discussion of "culture" see Paul Willis, "Shop Floor Culture, Masculinity and the Wage Form," in John Clarke, Chas. Critcher and Richard Johnson, eds., *Working Class Culture* (London: Hutchinson, 1979), pp. 185–98; Richard Johnson, "Histories of Culture/Theories of Ideology: Notes on an Impasse," in M. Barrett et. al., eds., *Ideology and Cultural Production* (New York: St. Martin's Press, 1979): 49–77.

5. These data will be reported in full at a later date.

6. Urban College, *Self-Study Report* (submitted to Middle States for accreditation), 1981, p. 2. The zip codes of students enrolled in Urban College during the

1979–80 academic year indicate that 90.3 percent live in the city. Of these, 72.1 percent live in the city center, while 18.2 percent live on the periphery. The remaining 9.7 percent live in the suburbs and surrounding towns.

7. These data were obtained through questionnaires administered to all students in Day division English classes. Questionnaires were administered by a carefully trained group of Urban College students in order to maximize accuracy in responses. Since forms were administered to students in English classes, results are skewed slightly toward newer students.

8. Urban College, *Self-Study*, p. 2. When tuition was imposed throughout the state system, the state's Tuition Assistance Plan (TAP) became operative. Under TAP, low-income students qualify for full tuition assistance. Only full-time students are eligible for TAP benefits.

9. These figures are based on the questionnaire described in footnote 7. Occupations were classified according to Donald Treiman's Standard International Occupational Prestige Scale. See Donald Treiman, *Occupational Prestige in Comparative Perspective* (New York: Academic Press, 1977). It is possible, of course, for "Production" workers to be skilled. Given low levels of education and historic job ceilings for blacks however, it can be assumed that a very small percentage of fathers are skilled laborers.

10. Data on mother's occupation suggest that mothers hold slightly more prestigious positions than fathers. This must be interpreted with caution, however, since "prestigious" jobs such as teacher aide or nurse's aide do not pay particularly well.

11. For a discussion of quasilegal activities, see Betty Lou Valentine, *Hustling and Other Hard Work* (New York: Free Press, 1978), Jagna Wojcicka Sharff, *Life on Doolittle Street: How Poor People Purchase Immortality*, Final Report, Hispanic Study Project, Department of Anthropology, Columbia University, 1980. The effect of the intersection between the "legitimate" and the "irregular" economy on student cultural form will be discussed at a later date.

12. See Richard Edwards, *Contested Terrain* (New York: Basic Books, 1979). Numerous studies also show that secondary jobs exhibit a persistently small return to education and this is particularly true for black workers. See Robert Buchele, "Jobs and Workers: A Labor Market Segmentation Perspective on the Work Experience of Middle Aged Men," unpublished paper submitted to the Secretary of Labor's Conference on the National Longitudinal Survey of the Pre-Retirement Years, Boston, 1975; Martin Carnoy and Russell Rumberger, *Segmented Labor Markets: Some Empirical Findings* (Palo Alto: Center for Economic Studies, 1975); David Gordon, "Class Productivity and the Ghetto: A Study of the Labor Market Stratification," Ph.D. diss., Harvard University, 1971; Paul Osterman, "An Empirical Study of Labor Market Segmentation," *Journal of Industrial and Labor Relations*, 1975, cited in Edwards, *Contested Terrain*, p. 170.

13. This information was obtained through questionnaires as well as interactions with students.

14. Glasgow has noted that the solidification of an industrial underclass represents one of the most significant class developments in the past two decades. As he notes, "the term *underclass* does not connote moral or ethical unworthiness, nor does it have any other pejorative meaning; it simply describes a relatively new population in industrial society." In the United States today, blacks constitute a large proportion of the permanently trapped urban poor. See Douglas G. Glasgow, *The Black Underclass* (New York: Vintage Books, 1981). See also Elliot

Liebow, *Tally's Corner* (Boston: Little Brown, 1967); Melvin Williams, *On the Street Where I Lived* (New York: Holt, Rinehart and Winston, 1981).

15. Numerous ethnographies, biographies, and autobiographies depict "street" life in the ghetto. See Claude Brown, *Manchild in the Promised Land* (Toronto: Macmillan, 1965); Malcolm Little, *The Autobiography of Malcolm X* (New York: Grove Press, 1966); Carol Stack, *All Our Kin* (New York: Harper & Row, 1974); Sharff, *Life on Doolittle Street*; Glasgow, *Black Underclass*; Valentine, *Hustling and Other Hard Work* (New York: The Free Press, 1978).

16. Howard London, *The Culture of a Community College* (New York: Praeger Publishers, 1978). Such comparisons must be made cautiously, however, especially in the case of Willis's "lads." The United States has had a less overt set of class antagonisms than Britain, and working-class cultures will differ somewhat simply on that basis. In addition, the lads attend school by law whereas community college students attend by choice. Despite these caveats, the comparisons promote fruitful discussion about cultural form and its relationship to the economy.

17. Fathers of students typically hold such jobs as construction worker, longshoreman, telephone worker, fork-lift driver, and industrial machinist.

18. These two elements of culture were selected since they emerged as core elements in all three studies.

19. Willis, *Learning to Labour*, p. 13.

20. The pattern for females is notably different. London also suggests that "older" students do not exhibit these behavioral manifestations of lived cultural form.

21. London, *Culture*, especially chapter 3.

22. See Willis, *Learning to Labour*, pp. 62–77 for a discussion of the teaching paradigm.

23. In point of fact the vast majority of teachers are white.

24. The struggle to overturn Jim Crow segregationist laws in the South is an important example here. See Harvard Sitkoff, *The Struggle for Black Equality 1954–1980* (New York: Hill and Wang, 1981). See also C. Vann Woodward, *The Strange Career of Jim Crow* (New York: Oxford University Press, 1966).

25. Willis, *Learning to Labour*, p. 26.

26. London, *Culture* p. 68.

27. This is an important element of the "hidden curriculum" and will be subject to more extended analysis at a later point.

28. The attendance policy allows two hours of absence for each hour of credit. This means that six absences are allowed for a three-credit course. Faculty reserve the right to count "lateness" as absence.

29. While there has been some attempt on the part of the administration to stop this practice, the attempt is not without contradictory effects. Since faculty and ultimately administrative jobs depend upon student headcount in the state system, it may not be in the college's best interest to deny admission to students even if they engage in this practice.

30. These data underestimate absenteeism since they depend upon faculty reporting of absenteeism. In-class observations indicate even greater absenteeism than Tables 1 or 2 suggest. A class in Fashion Merchandising began with close to 35 students; by 14 December 1979 between 7 and 12 students were attending the course. Twelve of an original 32 students were attending a Salesmanship class by 17 November. Twenty-four students were attending a Business Seminar (a remedial course) on 8 February; attendance had dropped to between 4 and 11 by 5 May.

Actual attendance in classes is even lower than that suggested by data presented in Tables 1 and 2.

31. Diane is approximately 50 years old. The older women in particular are largely exempt from the group logic examined here.

32. It can be assumed, because of grant requirements, that these students have always taken a full load.

33. Urban College Task Force, *Student Enrollment, Retention and Placement*, 1976–1981 Data Bank. These are estimates based on number of admits per given year and number of graduates two and three years later.

34. See Michael Apple, "Reproduction, Contestation and Curriculum"; Paul Willis, "Cultural Production is Different."

35. Bisseret has pointed to the manner in which sexist terms and metaphors dominate our linguistic usage. Willis's term "penetration" is a good example here. See Noelle Bisseret, *Education, Class Language and Ideology* (London: Routledge and Kegan Paul, 1979) as cited in Apple, "Reproduction, Contestation, and Curriculum," p. 44.

36. Willis, *Learning to Labour*, p. 119.

37. Ibid.

38. See Harry Braverman, *Labor and Monopoly Capital* (New York: Monthly Review Press, 1974); Michael Burawoy, "Toward a Marxist Theory of the Labor Process: Braverman and Beyond," *Politics and Society* 8, no. 3–4 (1978): 247–312. This is not of course without its contradictory effects. See Richard Edwards, *Contested Terrain*.

39. Willis, *Learning to Labour*, p. 119.

40. Jerome Karabel, "Community Colleges and Social Stratification: Submerged Class Conflict in American Higher Education," *Harvard Educational Review*, 42, no. 4 (1972): 521–62.

41. As Willis notes, capitalism can afford to yield individualism amongst the working class but it cannot yield division. While individualism is penetrated by working class cultural forms in school, these *same* forms actually produce division, thus ensuring the ideological hegemony of the dominant classes. See Willis, *Learning to Labour*, especially Chapters 5 and 6.

42. Overt physical challenges under slavery—insurrection and running away to freedom—not only were unlikely to succeed but were punishable by death or the selling of members of one's family. The conditions for overt collective action did not improve after the Civil War. Jim Crow laws were passed throughout the South, and the Ku Klux Klan mounted a terror campaign that severely discouraged overt resistance. See Eugene Genovese, *Roll, Jordan, Roll: The World the Slaves Made* (New York: Vintage Books, 1972); Sidney Wilhelm, *Who Needs the Negro?* (Garden City, New York: Anchor Books, 1971).

43. See Sitkoff, *The Struggle for Black Equality*.

44. Black resistance is often embedded in folklore for example. See Thomas Webber, *Deep Like the River* (New York: W. W. Norton and Company, 1978); and Lawrence Levine, *Black Culture and Black Consciousness* (New York: Oxford University Press, 1981.

45. I do not mean to imply here that there is no day-to-day resistance among the white working class. Clearly this is not true. My point is that there is a collective tradition that embodies forms of *overt* resistance among the white working class, whereas this is much less the case for American blacks. On day-to-day resistance among white working-class males and females, see Michael

Apple, "The Other Side of the Hidden Curriculum: Correspondence Theories and the Labor Process," *Interchange* 11, no. 3 (1980–81): 5–22.

46. Genovese, *Roll, Jordan, Roll*, provides an excellent discussion of cultural form as embodying elements of both accommodation and resistance at the same time. See especially his chapters on the black work ethic and language.

47. See ibid., pp 561–66, for a discussion of slave literacy and prohibitions associated with it.

48. For a detailed quantitative analysis of racial inequality in the United States see Michael Reich, *Racial Inequality* (Princeton: Princeton University Press, 1981).

49. Michael Olneck, "The Effects of Education," in Christopher Jencks, et. al., *Who Gets Ahead?* (New York: Basic Books, 1979) pp. 150–70. While Olneck did not assess the effects of an Associates degree per se, we can assume that black students with only Community college degrees are still at even more of a disadvantage relative to whites than blacks who continue their education at a four year school and complete the Bachelor's.

50. See Willis, *Learning to Labour*, pp. 120–21, for a discussion of this important point.

51. See Genovese, pp. 161–284, for a discussion of black Christianity.

52. It is important to point out here that the group logic does *not* embody an affirmation of underclass life and associated practices in the same way that cultural practices among working-class white males embody a voluntary giving of manual labor. Urban College Students are attending school to escape the underclass. The important point here is that the group logic operates to ensure that, as a group, they cannot escape. The vast majority of students end up as part of a permanently trapped population of poor people. I suspect that a comparable study among black secondary-school students would uncover a subjective identification with the urban underclass that parallels the subjective giving of manual labor described by Willis. This is an excellent topic for future research.

CHAPTER 11

Play in the Workplace

NANCY R. KING

Work and play are issues that dominate discussions about contemporary American life. The alienation of adults from both their work experiences and their leisure pursuits has created a search for new incentives on the job and an increased involvement in free-time activities. The relationship between work and leisure is a complex and interesting one. Although leisure is often defined as the time during which adults are free of the constraints of work, leisure pursuits are, in fact, influenced by the duration and timing of work, the organization of the workplace, and the nature of the work acitvity.[1]

The distinction between work and play that is taken for granted by most adults is not obvious to young children. It is the child's elementary-school experiences that offer important lessons in the differences between socially organized work and play. This distinction orients the children to the nature of appropriate participation during most classroom activities and shapes their understanding of the classroom reality.

School is the child's first workplace. Parents send their children to school to "work hard"; teachers strive to keep the children working, and the children themselves identify the important educational activities of the school as work.[2] The quality of the students' work habits is as closely evaluated as their mastery of the academic curriculum. The motivation to complete tasks assigned by others, the ability to concentrate in potentially distracting surroundings, the belief in the meaningfulness of an external reward system, and a desire to excel are among the lessons which children are expected to learn in school. Not only do such skills help children succeed in the classroom, but they will also help children succeed as adult workers. Thus, the child's training to be a successful member of the adult workforce begins to take shape as he or she works in elementary school.[3]

The school is a place of work for adults as well as for children. The teachers, custodial and cafeteria staff, secretaries, and principal are at work when they are at school. The child, then, spends many hours a day inside an *adult* workplace, and this dimension of elementary-school experience also helps to shape the child's understanding of and orientation toward adult work roles.

Although the school is a workplace, this is not to say that no play takes place there. It seems safe to assume that most workplaces, at one time or another, become places of play, surreptitious or sanctioned. In some cases, "play times" may be built into the schedule of the day as coffee breaks, lunch hours, or periods of time in the company gymnasium. Play of another sort may develop as workers converse informally, share jokes, or indulge in horseplay.

In the case of the school, it is especially likely for a number of reasons that play will have a place in the daily activities.[4] First, it is thought that for children, particularly young children, play is necessary to healthy growth and development. While this does not indicate that children should play in the classroom, it does indicate a reluctance to suppress entirely the children's spontaneous desire to play in school for fear of damaging them physically or emotionally. Second, play is believed to be a natural mode of learning for young children. Arranging the classroom curriculum as play entices the children to participate and creates an atmosphere of spontaneity and pleasure. Finally, periods of play serve as attractive rewards for children who have successfully completed their assigned tasks.

It is not safe for adults to assume that they know when schoolchildren are playing in the classroom. A study of kindergarten children in four public-school classrooms revealed that the children's definitions and the teachers' definitions of play do not necessarily accord.[5] Kindergarten children used the social context of their activities to help them determine if they were working or playing. If the activity was one in which they were required to participate, the children labeled their activities work. Children, squealing with delight as they marched to music, laughing with pleasure as they watched a movie, or eagerly choosing construction paper for their pictures, said they were working.

Only when the kindergartners perceived themselves to be free of adult supervision did they call their activities play. The children said they were playing when their activities were voluntary, when they were able to choose their own mates, materials, and projects, and when they were free to leave an activity at will. No assigned task was ever called play by any kindergartner, and "structured play" may be something of a contradiction in terms from the children's point of view.

Teachers in the four classrooms referred to more classroom activities as play than the children did. Criteria such as the degree of creativity and the amount of pleasure the children displayed helped teachers differentiate work from play. Neither of these criteria was used by the kindergarten children.

Teachers, then, cannot rely on their own definition of work and play in preparing "work" or "play" experiences for children. It is necessary to study the definitions of work and play used by children at each elementary grade level in order to understand how they interpret the curriculum with regard to these concepts. We cannot assume that adult perspectives will be helpful; nor can we assume that kindergarten perspectives will hold. An understanding of the elementary-school child's point of view requires the study of children in elementary school classrooms.

The Study

This exploratory study investigates the manner in which elementary-school children in grades one through five define their school activities as work or play. The following two groups of questions guide the research effort:

1. What are the criteria used by elementary-school children to differentiate work activities from play activities in school? How do these criteria relate to those used by kindergarten children?

2. Using the children's definitions, what is the relationship between work and play in school? More specifically, what is the nature of play in school, and what is its relationship to schoolwork?

The school in which this study took place is located on a major two-lane state highway in a large rural area. The school building opened in 1955, and the third and final addition was completed in 1975. The classrooms are self-contained units; each has a row of windows and a door opening onto a central hallway. Eighty-five percent of the 687 children enrolled in kindergarten through the fifth grade are bused to school. The school serves predominantly white middle-class families; some parents work in a large city some 20 miles from the school while others work locally in a number of small towns or on farms.

There are 23 full-time teachers including two kindergarten teachers, four teachers at each grade level one through four, and five fifth-grade teachers. Each kindergarten and first-grade class is taught by one teacher in the traditional model of a self-contained classroom. The children in grades two through five are grouped and regrouped for each subject. While some children spend most of their day with one teacher, most of the children get to know all the teachers at their grade level. Teachers try to have their classes ready to change classrooms at the end of each period, but there is some flexibility in the schedule, and there are no bells or rigid adherence to the clock.

In addition to studying academic subjects with their classroom teachers, the children study art, music, physical education, and media with specialized teachers. The school has an art room, a music room, a library, and a gymnasium. On days when a class does not have physical education, the classroom teachers are expected to take the children outside for 30 minutes. The first-grade teachers permit their classes to use the playground equipment during this time; teachers in grades two through five ordinarily have a period of organized games or races.

The children eat lunch in a large cafeteria/auditorium. After they eat, they go outside for recess. The outdoor facilities are spacious and include a large grassy area as well as a paved blacktop. There are two adult aides outside during recess; they rarely intrude on the children except to prevent fighting and dangerous activities. At the end of recess, the aides, with the help of a bullhorn, line the children up and quiet them down before they file into their homerooms for the beginning of afternoon classes.

The data for the study were collected from September 1980 through November 1980. Ten of the teachers' classrooms, grades one through five, were observed and a running narrative of classroom events was recorded. Sixty children, evenly divided between boys and girls, were interviewed. The children to be interviewed were selected to represent a wide range of academic accomplishment and classroom behavior. All the children interviewed had parental permission to participate in the study.

The children were observed in their classrooms and outside with their classroom teachers, in the art room, in the music room, outside with the physical education teacher, and at recess. Children at each grade level were observed for two or more consecutive days, and their classroom activities were noted. An interview schedule was developed for each child, based on the specific classroom events in which the child had been observed to participate. After each child was asked for examples of work and play in school, the researcher read the list of observed activities, and the child categorized each activity as either work or play. In some cases, the child was asked for reasons for a particular answer. In addition, the children were asked about their attitudes toward and use of time during recess.

None of the children interviewed was a reluctant respondent. Most of them were gregarious and added considerable additional information beyond their answers to the questions. Only two children asked what the data were to be used for, and both expressed relief that their teachers would not see their answers.

The Findings

In response to the question, "Did you work at school this week?" all of the children interviewed replied "Yes." Most children named three or four activities or subject areas as examples of work in school. The first graders and most of the second graders named specific activities such as watching "The Electric Company" on television, participating in kickball games, practicing soccer skills, doing a phonics ditto, and making posters in art. Third, fourth, and fifth graders tended to name content areas such as spelling, math, and reading. In each case, these were assigned and supervised by the teacher and each child's behavior or performance was evaluated. One fourth grader summarized his examples by saying "It's the things the teacher gives you that you have to do."

In response to the question, "Did you play at school this week?" all but three children, two fourth graders and one fifth grader, replied "Yes." Children at every grade level offered recess as an example of play. Other examples included required activities, such as kickball and academic classroom games, optional activities, such as using games when assigned tasks were completed, and surreptitious activities, such as "playing around" while waiting for the school bus.

From these initial responses, it is clear that the major criterion for categorizing an activity as work is that the activity is required. This accords with the criteria used by kindergarten children, who also labeled as work activities that were required. The activities listed by the grade-school children as work, then, would also have been labeled work by kindergartners. Definitions of play, on the other hand, differ. Both define as play many activities that are voluntary, that are not evaluated, and during which the children do not perceive themselves to be under direct adult supervision. In addition, however, elementary-school children included a variety of required activities that the kindergartners would have called work. The category of play, apparently, has been enlarged to include activities other than optional ones.

After the initial open-ended questions, each child was asked to categorize a number of activities in which he or she had been observed to participate. A look at these findings provides a more detailed picture of the manner in which elementary-school children differentiate work from play.

Whereas the responses of the kindergarten children were uniform, the responses of elementary-school children varied. Three groups of activities emerge from the elementary-school data: first, the group that all children agree are work; second, the group that all agree are play; and third, the group that some children call work and others call play.

The activities that all children agree are work fall into three categories:

first, listening to the teacher give directions; second, listening to or participating in large group academic lessons during which the teacher makes a didactic presentation; and third, doing required, individual academic tasks. There were three exceptions to the overall uniformity in the final category, and in each case the exception provides additional insight into the quality of work activities. Third graders involved in cutting and pasting pictures of Eskimo life from a ditto called the activity play, although it was a required, individual academic task. The pieces to be cut and pasted were identical, but the teacher encouraged the children to arrange their pieces differently so as to create a unique picture. Such activity was not usually part of social studies during the period of observation, and the children obviously enjoyed the lesson. The two other exceptions occurred in the fifth grade. In one case, children described a ditto in which they were required to underline the nouns as play, explaining that it was "very easy." In the other case, fifth graders required to write a poem described the activity as play because it was fun.

Recess is the only sanctioned school activity that all children agree is play. All of the children indicated that they like recess and some called it the best part of the school day. First and second graders said they like recess because they can "go outside," "run around," "scream and shout," and "talk to friends." Older children also talked about the freedom they have at recess in contrast to the constraints on their activities in the classroom. In addition to emphasizing the freedom to make decisions, and the opportunity for physical activity and social contacts, many children made statements such as "Recess is our time to play," and "School is mostly work, but recess is play." When asked how recess resembles the rest of the school day, many children, particularly younger children, could not think of any way recess is like the rest of the day. Those children who did respond, talked in terms of constraints on their recess activity. For example, some said that lining up to reenter the building was a similarity.

The only other activity that all children agreed was play was surreptitious talking and whispering to other children and other illicit behavior such as clowning around, and silly laughing. These activities are not sanctioned by the teachers, who view them as a nuisance and a disruption.

An analysis of activities labeled work by some children and play by others provides a clear picture of the subtle distinctions elementary-school children make between work and play. The meanings of these categories remain opaque, however, until we turn to the reasons given by the children for the manner in which they categorize their activities. First graders speak about work in a serious tone of voice and their categorization of classroom activities reveals four major characteristics of work.

First, work activities are required, supervised, and assigned by the teacher. Second, work activities are associated with learning. One child, for example, said that watching "The Electric Company" on television was work because "Even though it's fun, we *are* learning." Third, the children associate work with activities that are difficult or "hard," and, finally, with activities that are constraining. Children who said that listening to the teacher read a story was work pointed to the fact that they had to "sit still and be quiet" as their reason. These four characteristics, in one form or another, continue to be identified with classroom work throughout the elementary grades.

By the second grade, work is closely identified with academic content, and with difficult tasks; for example, all the children said that threading their needles in art was work "because it's hard to do," and some said that the art project was work because "I can't sew good." Activities requiring skill were associated with work, as were activities that children did not want to do, such as clean-up. Children labeled many activities work because "you *have* to do it," but since required activities were also labeled play, this criterion no longer has the prominence it did in kindergarten.

Third graders identify work activities with being quiet, with concentrating, with learning, and with activities that are difficult or carry the possibility of failure. One child, for example, said that being at bat in a kickball game was work because "it's hard and you might miss." The children also point to the fact that work activities are required by the teacher. Older elementary-school children make the same distinctions as younger children do, highlighting the required, serious, difficult, and somewhat unpleasant characteristics of activities they labeled work.

First graders respond to events they call play with smiles and squeals, and pleasure emerges for the first time in the first-grade responses as a criterion useful in the distinction between work and play. The most common reason for labeling an activity play becomes "Because I like to do that." The physical location also appears as a criterion for the first time, and play activities are associated with being outside of the school building. The first graders' responses indicate that the category of play may include different types of play, or that activities may have varying degrees of play. For example, one child called watching "The Electric Company" play, but said that using the playground equipment was "*really* play." Similarly, another child who categorized singing in music as play, said that the school day includes recess because, "The kids have been working all day, and they need a chance to play."

By the second grade the association of play activities with enjoyment is so strong that many children spontaneously categorize activities as "fun" and then change their response to "play" when asked again to label the activity as either work or play. Second graders are the first to use as one of their differentiating criteria the opportunity to interact with peers. Play is also associated with activities that are not demanding or that the children have mastered, as well as with voluntary activities that are not evaluated by the teacher. For example, one child responded to an activity by saying, "Doing a center is play because you can choose which one you want and there's no checking [to see] if you get it wrong."

Interestingly enough, play is associated with both energetic physical activity and passive inactivity. Second graders label as play activities that permit them to run around outside or to move about in the classroom. They also label passive classroom activities as play for reasons such as "We didn't have to do anything," and "All we do is sit there." In some cases, children indicated that play activities were less important than work with responses such as "That was play because it was just for fun," or "That was only play," while work activities were described as "*not* just for fun, they're to *learn* something."

By the third grade, having fun and being able to talk emerge as the two most important criteria used to designate activities as play, and fourth graders continue to associate play with fun and success, and with activities that are easy or undemanding.

The criteria used by fifth graders are numerous and complex, and the children draw fine distinctions in differentiating between work and play. For example, one child said, "Studying vocabulary words is play if I'm in the mood, and work if it's boring." "Changing classrooms is either work or play," said one child, "depending on where you are going. If I like the next class, it's play, but if I don't like it, it's work." Some children called changing classes work "because you have to carry all those heavy books," while others called it play "because you can talk to your friends." Activities that are easy to do are called play, but activities that are too easy, and consequently are boring, are called work. Fifth graders also compare activities with other activities in order to differentiate work from play. For example, many children called watching a television program play "because it was instead of science, and science is work."

By the fifth grade, then, the criteria differentiating work from play have become predominantly personal. Play is associated with activities that are fun, interesting, easy but not boring, undemanding, and unevaluated. Work is associated with required activities that are unpleasant, difficult, or boring. Work activities are also supervised and evaluated and have to do with learning skills or academic content.

In summary, then, there is a clear trend toward labeling an increasingly diverse number of activities as play as the children move through the elementary grades. In kindergarten, work was the category for all activities that were not clearly play. In elementary school, however, play is the category for all activities that are not clearly work. The kindergartners rely on the social context to provide indications about whether an activity is work or play. Elementary-school children invoke a personal standard. By the first grade, children have lost the certainty the kindergartners have about whether an activity is work or play. First graders seem confused by some questions; they take more time to think, and they qualify their answers. They seem torn between using the social context as their most important clue, or using their personal attitude toward an activity as the differentiating factor. By the fifth grade, the children's uncertainty is past, and they rely almost exclusively on the psychological context. The essence of play in kindergarten is that it is voluntary and self-directed. The essence of play by the fifth grade is that it is fun and undemanding.

Discussion

It is clear from the data that specific activities do not have intrinsic characteristics that define them as work or play. The social and psychological contexts of activities are the significant determinants. Through the elementary grades, there is a steady proliferation of criteria, which, in addition to becoming increasingly complex and subtle, shift from complete reliance on the social context to primary reliance on the psychological context. As personal attitudes and reactions become of paramount importance, the children's responses to particular activities vary. Activities that are fun or easy for one child may, after all, be unpleasant or boring to another. Consequently, no clear pattern of responses emerges from the data; the pattern is evident only as the children share their criteria.

Although the number of activities called play increases significantly in the elementary grades, this does not indicate that elementary children have more fun in school than kindergartners do. Since the amount of pleasure they took in an activity was not a differentiating criterion for kindergartners, they labeled many enjoyable activities work. Fifth graders, on the other hand, use pleasure as the most significant criterion, and the activities they enjoy are always called play. It is ironic that while the kindergarten curriculum ordinarily reflects early childhood education's interest in play, kindergarten children label few activities play. By the fifth grade, where the curriculum is largely work-oriented, the children label more activities play.

This trend toward labeling an increasing number of activities play flies in the face of our commonsense view of what the curriculum includes. As adults, we recall our early experiences in light of the criteria we presently use to categorize activities. We reconstruct the curriculum from our present perspective, and children do the same. During his interview, a second grader spontaneously remarked, "There's not much play in second grade. There was more in first grade, and it's all we did in kindergarten." That is not, of course, what the kindergartners think.

The increasing number of play responses through the elementary grades reflects, in part, the children's acceptance of adult perspectives on the difference between work and play. It is common for adults, when differentiating between work and play, to consider the degree of pleasure they take in an activity. It is not surprising, then, that children, as they grow older, come to share a similar perspective. While teachers may not actively strive to teach children the salient differences beteen work and play, children have ample opportunity to learn about adult perspectives on these differences in their daily contact with adults in the classroom. The more successful that children are in sharing the teacher's perspective, the more intelligible and predictable classroom life becomes.

The children in this study were made aware of adult perspectives in informal conversations with adults and in spontaneous comments teachers made to their classes. For example, a second-grade teacher told her class, "You were very good outside while we were playing." Later in the morning, she illustrated the meanings of two vocabulary words by saying, "Play. Most of you enjoy playing most of all. Harder. Each day your work gets a little harder." A third-grade teacher announced to her class, "Tomorrow we will finish working on dittoes and workbooks. Now we are going out to play with Mrs. C.'s class." To illustrate a point in language arts, a fourth-grade teacher said, "I went to school today, and I did some work, and I had some fun too."

In summary, play, which for young children refers only to voluntary self-directed activities, refers to a wide range of required as well as voluntary activities for elementary-school children. Play activities come to include goals and interests beyond those of the child participants. Whereas kindergarten children protected their play from any such encroachment by redefining traditional play activities as work whenever the teacher incorporated them into the curriculum, grade-school children label many required academic activities play.

In kindergarten, the category of work was broad and included activities that the children found tedious as well as ones they enjoyed. By the fifth grade, the category has narrowed and includes only required, difficult, boring, or tedious activities. Since pleasure has become an index of play, the category of work is bereft of pleasurable activities, and playfulness and enjoyment are no longer common to work experiences.

The Category of Work

The category of work includes those activities that the children gave as examples of work in response to the open-ended questions in the beginning of the interview and that they continued to label as work in response to questions about specific, observed activities. Work activities are associated with learning and usually require concentration, control, individual accomplishment, and quiet. They are seen as the real business of the school and are considered more important than play in the sense that they are of more consequence, are more serious, and are more closely related to the goals of schooling.

The importance of work was emphasized by the fact that these activities are assigned, required, directed, and evaluated by the teacher. In addition, the teachers emphasized the importance of work to their classes verbally. For example, a second-grade teacher told a child to complete the required portion of a spelling assignment before going on to the optional activities by saying, "Work on the things you *have* to get done first." The same teacher, when giving a vocabulary test, said, "Glad. I am glad when you do all your work." Another second-grade teacher told a reading group, "We're not going to race [a vocabulary word game]; we're going to get right into our story—we have no time to fool around today." At every grade level, children were required to finish assigned tasks before using games or other materials. In encouraging the children to finish an activity, a fourth-grade teacher said, "Remember, no one can play on the soccer team who doesn't have their work done."

The demands of work, then, control the timing and duration of the children's play in school. In addition, the nature of work influences the nature of play. As we shall see, many of the children's activities during play are a response to the requirements of their work.

Categories of Play

Three distinct categories of play emerge from an examination of the children's responses. I have called these categories instrumental play, recreation, and illicit play.

The first category of play, instrumental play, includes those activities that the children offered as examples of work in response to the open-ended questions at the beginning of the interview, but categorized as play in response to questions concerning their observed activities.

Some of these activities were called play because they included energetic, pleasurable involvement on the part of the children. Others were called play because they required little effort and were pleasurable simply because they were undemanding. These activities were ordinarily carried out in the classroom and usually involved academic content. They were required and assigned by the teacher, but they were not always evaluated. The teachers arranged these activities as games or in settings that permitted or encouraged considerable interaction between the children. In addition, this category includes outdoor games that were organized and supervised by the teacher, and required activities in art, music, and physical education that were not overtly academic.

Although the children call this group of activities play,[6] there are important differences between these activities and the spontaneous play of young children. Most significantly, these activities are not voluntary or self-directed, and they serve obvious purposes beyond the satisfaction of the participant. Participation in these activities is obligatory and each child's performance is evaluated by standards extrinsic to the participants themselves. The teacher organizes the activities so that elements of play are included, but it is the teacher who controls the situation, and the playful elements are never allowed to obscure the academic message. In a typical instance, during a vocabulary game, a second-grade teacher commented, "If you can't be quiet during the game, you'll have to go back to your seats."

Sometimes these activities were interrupted for other reasons. During a television program, for example, first graders were called, one by one, to a table at the back of the room to check their reading workbook assignment with a classroom aide. Such interruptions illustrate the fact that these activities were somewhat less important than work activities.

The category of instrumental play exemplifies the efforts of teachers to fuse work and play in the curriculum by embodying academic content in instructional forms ordinarily associated with children's play. Teachers provide games and other unusually relaxing or exciting curricular events in order to involve the children more easily, to relieve the tedium, and to help the children enjoy themselves in school. Amusements, then, become part of the curriculum and having fun becomes part of mastering the academic content. Simultaneously, achievement measured by extrinsic standards becomes part of play.

The second category of play, recreation, includes those sanctioned activities that the children gave as examples of play in the open-ended questions and continued to call play as they categorized the observed activities. Activities at recess make up the greater part of this category. The children's interview responses indicate that their recess activities more closely resemble their notion of "real play" than do their activities during instrumental play. Recess resembles spontaneous play to the extent that the children perceive themselves to be free of adult supervision and direction. This freedom is one of the most appealing characteristics of recess. However, play at recess is, in fact, controlled indirectly. For example, recess is not, strictly speaking, voluntary, and the time and space allocated to recess are dictated by the work orientation of the school. Recess is placed outside the daily classroom schedule and outside the school building.

Recreation differs from spontaneous play in two additional ways. First, recess is a reward; it is something to be earned by completing assigned tasks and behaving in an appropriately cooperative manner during classroom activities. Children were reminded periodically that their failure to achieve work-related goals would result in the loss of recess. In a typical example, a teacher told her class, "Some people didn't get enough spelling done. I'd hate to keep you in at recess, but I will if I have to." Similarly, another teacher warned a group that was getting restless before lunch, "It's almost lunch time and you have an assignment to do. If you can't work quietly, you'll have to stay in after lunch." One of the children interviewed said he rarely went out for recess because he rarely finished his assigned work and because he was often disruptive and noisy in class. He proudly announced, however, that he was going outdoors on the day of the interview because he had gotten an "A" on his spelling test.

The second major difference between spontaneous play and recreation is that the goals of recreation are not entirely intrinsic. The children themselves are aware that recess serves goals beyond those of the participants. In response to the question, "Why do you suppose there is recess at school?" some children pointed to reasons of health with responses such as, "So kids can get exercise," and "So we get fresh air and a suntan on our faces." Other children indicated that recess was a necessary break from work, saying, for example, "So kids get a break from work. You can't just have solid work—kids would get too tired to think and start being bad." Still other children believed that recess was included in the schedule to meet the teachers' needs. These children responded with answers such as, "So teachers can eat lunch and get a rest." and "Because the teachers want you to like them." These responses are close to the staff's reasons for including recess in the daily schedule. The staff believes that recess serves the children's needs for exercise, fresh air, and a period of relatively unrestricted free time outside of the school building.

Illicit play, the final category of play, includes unsanctioned interaction during classroom events. For example, surreptitious talking, whispering, poking other children, clowning, and laughing are called play. Such play is spontaneous and occurs in defiance of the rules and regulations of the classroom. The children realize that their illicit play involves unsanctioned behavior, and they are ordinarily careful to conceal it from the teacher. One third-grade boy was so successful at concealment that he managed to tie a girl's shoelaces to the rungs of her chair without attracting the notice of either the teacher or the girl. Illicit play is intrinsically motivated by the participants, and embodies their messages and meanings. The children shared jokes, tried on each other's bracelets, and attracted the attention of friends in order to exchange information and participate in interaction of a personal nature. One third-grade girl emphasized the personal quality of illicit play when she said, "If I whisper to Carol about our worksheet then it's work, but if I whisper to Carol about other stuff, then it's play."

While such activity was observed in every classroom at one time or another, it was never observed to disrupt classroom events for more than a moment. In some cases, teachers ignored the interruption; in other cases, teachers reminded children to focus on their work, or moved offending children's desks away from the group. In every observed instance, the teachers' remarks or actions were sufficient, and the children discontinued their play.

Relation between Work and Play

The categories of play, taken together, complement and support the work orientation of the school. Play activities provide a respite from difficult or tedious work, and children are expected to return to their assigned tasks with renewed vigor after a period of play. Play also serves as a reward for those who complete their work. The children look forward to it, and rather than grumbling excessively or refusing to work, they complete their required assignments, in part, so that they will be able to participate in it. The children learn that it is play that provides pleasure, social contact, physical activity, and the opportunity for personal expression. Consequently, they do not expect their work to be organized so as to provide similar opportunities. Play in school diverts the children's attention from the tedium of some of their work, and channels their energies and frustrations into acceptable activities that permit the work situation to be endured without serious challenge.

Within this general orientation, each of the three forms of play found in school has a somewhat different relationship to the category of work. First, instrumental play serves as an extension or a continuation of work.[8] Activities are focused on academic pursuits, are associated with learning, and are carried out in a social context identical to the context of work experiences. The activities are required, and the teacher directly controls and supervises the children's interaction. Although the children are often allowed greater latitude in their conduct, and the manner in which they fulfill an assignment may be unique or exciting (as in a game), unusually interesting (as in a science experiment), or unusually relaxing (as in a movie), these benefits are entirely within the control of the teacher.

Instrumental play, then, becomes a variety of play in the elementary school when pleasure is no longer a part of the experience of work. It is play as a direct extension of work.

Recreation, on the other hand, is play as compensation for work. Recess, the major example of recreation in school, serves as an opportunity for the children to seek out the experiences they are denied in the work context. During recess children exercise relative freedom in the selection of their activities; they indulge in exuberant play, scream and shout, talk to their friends, chase each other, and organize games. From the children's point of view, recess is entirely different from work; it is a sanctioned escape from the rigors of the work situation.

Finally, illicit play is play as resistance to the dominant social order and the demands of the work situation. Children's actions during illicit play clearly oppose the coercive nature of the explicit rules and implicit expectations of the classroom. Individual children who resist the requirements of the work situation are viewed as disruptive, and they are punished. Ordinarily, their punishment is the denial of recess. In thus prohibiting them from interacting freely with others, the teachers prevent alternative perspectives with regard to classroom conduct from spreading throughout the group of children. Only children sufficiently well socialized to recognize and accept the limitations on their playful behavior are permitted to participate in recess. The loss of recess also warns other children about the consequences of indulging in illicit play, and provides the teacher with an opportunity to reiterate classroom regulations.

Even as play reinforces the established pattern of work, it carries great potential for resistance by the children as a group. This possibility is clearest in examples of illicit play. The children themselves understand that their behavior during illicit play is in defiance of the classroom rules. Such play involves the children's personal interests rather than the official content of the curriculum, and the children realize that their success in interacting around their personal concerns is at the expense of the teacher's agenda. Illicit play, which focuses on personal interests and peer contacts in a secretive conspiratorial manner, has the potential to create a sense of solidarity among the children. Teachers ordinarily put a stop to disruptive activities, in part, so that the disruption will not spread to the whole class.

Recreation also includes the possibility of resistance. Recess, as an example of recreation, is the period of sanctioned play that allows the children the most extensive possibilities for autonomy and self-expression. During recess, they develop a social organization that reflects their needs and interests.[9] As they interact, informal groups spontaneously emerge and form the core of a children's culture. The informal group is the basic unit that is able to develop, embody, and maintain cultural meanings alternative to those of the dominant social order.[10] Children, in small groups, have the power to reinterpret their daily activities and to sustain and expand these alternative interpretations. The activity of the group provides an acceptable manner and recess provides an acceptable time and place to act upon these alternative world views.

The children's play at recess, then, poses a potential threat to the existing social order because it permits them to imagine, design, and enact an alternative. The freedom to organize their own time, to select their mates, and to plan and carry out their own activities gives them power and autonomy they do not have during work, and demonstrates that they are capable and creative in the management of their own affairs. This experience shows the children that the social order during work is not the only possibility.

The potential of the children's play experiences during recess to create a viable cultural alternative goes unrealized for a number of reasons. Adults control children's access to these play experiences, and one task teachers perform is to keep the child-oriented social order that is prevalent during recess from extending beyond the boundaries of the time and space allotted to it. Recess is clearly separated from the rest of the school day, and it is significant that it is held outdoors. The children must line up and become quiet before reentering the school building. Behavior appropriate to work is thus reestablished before the children return to their classrooms.

Children do not perceive their potential to change the social order or work orientation of the classroom. They do not expect to maintain the play culture they develop during recess, or to extend their playfulness beyond the imposed boundaries. Recess provides a pleasurable respite from classroom work, and they value highly the opportunity to participate in it. Consequently, they cooperate in classroom activities in order to earn the freedom to play, and their desire to organize and direct their own activities is satisfied when they are permitted to go out for recess. As the children place their expectations for fun, physical exercise, and social interaction on recess, their play, while carrying the seeds of social change, becomes, in fact, a substitute for that change. The children focus on enhancing their play experiences; they do not consider in any serious way the possibility of shaping their work experiences.

Children's and Adult's Play

The forms of play found in school resemble those found in the lives of many adults. Although work and play may be integrated in the lives of some adults, adult play is ordinarily distinct from work and relegated to a separate time and space. Stanley Parker has discussed the possible relationships between work and leisure in the lives of adults, and elements of his analysis find counterparts in the findings of this study.[11] Some adults seek play activities that are entirely different from their work activities and use their leisure to recuperate from the difficulty or monotony of their work. In the school setting, recess is analogous.

Some adults participate in play activities that clearly serve their career goals or are an extension of their work. Playing golf with a prospective client, and taking a course for purposes of career advancement are examples of such leisure. In the classroom, instrumental play provides opportunities for children to participate in this kind of play. Just as children are introduced to adult forms of work in school, then, they are also introduced to adult forms of play.

Interestingly enough, adult play, as well as children's, also has a role in resisting the organization of work and the dominant social order. There is a potentially rebellious and radical element in adult play. Harvey Cox discusses one form of radical play in his book, *The Feast of Fools*.[12] Cox maintains that fantasy and festivals are a form of social criticism, in that they deny the inevitability of existing social structures and, in the context of joyous celebration, enable people to envision "radically alternative life situations."[13]

Other forms of potentially radical play have been discussed with reference to industrial workplaces.[14] Boring routine work is punctuated by informal conversations among workers, snacks, trips to the vending machine, practical jokes, and horseplay. Such play provides relief from the monotony of the work situation without, ordinarily, disrupting work schedules. At times, however, such play can escape its boundaries and disrupt the work routine. Although they are "only playing," the potential of workers to reorganize their work situation is demonstrated at such times.

Thus, in their play, the relatively powerless create a freer and more autonomous position for themselves, and such play includes an implicit critique of existing social forms.[15] In providing some respite from reality, play permits people an opportunity to observe and reflect upon dimensions of their daily lives that are ordinarily hidden from view. The playful creation of alternative realities enables them to deny the inevitability of existing conditions.

Social reformers in the past recognized the radical dimension of children's play, and the play movement of the 1920s was, in part, a response to the counter-hegemonic elements obvious in the street games and play of immigrant children.[16] Young adults today focus their struggle for control over their lives on their leisure. Their play provides them an arena for self-expression and a means by which to create their own culture in opposition to the dominant culture in which they live.[17]

The radical potential of play, however, is largely unrealized. Adult play, in the form of leisure activities and recreation, serves as a reward and compensation for participation in the social relations of the workplace. Such play is separate from the reality of work and does not provide solutions to the tensions and demands of the work situation.[18] It offers nothing more than temporary relief and becomes apolitical, promoting "an escape from rather than a confrontation with the established arrangements."[19]

Conclusion

The natural, spontaneous, flowing play of the child is not what one sees in the elementary school. Play in school is play in a workplace, confined to particular times and designated spaces, and controlled by the teacher. From the children's point of view, the primary characteristic of play experiences is that they are fun. Three forms of play appear in daily classroom interaction: instrumental play, recreation, and illicit play.

The children's definitions indicate that the category of work has lost all playful elements and the category of play has lost its purity. This was not true of the definitions that kindergartners gave of their school activities. The dichotomy between work and playfulness (and, to some extent, between play and playfulness) first appears in the elementary school.

Spontaneous children's play is not possible within the constraints of the classroom. Play becomes routinized, organized, and controlled, and this institutionalization distorts the capacity of classroom play to embody the autonomous personal expressions of the players. This is less a conscious effort on the part of the teachers than a consequence of including play in a workplace. The distortions in the capacity of play to carry the meanings of the children are a consequence of the primacy of the work goals of the curriculum. In order to maintain the order and discipline necessary to achieve these goals, the children's play is shaped and controlled. This redefinition of the meaning of play is not achieved without some negotiation between the children and the adults. While the demands of work prevail, the potential of play to challenge and critique is not lost.

Notes

1. Books as different in orientation as the following three all focus on work as a central construct in the understanding of both society and individuals. Lee Braude, *Work and Workers* (New York: Praeger Publishers, 1975); Harry Braverman, *Labor and Monopoly Capital* (New York: Monthly Review Press,

1974); *Work in America*, Report of a Special Task Force to the Secretary of Health, Education, and Welfare (Cambridge, Mass.: The MIT Press, 1973).

2. The categories of work and play are children's categories for defining and differentiating their school experiences. See Nancy R. King, "The Hidden Curriculum and The Socialization of Kindergarten Children," Ph.D. diss., University of Wisconsin-Madison, 1976.

3. Walter Neff, *Work and Human Behavior* (New York: Atherton Press, 1968). Samuel Bowles and Herbert Gintis, *Schooling in Capitalist America* (New York: Basic Books, 1976). Jean Anyon, "Social Class and School Knowledge," *Curriculum Inquiry* 11, no. 1 (Spring 1981): 3–42.

4. See, for example, Joan Cass, *Helping Children Grow Through Play* (New York: Schocken Books, 1973); and Mary Reilly, ed., *Play as Exploratory Learning* (Beverly Hills: Sage Publications, 1974).

5. The following material is taken from Nancy R. King, "Play: The Kindergartners' Perspective," *The Elementary School Journal* 80, no. 2 (1979): 81–87.

6. It must be remembered that, because they categorized these activities according to personal standards, the children's responses varied.

7. Martha Wolfenstein, "The Emergence of Fun Morality," in Eric Larrabee and Rolf Meyersohn, eds., *Mass Leisure* (Glencoe, Ill.: The Free Press, 1958), pp. 86–96.

8. Stanley Parker, *The Sociology of Leisure* (New York: International Publications Service, 1976), p. 72. Parker discusses a variety of relationships between leisure and work focused on adult leisure outside the workplace.

9. Barry Glassner, "Kid Society," *Urban Education* 11, no. 1 (April 1976): 5–21.

10. Paul Willis, *Learning to Labour* (Westmead, England: Saxon House, 1977), p. 26.

11. Stanley Parker, *The Future of Work and Leisure* (London: MacGibbon & Kee, 1971), p. 103.

12. Harvey Cox, *The Feast of Fools* (New York: Harper & Row, 1969).

13. Ibid, p. 7.

14. See, for example, Donald Roy, "Banana Time: Job Satisfaction and Informed Interaction," *Human Organization* 18, no. 4 (Winter 1959–1960): 158–68, and Bill Watson, "Counter-Planning on the Shop Floor," *Radical America* 5, no. 3 (May–June 1971): 77–85.

15. For a discussion of the radical potential of play see Francis Hearn, *Domination, Legitimation and Resistance* (Westport, Connecticut: Greenwood Press, 1978); and Jurgen Moltmann, *Theology of Play* (New York: Harper & Row, 1972).

16. Cary Goodman *Choosing Sides* (New York: Schocken Books, 1979).

17. John Clarke, "Style," in Stuart Hall and Tony Jefferson, eds., *Resistance Through Rituals* (London: Hutchinson, 1975), pp. 175–91.

18. Paul Willis, *Profane Culture* (Boston: Routledge & Kegan Paul, 1978).

19. Francis Hearn, "Toward a Critical Theory of Play," *Telos* 5 no. 30 (winter 1976–77): 156.

Index